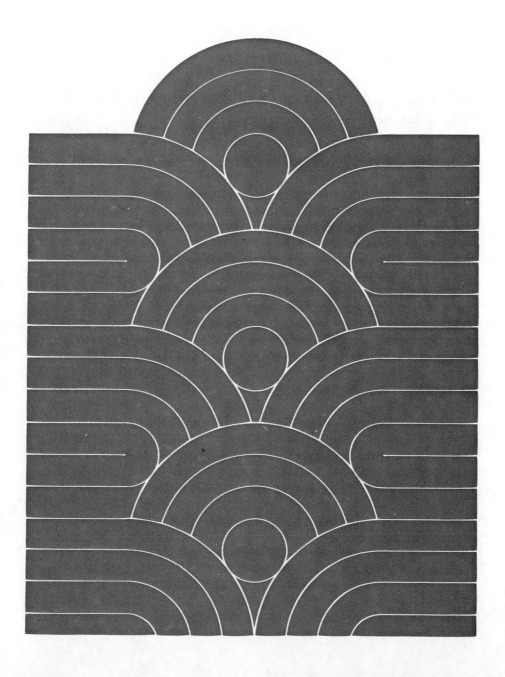

Classical Man

Edited by

Norman Ravitch

University of California, Riverside

Wadsworth Publishing Company, Inc.
Belmont, California

This book has been printed on recycled paper.

Designer: Steve Renick
Cover Designer: Joe Fay
Editor: Mara Niels/Kevin Gleason

ISBN-0-534-00227-7
L. C. Cat. Card No.:72-89431
Printed in the United States of
America

1 2 3 4 5 6 7 8 9 10—77 76 75
74 73

*To my wife, Sally,
with much love*

Preface

It would seem difficult to justify yet another book of source readings in the history of Western thought and culture. Many such collections are already available to the college student, and most of them fulfill the minimal needs of introductory courses. While the available editions differ somewhat in their selections and in the space and emphasis they give to various important thinkers from the Greeks to the Present, they do not differ in significant ways. Most of them share the virtue of representativeness and the vice of aimlessness.

During a decade of teaching Western civilization in college and a few years as director of a Western civilization program, I have endured the common succession of minor revisions and occasional major changes in what is basically a conventional course. Sometimes any change has been for the good, but usually the changes have not really mattered. Course changes in the direction of a topical or thematic rather than a "great books" approach to the thought and culture of Western man are by now common enough, but they may suffer from a too narrow concentration. Regardless of their individual experience, I think all teachers of Western civilization would concur that any course and collection of source readings should have some very specific aims.

I have found most satisfactory the organization of the ideas of Western man through the images of Classical, Christian, and Modern man. Western civilization was taught along these lines for several years at the Riverside campus of the University of California, and I believe that on balance it was an effective course from both faculty and student points of view. This experience is behind this new source book, *Images of Western Man.* If we consider the renewed interest among youth today in religion and the religious perspective, I believe we can find justification for devoting one-third of the sources of Western civilization to Christian man, an appropriate corrective to the more common emphasis on social and economic thought.

Among those who have helped me with their suggestions and criticisms, I must first thank many on the faculty of the University of California, Riverside, who worked in the Western civilization program under my general direction. Without their cooperation our course would not have succeeded and this book would never have been published.

I am also indebted for their generous comments and suggestions to Professors J. D. Bing, University of Tennessee; Richard Cosgrove, University of Arizona; Allan Dirrim, California State University, San Fernando; Everett Ferrill, Ball State University; James Fitts, California State Polytechnic University, San Luis Obispo; Frank Frost of the University of California, Santa Barbara; William Hitchcock, University of California, Santa Cruz; James Marcum, Oklahoma Baptist University; and James Richards, Macon Junior College. My editor, Mr. Michael Helm, who took over someone else's task *in media res,* has been a careful and encouraging man to work with, and I am grateful for his confidence. And Mara Niels was energetic and attentive in editing and preparing the manuscript for publication. Finally, I should like to thank a countless number of students from whom I have learned much more than they could have believed. I hope this collection of readings provides some coherence for many students to come.

Contents

General Introduction   *1*

Introduction   *3*

1   The Greek Historians: *The Greeks at War*   6
Herodotus: *The Greeks at War against Strangers*   9
Thucydides: *The Greeks at War among Themselves*   42

2   The Greek Dramatists: *Justice—The Blood Feud or Social Order?*   86
Aeschylus: *Agamemnon*   88; *The Eumenides*   136

3   The Greek Dramatists: *Morality—Individual Responsibility or Obedience to Law?*   148
Sophocles: *Antigone*   149

4   Classical Philosophy: *The Good Is the Rational*   195
Plato: *The Phaedo*   196

5   Classical Philosophy: *The Good Life*   210
Aristotle: *The Nicomachean Ethics*   211

6   Classical Philosophy: *Inner Tranquility in the Midst of Disorder*   224
Cicero: *The Tusculan Disputations*   225

Contents of volumes II and III   *232*

General Introduction

History is a subject to which we are introduced shortly after mastering basic reading skills, and some study of history accompanies most of our formal education. A few of us develop an abiding interest in the historical past, while a majority loses its interest upon leaving school for good. However, the more we study history—political, social, economic, cultural, and intellectual—the more we realize that this discipline is more than the study of what happened. We become aware that history is the "remembered past."* Not everything in history can be known, and not everything needs to be remembered. But we do need to remember what men have regarded as meaningful in understanding themselves, their world, and their individual and collective future. With increasing knowledge and sophistication, history becomes an attempt to see the human condition with understanding and insight.

All history as a result becomes to some extent "intellectual" in that it seeks to help us understand the questioning mind of man. The study of culture and ideas is especially the quest for understanding man's place in the universe. Such a study must necessarily be somewhat arbitrary or artificial since it seeks to extract meaning and meaningful patterns from man's complex past. One useful but by no means definitive way of dividing the cultural and intellectual past of Western civilization is into three historical and thematic images: the self-awareness of the ancient Graeco–Romans we may call the image of classical man; the world-view of the great Judaeo–Christian religious tradition, Christian man; and the secular and scientific outlook of Europeans and their descendants during the last several hundred years, modern man.

Such a threefold division of Western civilization's past may be arbitrary, but it can suggest insights into three fundamental ways in which Western man has asked and answered questions about himself. Is man part of nature or above it? Can he control nature or is he controlled by it? Is he basically good or evil? Is he at the center of the universe or on its periphery? Is his life meaningful or meaningless? Classical man saw himself as basically *rational* and *philosophical,* with the potential of rising above the dictates of

---

*John Lukacs, *Historical Consciousness or the Remembered Past* (New York: Harper & Row, Publishers, 1968).

merely physical nature. Christian man has presented himself as a creature of God and has explained his nature and destiny through religious myths and symbols, a *mythopoeic* explanation of human nature. Modern man has generally viewed himself as part of nature but able to understand and control nature; he is *scientific* in outlook. These three images of Western man have at times opposed one another, at times been combined in various mixtures and patterns. All three exist in the contemporary world, each offering useful insights into the nature and destiny of man and each seeking to explain his predicament. An investigation of the best examples of these different approaches to the human condition can help contemporary man to understand himself.

The images of classical man, Christian man, and modern man are all valid; they are also limited. The student of human nature and history can profit by confronting them, comparing and contrasting them, and making up his own mind about self-image.

Introduction

The image of classical man is the product of the history, thought, and culture of the Graeco–Roman civilization of the ancient world. From the point of view of Western man, the civilization of Greece and Rome began some several hundred years after 1000 B.C. and lasted about one thousand years until the Roman Empire had become sufficiently Christianized and barbarized so as to no longer seem classical. The Greeks and Romans and the peoples who were subject to their rule along the Mediterranean coast and in the hinterlands lived in the first half of this thousand-year period in various *poleis* or city–state republics under various degrees of rule by monarchs, aristocracies, and popular democracies. The conquests of Alexander the Great and of the Roman Republic (fourth through first centuries B.C.) served to organize the Mediterranean world into a vast empire ruled increasingly by military power. The Roman Empire was the model of the splendor, organization, and universality of ancient imperialism, as well as of its brutality, despotism, and vulgarity. Ancient civilization ended in the material breakdown of the Roman Empire through economic, political, and military failure and the spiritual weakening of pagan thought and religion accompanied by the victory of Christianity. In this ancient civilization, it was generally the Greeks who achieved the most notable successes in philosophy, literature, and the sciences, while the Romans displayed great practical skill in law, politics, and engineering. Other peoples in the Graeco–Roman world are usually judged according to how much they became assimilated to Graeco–Roman civilization; otherwise they are ignored. Thus, classical man was a Greek or a Roman, and Greek culture has generally been preferred to Roman as more original and creative. The term "classical man," thus, almost always refers to Greek culture.

Western man's attitude towards classical man has ranged from the worshipful appreciation from Renaissance intellectuals of the fifteenth and sixteenth centuries to the condescension of modern, scientifically oriented man, who seems to share the attitude of Francis Bacon (d. 1626) that whatever the achievements of classical man, modern man knows far more about nature than did his ancestors in the Graeco–Roman world. Medieval Christian Europe felt both admiration and suspicion for the pagan culture of antiquity and generally sought to tame classical man for pious Christian purposes. But, for the most part, classical man has been idealized in Western civilization. Classical thought—philosophical, ethical, aesthetic—was made the foundation of the liberal arts education, and for hundreds of years it has been the education of the Western gentleman. Classical man is not simply the chronological starting point for an investigation of Western man. It is also the plentiful source of values and insights into the human condition which men have found relevant in many different epochs of Western and world history.

To discover the image of classical man, one turns to the poets, historians, philosophers, and literary men of Graeco–Roman antiquity, even though their world spanned a millenium and a variety of political forms and philosophical persuasions. One can only generalize about the most persistent and consistent insights of antiquity as they have continued to be important and influential in the very different modern world. Such generalizations will perhaps dissatisfy many, but they need, nevertheless, to be attempted.

Classical man was profoundly pessimistic about the meaning of human life. His myths, both religious and social, taught him that man was a creature capable of rational behavior who, more often than not, became the victim of urges and passions he could not control. The principles of order and reason were represented for him by the highest of the Olympian gods or by the divine laws of the universe, and man came into conflict with these principles because of his human nature. Defiance of the laws of the gods always led classical man to disaster, even when there was some merit in his disobedience. True wisdom was resigned acceptance of the way the universe was, but neither happiness nor satisfaction followed such acceptance, and it was in any case difficult for man, slave to his passions and excesses, to accomplish this. In particularly pessimistic times, classical man identified goodness with a sort of disembodied reason, and he associated evil with the limitations of the body and human nature; this resulted in an almost un-Western form of dualism or disharmony between body and soul. Plato's thought at this point approached Oriental mysticism. In less pessimistic times, classical man counselled happiness through the pursuit of the intellect, but such activity was reserved for the few who had the leisure and aptitude for such study and contemplation. Whether pessimistic about the universe or a degree more hopeful, classical man remained thoroughly aristocratic in that he doubted that the majority of men could be anything but the playthings of the gods, of fate, or of other men. Wisdom, resignation, a degree of understanding and happiness—these were for the very few. The total identification of goodness with reason, making virtue entirely intellectual, encouraged classical man to seek to avoid contaminating contact with the everyday world of activity and to hunger after contemplation. At times classical man seemed more intent on learning how to die than how to live.

To balance this pessimism, however, note that the political organization of classical man avoided any split between the political and spiritual obligations of man. The city–state, or *polis,* was, at its zenith in early Athens, Sparta, and Rome, the object of the highest religious and political loyalty of the citizen. The vast empires which succeeded the city–states continued the total identification of the state with the divinity, sometimes in repulsive and alien ways. Classical man was thus asked to pay the price of individual liberty and moral autonomy in exchange for the security of a total society. In his drama, philosophy, and political life, classical man raised virtually all the basic questions one can ask about his predicament and destiny, but he offered no solution for all men. Yet classical man remains a compelling interest for all time because of his brilliant insight into the human condition.

1

The Greek
Historians:
The
Greeks at War

One important sign of civilization is a people's self-awareness and desire to understand its past and commit its experience to posterity. Writing down history is a most important step in the development of a civilization; the Greeks of the fifth century B.C. seem to have invented written history. Except for the ancient Hebrews—who did write history, though for less secular purposes—no people of antiquity had the Greeks' scientific and humanistic interest in their own past. What passed for history among the ancient Near Eastern peoples was largely mythical and religious. The Greeks of the fifth century B.C., on the other hand, developed some very modern notions of historical inquiry.

The two most important and memorable events to take place in the Hellenic world in the fifth century were the Persian invasion (499–479) and the great Peloponnesian War between Athens and Sparta (431–404); these events have become memorable indeed because they were described by the two greatest historians Greece ever produced, Herodotus and Thucydides. In what they chose to remember, to analyze, and to interpret, Herodotus and Thucydides reveal the attitudes of classical man towards the perennial questions of mortal man's relationship to the vast universe.

In the late sixth and early fifth centuries B.C., the rise and fall of great empires in Western Asia had a critical impact upon the lives of the Greek peoples who were grouped into various city–states or *poleis* in the Balkan Peninsula, on the islands of the Aegean Sea, and on the coast of Asia Minor. Under the leadership of Cyrus the Great and his successors, a good portion of Western Asia fell under the rule of the Perisans. This brought the Persians and the Greeks into contact and conflict; while to the vast Persian Empire the Greeks might have seemed little more than irritants on the Western frontiers, to many of the Greeks Persian rule constituted a threat. In 499 Greek cities in Asia Minor (Ionia) revolted against Persian overlordship; this brought on a Persian invasion of the Greek homeland—an invasion which the Greeks, led by the Athenians and Spartans, successfully repulsed between 490 and 479. It was this war and the nature of the different peoples involved that became the subject of Herodotus' *History.*

Among the Greeks warring against the invading Persians, the Spartans were most courageous and skillful, but the Athenians had the more insightful view of the threat which Persian power held for the Greeks and their cherished freedom. After the Persians had failed in their invasion of Greece, Athens led in the liberation of those Greek cities still living under Persian rule, and the might and leadership built up by Athens resulted in an Athenian Empire of over 150 separate city–states. Athenian power was largely naval, and it was supported by thriving commercial activity in all parts of the Eastern Mediterranean. Far from being considered the saviors of Greece, the Athenians came to be viewed as bent upon ruling all the Greeks. The Spartans, representing a more conservative and agricultural outlook, took the leadership of those Greeks fearing the revolutionary inclinations of the Athenians towards Greek political unification. The resulting war between the Athenians and Spartans and their respective clients, satellites, and allies, was the great civil war, the Peloponnesian War, about which Thucydides wrote. The war lasted until the end of the fifth century, and it utterly destroyed the Greeks' ability to rule themselves either democratically or aristocratically. Greece in the fourth century finally yielded to the imperial rule of Alexander the Great, which was a prelude for imperial domination by Rome, destined to last for many centuries.

Herodotus (c. 484–425) was a Greek from Halicarnassus in Asia Minor, a region where Greeks easily came into contact with foreign peoples of great antiquity and culture. This proximity of Greeks and foreigners in Asia Minor undoubtedly encouraged curiosity about eras before the present and peoples other than the relatively few and backward Greeks. Herodotus travelled widely, including visits to the domains of the Egyptians and the Persians, and he had access to the royal annals of these peoples. He also met former participants in the Persian War and heard their accounts of what had occurred. The result of his researches may fall somewhat short of a thoroughly scientific discussion of the war, but Herodotus' immense interest in the customs and beliefs of the various peoples of the Near East—his comparative *ethnography,* if one wishes to use a modern term—was extraordinarily scientific in scope. Like any historian, Herodotus had to do more than record what had happened; he had to make some sense of endless events and details. He chose to write the history of the Greek encounter with the Persians as a struggle between freedom and slavery. The Egyptians and the Persians were unquestionably richer in goods and in creative imagination than the rustic Greeks, but they were not capable of political freedom. The Greeks fought for freedom, and in their victory over the Persians, European freedom triumphed over oriental despotism. This theme of Herodotus has been very influential in the development of European self-awareness and racial self-consciousness. Herodotus also sought to portray the defeat of the Persians as the personal tragedy of the Persian ruler Xerxes whose overweening pride and arrogance brought the destruction of the gods down on him. Herodotus, then, wrote his *History* to celebrate the virtues of political freedom and personal moderation —characteristically Greek ideals—in a world subject to the rule of naked power and human arrogance.

Thucydides (471 or 460–399) was an Athenian citizen of high social status who participated in the Peloponnesian War and was exiled for political and military error. Like Herodotus, Thucydides was able to interview eyewitnesses to the events of the great Greek civil war and to travel among participants from both sides. But unlike Herodotus, Thucydides narrowed his historical vision considerably, focusing mostly on war, diplomacy, and politics and little on cultural and spiritual factors. Thucydides reflected an increasing Greek materialism; he sought to explain human behavior in a secular and material way. When he cited Homer, the great poet of Hellenic antiquity, he tended to demythologize Homer's explanations and offered economic rather than mythical interpretations for the course of the Trojan War and the political changes in the Greek city–states. Thucydides believed that what motivated men was nothing so elevated as justice, but rather "fear, honor, and interest." Convinced of such material and constant human motivations and that human nature is unchangeable, Thucydides believed that history could be expected to repeat itself; his *Peloponnesian War* was designed to find the permanent lessons of history for future use. Thucydides interpreted the great war between the Greeks as the story of the rise and fall of the Athenian state, a state marked by revolutionary innovation, political democracy, and imperialism. In the end, Thucydides discusses the political failure of Athens: its democracy depended on enlightened leadership, as represented by Pericles (461–429). After Pericles' death, the ugly side of democracy revealed itself all too clearly, and in the decline of Athens the Greeks also lost the possibility of uniting themselves on the basis of consent and freedom. In Thucydides' remarkable and inventive recreation of Athenian political life we have an enduring portrait of classical man as he strove for power and freedom.

While Herodotus and Thucydides represented different genera-tions and different approaches to history, both saw in history enduring lessons for the political and spiritual enlightenment of man. And they both saw tragedy for men and nations who violated these ideals.

Herodotus:
The Greeks
at War against Strangers

This is a publication of the researches of Herodotus of Halicarnassus, in order that the actions of men may not be effaced by time, nor the great and wondrous deeds displayed both by Greeks and barbarians deprived of renown:—and amongst the rest, for what cause they waged war upon each other.

1. The learned among the Persians assert that the Phoenicians were the original authors of the quarrel; for that they having migrated from that which is called the Red Sea to the Mediterranean, and having settled in the country which they now inhabit, forthwith applied themselves to distant voyages; and that having exported Egyptian and Assyrian merchandise, they touched at other places, and also at Argos. Now Argos at that period in every respect surpassed all those states which are now comprehended under the general appellation of Greece. *They say,* that on their arrival at Argos, the Phoenicians exposed their merchandise to sale, and that on the fifth or sixth day after their arrival, and when they had almost disposed of their cargo, a great number of women came down to the sea-shore, and among them the king's daughter, whose name, as the Greeks also say, was Io daughter of Inachus. *They add,* that while these women were standing near the stern of the vessel, and were bargaining for such things as most pleased them, the Phoenicians, having exhorted one another, made an attack upon them; and that most of the women escaped, but that Io, with some others, was seized: and that they, having hurried them on board, set sail for Egypt. 2. Thus the Persians say that Io went to Egypt, not agreeing *herein* with the Phoenicians; and that this was the beginning of wrongs. After this, that certain Grecians, (for they are unable to tell their name,) having touched at Tyre in Phoenicia, carried off the king's daughter Europa. These must have been Cretans. Thus far they say that they had only retaliated; but that after this the Greeks were guilty of the second provocation; for that having sailed down in a vessel of war to Aea, a city of Colchis on the river Phasis, when they had accomplished the more immediate object of their expedition, they carried off the king's daughter Medea; and that the king of Colchis, having despatched a herald to Greece, demanded satisfaction for the rape, and the restitution of the princess; but the Greeks replied, that as they of Asia had not given any satisfaction for the rape of Io, neither would they give any to them. 3. They say too, that in the second

Herodotus' History, Henry Cary, trans. (London: George Bell & Sons, 1894), pp. 1-3, 11-15, 59-63, 94-96, 101-104, 108-110, 407-419, 454-455, 479-489, 516-525.

generation after this, Alexander the son of Priam, having heard of these events, was desirous of obtaining a wife from Greece by means of violence, being fully persuaded that he should not have to give satisfaction, for that the Greeks had not done so. When therefore he had carried off Helen, *they say,* that the Greeks immediately sent messengers to demand her back again, and require satisfaction for the rape; but that they, when they brought forward these demands, objected to them the rape of Medea; "that they who had not themselves given satisfaction, nor made it when demanded, now wished others to give it to themselves." 4. Thus far then *they say* that there had only been rapes from each other; but that after this the Greeks were greatly to blame, for that they levied war against Asia before the Asiatics did upon Europe. Now, to carry off women by violence the Persians think is the act of wicked men, but to trouble oneself about avenging them when so carried off is the act of foolish ones; and to pay no regard to them when carried off, of wise men: for that it is clear, that if they had not been willing, they could not have been carried off. Accordingly the Persians say, that they of Asia made no account of women that were carried off; but that the Greeks for the sake of a Lacedaemonian woman assembled a mighty fleet, and then having come to Asia overthrew the empire of Priam. That from this event they had always considered the Greeks as their enemies: for the Persians claim Asia and the barbarous nations that inhabit it, as their own, and consider Europe and the people of Greece as totally distinct.

5. Such is the Persian account; and to the capture of Troy they ascribe the commencement of their enmity to the Greeks. As relates to Io, the Phoenicians do not agree with this account of the Persians: for they affirm that they did not use violence to carry her into Egypt; but that she had connexion at Argos with the master of a vessel, and when she found herself pregnant, she, through dread of her parents, voluntarily sailed away with the Phoenicians, to avoid detection. Such then are the accounts of the Persians and Phoenicians: I, however, am not going to inquire whether the facts were so or not; but having pointed out the person whom I myself know to have been the first guilty of injustice towards the Greeks, I will then proceed with my history, touching as well on the small as the great estates of men: for of those that were formerly powerful many have become weak, and some that were powerful in my time were formerly weak. Knowing therefore the precarious nature of human prosperity, I shall commemorate both alike. . . .

29. When these nations were subdued, and Croesus had added them to the Lydians, all the other wise men of that time, as each had opportunity, came from Greece to Sardis, which had then attained to the highest degree of prosperity; and amongst them Solon an Athenian, who having made laws for the Athenians at their request, absented himself for ten years, having sailed away under pretence of seeing the world, that he might not be compelled to abrogate any of the laws he had established: for the Athenians could not do it themselves, since they were bound by solemn oaths to observe for ten years whatever laws Solon should enact for them. 30. Solon therefore having

gone abroad for these reasons, and for the purposes of observation, arrived in Egypt at the court of Amasis, and afterwards at that of Croesus at Sardis. On his arrival he was hospitably entertained by Croesus, and on the third or fourth day, by order of the king, the attendants conducted him round the treasury, and showed him all their grand and costly contents; and when he had seen and examined every thing sufficiently, Croesus asked him this question "My Athenian guest, your great fame has reached even to us, as well of your wisdom as of your travels, how that as a philosopher you have travelled through various countries for the purpose of observation; I am therefore desirous of asking you, who is the most happy man you have seen?" He asked this question, because he thought himself the most happy of men. But Solon, speaking the truth freely, without any flattery, answered, "Tellus the Athenian." Croesus, astonished at his answer, eagerly asked him, "On what account do you deem Tellus the happiest?" He replied, "Tellus, in the first place, lived in a well-governed commonwealth; had sons who were virtuous and good; and he saw children born to them all, and all surviving: in the next place, when he had lived as happily as the condition of human affairs will permit, he ended his life in a most glorious manner. For coming to the assistance of the Athenians in a battle with their neighbours of Eleusis, he put the enemy to flight, and died nobly. The Athenians buried him at the public charge in the place where he fell, and honoured him greatly."

31. When Solon had roused the attention of Croesus by relating many and happy circumstances concerning Tellus, Croesus, expecting at least to obtain the second place, asked, whom he had seen next to him. "Cleobis," said he, "and Biton, for they being natives of Argos, possessed a sufficient fortune, and had withal such strength of body, that they were both alike victorious in the public games; and moreover the following story is related of them: when the Argives were celebrating a festival of Hera, it was necessary that their mother should be drawn to the temple in a chariot; but the oxen did not come from the field in time, the young men therefore, being pressed for time, put themselves beneath the yoke, and drew the car in which their mother sate; and having conveyed it forty-five stades, they reached the temple. After they had done this in sight of the assembled people, a most happy termination was put to their lives; and in them the Deity clearly showed, that it is better for a man to die than to live. For the men of Argos, who stood round, commended the strength of the youths, and the women blessed her as the mother of such sons; but the mother herself, transported with joy both on account of the action and its renown, stood before the image and prayed, that the goddess would grant to Cleobis and Biton, her own sons, who had so highly honoured her, the greatest blessing man could receive. After this prayer, when they had sacrificed and partaken of the feast, the youths fell asleep in the temple itself, and never awoke more, but met with such a termination of life. Upon this the Argives, in commemoration of their piety, caused their statues to be made and dedicated at Delphi." 32. Thus Solon adjudged the second place of felicity to these youths. But Croesus, being enraged, said, "My

Athenian friend, is my happiness then so slighted by you as nothing worth, that you do not think me of so much value as private men?" He answered; "Croesus, do you inquire of me concerning human affairs—of me, who know that the divinity is always jealous, and delights in confusion. For in lapse of time men are constrained to see many things they would not willingly see, and to suffer many things *they would not willingly suffer.* Now I put the term of man's life at seventy years; these seventy years then give twenty-five thousand two hundred days, without including the intercalary month; and if we add that month to every other year, in order that the seasons arriving at the proper time may agree, the intercalary months will be thirty-five more in the seventy years, and the days of these months will be one thousand and fifty. Yet in all this number of twenty-six thousand two hundred and fifty days, that compose these seventy years, one day produces nothing exactly the same as another. Thus, then, O Croesus, man is altogether the sport of fortune. You appear to me to be master of immense treasures, and king of many nations; but as relates to what you inquire of me, I cannot say, till I hear you have ended your life happily. For the richest of men is not more happy than he that has a sufficiency for a day, unless good fortune attend him to the grave, so that he ends his life in happiness. Many men, who abound in wealth, are unhappy; and many, who have only a moderate competency, are fortunate. He that abounds in wealth, and is yet unhappy, surpasses the other only in two things; but the other surpasses the wealthy and the miserable in many things. The former indeed is better able to gratify desire, and to bear the blow of adversity. But the latter surpasses him in this; he is not indeed equally able to bear misfortune or *satisfy* desire, but his good fortune wards off these things from him; and he enjoys the full use of his limbs, he is free from disease and misfortune, he is blessed with good children and a fine form, and if, in addition to all these things, he shall end his life well, he is the man you seek, and may justly be called happy; but before he die we ought to suspend our judgment, and not pronounce him happy, but fortunate. Now it is impossible for any one man to comprehend all these advantages: as no one country suffices to produce every thing for itself, but affords some and wants others, and that which affords the most is the best; so no human being is in all respects self-sufficient, but possesses one advantage, and is in need of another; he therefore who has constantly enjoyed the most of these, and then ends his life tranquilly, this man, in my judgment, O king, deserves the name of happy. We ought therefore to consider the end of every thing, in what way it will terminate; for the Deity having shown a glimpse of happiness to many, has afterwards utterly overthrown them. . . ."

131. The Persians, according to my own knowledge, observe the following customs. It is not their practice to erect statues, or temples, or altars, but they charge those with folly who do so; because, as I conjecture, they do not think the gods have human forms, as the Greeks do. They are accustomed to ascend the highest parts of the mountains, and offer sacrifice to Zeus, and they call the whole circle of the heavens by the name of Zeus. They sacrifice to the sun and moon, to the earth, fire, water, and the winds. To these alone

they have sacrificed from the earliest times: but they have since learnt from the Arabians and Assyrians to sacrifice to Aphrodite Urania, whom the Assyrians call Aphrodite Mylitta, the Arabians, Alitta, and the Persians, Mitra. 132. The following is the established mode of sacrifice to the above-mentioned deities: they do not erect altars nor kindle fires when about to sacrifice; they do not use libations, or flutes, or fillets, or cakes; but, when any one wishes to offer sacrifice to any one of these deities, he leads the victim to a clean spot, and invokes the god, usually having his tiara decked with myrtle. He that sacrifices is not permitted to pray for blessings for himself alone; but he is obliged to offer prayers for the prosperity of all the Persians, and the king, for he is himself included in the Persians. When he has cut the victim into small pieces, and boiled the flesh, he strews under it a bed of tender grass, generally trefoil, and then lays all the flesh upon it: when he has put every thing in order, one of the Magi standing by sings an ode concerning the original of the gods, which they say is the incantation; and without one of the Magi it is not lawful for them to sacrifice. After having waited a short time, he that has sacrificed carries away the flesh and disposes of it as he thinks fit. 133. It is their custom to honour their birth-day above all other days; and on this day they furnish their table in a more plentiful manner than at other times. The rich then produces an ox, a horse, a camel, and an ass, roasted whole in an oven; but the poor produce smaller cattle. They are moderate at their meals, but eat of many after dishes, and those not served up together. On this account the Persians say, "that the Greeks rise hungry from table, because nothing worth mentioning is brought in after dinner, and that if any thing were brought in, they would not leave off eating." The Persians are much addicted to wine; they are not allowed to vomit or make water in presence of another. These customs are observed to this day. They are used to debate the most important affairs when intoxicated; but whatever they have determined on in such deliberations, is on the following day, when they are sober, proposed to them by the master of the house where they have met to consult; and if they approve of it when sober also, then they adopt it; if not, they reject it. And whatever they have first resolved on when sober, they reconsider when intoxicated. 134. When they meet one another in the streets, one may discover by the following custom, whether those who meet are equals. For instead of accosting one another, they kiss on the mouth; if one be a little inferior to the other, they kiss the cheek; but if he be of a much lower rank, he prostrates himself before the other. They honour, above all, those who live nearest to themselves; in the second degree, those that are second in nearness; and after that, as they go further off, they honour in proportion; and least of all they honour those who live at the greatest distance; esteeming themselves to be by far the most excellent of men in every respect; and that others make approaches to excellence according to the foregoing gradations, but that they are the worst who live farthest from them. During the empire of the Medes, each nation ruled over its next neighbour, the Medes over all, and especially over those that were nearest to them; these again, over the bordering people, and the last in like manner over their next neighbours; and in the same gradations the Persians honour; for that nation went on extending its government and guardianship. 135. The Persians are of all nations most ready to adopt foreign customs; for they wear the Medic costume, thinking it handsomer than their own; and in war they use the Egyptian cuirass. And they practise all kinds of indulgences with which they become acquainted; amongst others, they have learnt from the Greeks a passion for boys: they marry, each of them, many wives; and keep a still greater number of concubines. 136. Next to bravery in battle, this is considered the greatest proof of manliness, to be able to exhibit many children; and to such as can exhibit the greatest number, the king sends presents every year; for numbers are considered strength. Beginning from the age of five years to twenty, they instruct their sons in three things only; to ride, to use the bow, and to speak truth. Before he is five years of age, a son is not admitted to the presence of his father, but lives entirely with the women: the reason of this custom is, that if he should die in childhood, he may occasion no grief to his father.

137. Now I much approve of the above custom, as also of the following, that not even the king is allowed to put any one to death for a single crime, nor any private Persian exercise extreme severity against any of his domestics for one fault, but if on examination he should find that his misdeeds are more numerous and greater than his services, he may in that case give vent to his anger. They say that no one ever yet killed his own father or mother, but whenever such things have happened they affirm, that if the matter were thoroughly searched into, they would be found to have been committed by supposititious children or those born in adultery, for they hold it utterly improbable that a true father should be murdered by his own son. 138. They are not allowed even to mention the things which it is not lawful for them to do. To tell a lie is considered by them the greatest disgrace; next to that, to be in debt; and this for many other reasons, but especially because they think that one who is in debt must of necessity tell lies. Whosoever of the citizens has the leprosy or scrofula, is not permitted to stay within a town, nor to have communication with other Persians; and they say that from having committed some offence against the sun a man is afflicted with these diseases. Every stranger that is seized with these distempers many of them even drive out of the country; and they do the same to white pigeons, making the same charge against them. They neither make water, nor spit, nor wash their hands in a river, nor defile the stream with urine, nor do they allow any one else to do so, but they pay extreme veneration to all rivers. 139. Another circumstance is also peculiar to them, which has escaped the notice of the Persians themselves, but not of us. Their names, which correspond with their personal forms and their rank, all terminate in the same letter which the Dorians call *San,* and the Ionians *Sigma.* And if you inquire into this you will find, that all Persian names, without exception, end in the same letter. 140. These things I can with certainty affirm to be true, since I myself know them. But what follows, relating to the dead, is only secretly mentioned and not openly; viz. that the

dead body of a Persian is never buried until it has been torn by some bird or dog; but I know for a certainty that the Magi do this, for they do it openly. The Persians then, having covered the body with wax, conceal it in the ground. The Magi differ very much from all other men, and particularly from the Egyptian priests, for the latter hold it matter of religion not to kill any thing that has life, except such things as they offer in sacrifice; whereas the Magi kill every thing with their own hands, except a dog or a man; and they think they do a meritorious thing, when they kill ants, serpents, and other reptiles and birds. And with regard to this custom, let it remain as it existed from the first. I will now return to my former subject.

Book II. Euterpe

... 2. The Egyptians, before the reign of Psammitichus, considered themselves to be the most ancient of mankind. But after Psammitichus, having come to the throne, endeavoured to ascertain who were the most ancient, from that time they consider the Phrygians to have been before them, and themselves before all others. Now, when Psammitichus was unable, by inquiry, to discover any solution of this question, who were the most ancient of men, he devised the following expedient. He gave two new-born children of poor parents to a shepherd, to be brought up among his flocks in the following manner: he gave strict orders that no one should utter a word in their presence, that they should lie in a solitary room by themselves, and that he should bring goats to them at certain times, and that when he had satisfied them with milk he should attend to his other employments. Psammitichus contrived and ordered this, for the purpose of hearing what word the children would first articulate, after they had given over their insignificant mewlings; and such accordingly was the result. For when the shepherd had pursued this plan for the space of two years, one day as he opened the door and went in, both the children falling upon him, and holding out their hands, cried "Becos." The shepherd, when he first heard it, said nothing; but when this same word was constantly repeated to him whenever he went and tended the children, he at length acquainted his master, and by his command brought the children into his presence. When Psammitichus heard the same, he inquired what people call any thing by the name of "Becos;" and on inquiry he discovered that the Phrygians call bread by that name. Thus the Egyptians, convinced by the above experiment, allowed that the Phrygians were more ancient than themselves. 3. This relation I had from the priests of Hephaestus at Memphis. But the Greeks tell many other foolish things, and moreover that Psammitichus, having had the tongues of some women cut out, then had the children brought up by these women. Such is the account they gave of the nurture of the children. I heard other things also at Memphis in conversation with the priests of Hephaestus. And on this very account I went also to Thebes, and to

Heliopolis, in order to ascertain whether they would agree with the accounts given at Memphis; for the Heliopolitans are esteemed the most learned in history of all the Egyptians. The parts of the narration that I heard concerning divine things, I am not willing to relate, except only their names; and with these I suppose all men are equally well acquainted: but what more I shall relate of these matters, I shall relate from a necessity to keep up the thread of my story.

4. But as concerns human affairs, they agree with one another in the following account: that the Egyptians were the first to discover the year, which they divided into twelve parts; and they say that they made this discovery from the stars: and so far, I think, they act more wisely than the Grecians, in that the Grecians insert an intercalary month every third year, on account of the seasons; whereas the Egyptians, reckoning twelve months of thirty days each, add five days each year above that number, and so with them the circle of the seasons comes round to the same point. They say also, that the Egyptians were the first who introduced the names of the twelve gods, and that the Greeks borrowed those names from them; that they were the first to assign altars, images, and temples to the gods, and to carve the figures of animals on stone; and most of these things they proved were so in fact. They added, that Menes was the first mortal who reigned over Egypt, and that in his time all Egypt, except the district of Thebes, was a morass, and that no part of the land that now exists below Lake Myris was then above water: to this place from the sea is a seven days' passage up the river. 5. And they seemed to me to give a good account of this region. For it is evident to a man of common understanding, who has not heard it before, but sees it, that the part of Egypt which the Greeks frequent with their shipping, is land acquired by the Egyptians, and a gift from the river; and the parts above this lake, during a three days' passage, of which, however, they said nothing, are of the same description. For the nature of the soil of Egypt is of this kind; when you are first sailing to it, and are at the distance of a day's sail from land, if you cast the lead you will bring up mud, and will find yourself in eleven fathoms water: this so far shows that there is an alluvial deposit. . . .

19. But the Nile, when full, inundates not only Delta, but also part of the country said to belong to Libya and Arabia, to the extent of about two days' journey on either side, more or less.

Respecting the nature of this river, I was unable to gain any information, either from the priests or any one else. I was very desirous, however, of learning from them why the Nile, beginning at the summer solstice, fills and overflows for a hundred days; and when it has nearly completed this number of days, falls short in its stream, and retires; so that it continues low all the winter, until the return of the summer solstice. Of these particulars I could get no information from the Egyptians, though I inquired whether this river have any peculiar quality that makes it differ in nature from other rivers. Being anxious, then, of knowing what was said about this matter, I made inquiries, and also how it comes to pass, that this is the only one of all rivers that does not send forth breezes from its surface. 20. Nevertheless, some of the Greeks, wishing to be distinguished for their wisdom, have attempted to account for these inundations in three different ways: two of these ways are scarcely worth mentioning, except that I wish to show what they are. One of them says that the Etesian winds are the cause of the swelling of the river, by preventing the Nile from discharging itself into the sea. But frequently the Etesian winds have not blown, yet the Nile produces the same effects; besides, if the Etesian winds were the cause, all other rivers that flow opposite to the same winds, must of necessity be equally affected and in the same manner as the Nile; and even so much the more, as they are less and have weaker currents: yet there are many rivers in Syria, and many in Libya, which are not all affected as the Nile is. 21. The second opinion shows still more ignorance than the former, but, if I may so say, is more marvellous. It says that the Nile, flowing from the ocean, produces this effect; and that the ocean flows all round the earth. 22. The third way of resolving this difficulty is by far the most specious, but most untrue. For by saying that the Nile flows from melted snow, it says nothing, for this river flows from Libya through the middle of Ethiopia and discharges itself into Egypt; how therefore, since it runs from a very hot to a colder region, can it flow from snow? Many reasons will readily occur to men of good understanding, to show the improbability of its flowing from snow. The first and chief proof is derived from the winds, which blow hot from those regions: the second is, that the country, destitute of rain, is always free from ice; but after snow has fallen, it must of necessity rain within five days; so that if snow fell, it would also rain in these regions. In the third place, the inhabitants become black from the excessive heat; kites and swallows continue there all the year; and the cranes, to avoid the cold of Scythia, migrate to these parts as winter quarters: if then ever so little snow fell in this country through which the Nile flows, and from which it derives its source, none of these things would happen, as necessity proves. 23. But the person who speaks about the ocean, since he has referred his account to some obscure fable, produces no conviction at all; for I do not know any river called the Ocean; but suppose that Homer, or some other ancient poet, having invented the name, introduced it into poetry.

24. Yet if, after I have found fault with the opinions advanced *by others,* it becomes me to declare my own concerning so obscure a question, I will describe what, in my opinion, causes the Nile to overflow in summer. During the winter season, the sun, being driven by storms from his former course, retires to the upper parts of Libya: this in few words comprehends the whole matter; for it is natural that that country which this god is nearest to, and over which he is, should be most in want of water, and that the native river streams should be dried up. 25. But to explain my meaning more at length, the case is this: the sun passing over the upper parts of Libya, produces the following effect; as the air in these regions is always serene, and the soil always hot, since there are no cold winds passing over, he produces just the same effect, as he usually does in the summer, when passing through the middle of the firmament; for he attracts the water to himself, and having so attracted it,

throws it back upon the higher regions; there the winds, taking it up and dispersing it, melt it: and therefore, with good reason, the winds that blow from this country, from the south and south-west, are by far the most rainy of all. I do not think, however, that the sun on each occasion discharges the annual supply of water from the Nile, but that some remains about him. When, however, the winter grows mild, the sun returns again to the middle of the heavens, and from that time attracts water equally from all rivers. Up to this time those other rivers, having much rain-water mixed with them, flow with full streams: but as the country has been watered by showers and torn up by torrents, when the showers fail them, and they are attracted in summer by the sun, they become weak, but the Nile, being destitute of rain, and attracted by the sun, is the only river that with good reason flows much weaker, than usual at this time, than in summer; for in summer it is attracted equally with all other waters, but in winter it alone is hard pressed. Thus I consider that the sun is the cause of these things. 26. The same cause in my opinion occasions also the dryness of the air in these parts, the sun scorching every thing in his passage: in consequence of this, heat always prevails in the upper parts of Libya. But if the order of the seasons were changed, and that part of the heaven where the north and winter are now placed could be made the position of the south and mid-day, and the north were transferred to the south, if such a change were made, the sun, driven from the middle of the firmament by the winter and the north wind, would go to the upper parts of Europe, as he now does through those of Libya; and I suppose he would produce in his passage the same effects on the Ister, which he now does on the Nile. 27. Then with regard to the reason why no breezes blow from the Nile; my opinion is, that it is very improbable they should blow from hot countries, for they generally blow from some cold one.

28. But I leave these things as they are, and as they were at the beginning. With respect to the sources of the Nile, no man of all the Egyptians, Libyans, or Grecians with whom I have conversed, ever pretended to know any thing; except the registrar of Minerva's treasury at Sais in Egypt. He indeed seemed to be trifling with me, when he said he knew perfectly well; yet his account was as follows: "That there are two mountains rising into a sharp peak, situated between the city of Syene in Thebais and Elephantine; the names of these mountains are, the one Crophi, the other Mophi; that the sources of the Nile, which are bottomless, flow from between these mountains; and that half of the water flows over Egypt, and to the north, the other half over Ethiopia and the south. That the fountains of the Nile are bottomless, he said, Psammitichus king of Egypt proved by experiment; for having caused a line to be twisted many thousand fathoms in length, he let it down, but could not find a bottom." Such then was the opinion the registrar gave, if indeed he spoke the real truth; *proving,* in my opinion, that there are strong whirlpools and an eddy here; so that the water beating against the rocks, a sounding line, when let down, cannot reach the bottom. . . .

35. I now proceed to give a more particular account of Egypt; it

possesses more wonders than any other country, and exhibits works greater than can be described, in comparison with all other regions; therefore more must be said about it. The Egyptians, besides having a climate peculiar to themselves, and a river differing in its nature from all other rivers, have adopted customs and usages in almost every respect different from the rest of mankind. Amongst them the women attend markets and traffic, but the men stay at home and weave. Other nations, in weaving, throw the wool upwards; the Egyptians, downwards. The men carry burdens on their heads; the women, on their shoulders. The women stand up when they make water, but the men sit down. They ease themselves in their houses, but eat out of doors; alleging that, whatever is indecent, though necessary, ought to be done in private; but what is not indecent, openly. No woman can serve the office for any god or goddess; but men are employed for both offices. Sons are not compelled to support their parents unless they choose, but daughters are compelled to do so, whether they choose or not. 36. In other countries the priests of the gods wear long hair; in Egypt they have it shaved. With other men it is customary in mourning for the nearest relations to have their heads shorn; the Egyptians, on occasions of death, let the hair grow both on the head and face, though till then used to shave. Other men live apart from beasts; but the Egyptians live with them. Others feed on wheat and barley, but it is a very great disgrace for an Egyptian to make food of them; but they make bread from spelt, which some call zea. They knead the dough with their feet; but mix clay and take up dung with their hands. Other men leave their private parts as they are formed by nature, except those who have learnt otherwise from them; but the Egyptians are circumcised. Every man wears two garments; the women, but one. Other men fasten the rings and sheets of their sails outside; but the Egyptians, inside. The Grecians write and cipher, moving the hand from left to right; but the Egyptians, from right to left: and doing so they say they do it right-ways, and the Greeks left-ways. They have two sorts of letters, one of which is called sacred, the other common.

37. They are of all men the most excessively attentive to the worship of the gods, and observe the following ceremonies. They drink from cups of brass, which they scour every day; nor is this custom practised by some and neglected by others, but all do it. They wear linen garments, constantly fresh washed, and they pay particular attention to this. They are circumcised for the sake of cleanliness, thinking it better to be clean than handsome. The priests shave their whole body every third day, that neither lice nor any other impurity may be found upon them when engaged in the service of the gods. The priests wear linen only, and shoes of byblus, and are not permitted to wear any other garments, or other shoes. They wash themselves in cold water twice every day, and twice every night; and, in a word, they use a number of ceremonies. On the other hand, they enjoy no slight advantages, for they do not consume or expend any of their private property; but sacred food is cooked for them, and a great quantity of beef and geese is allowed each of them every day, and wine from the grape is given them; but they may not taste of fish. Beans the

Egyptians do not sow at all in their country, neither do they eat those that happen to grow there, nor taste them when dressed. The priests, indeed, abhor the sight of that pulse, accounting it impure. The service of each god is performed, not by one, but by many priests, of whom one is chief priest; and, when any one of them dies, his son is put in his place. 38. The male kine they deem sacred to Epaphus, and to that end prove them in the following manner. If the examiner finds one black hair upon him, he adjudges him to be unclean; and one of the priests appointed for this purpose makes this examination, both when the animal is standing up and lying down; and he draws out the tongue, to see if it is pure as to the prescribed marks, which I shall mention in another part of my history. He also looks at the hairs of his tail, whether they grow naturally. If the beast is found pure in all these respects, he marks it by rolling a piece of byblus round the horns, and then having put on it some sealing earth, he impresses it with his signet; and so they drive him away. Any one who sacrifices one that is unmarked, is punished with death. In this manner the animal is proved. 39. The established mode of sacrifice is this: having led the victim, properly marked, to the altar where they intend to sacrifice, they kindle a fire. Then having poured wine upon the altar, near the victim, and having invoked the god, they kill it; and after they have killed it, they cut off the head; but they flay the body of the animal: then having pronounced many imprecations on the head, they who have a market and Grecian merchants dwelling amongst them, carry it there, and having so done, they usually sell it; but they who have no Grecians amongst them, throw it into the river: and they pronounce the following imprecations on the head: "If any evil is about to befall either those that now sacrifice, or Egypt in general, may it be averted on this head." With respect, then, to the heads of beasts that are sacrificed, and to the making libations of wine, all the Egyptians observe the same customs in all sacrifices alike: and from this custom no Egyptian will taste of the head of any animal. . . .

Book VII. Polymnia

When the news of the battle fought at Marathon reached Darius, son of Hystaspes, who was before much exasperated with the Athenians on account of the attack upon Sardis, he then became much more incensed, and was still more eager to prosecute the war against Greece. Having therefore immediately sent messengers to the several cities, he enjoined them to prepare an army, imposing on each a much greater number than they had furnished before, and ships, horses, corn, and transports. When these orders were proclaimed round about, Asia was thrown into agitation during the space of three years, the bravest men enrolled and prepared for the purpose of invading Greece. But in the fourth year the Egyptians, who had been subdued by Cambyses, revolted from the Persians; whereupon Darius only became more eager to march against both. 2. When Darius was preparing for his expeditions against Egypt and Athens, a violent dissension arose between his sons concerning the sovereignty; for by the customs of the Persians he was obliged to nominate his successor, before he marched out on any expedition. Now Darius, even before he became king, had three sons born to him by his former wife, the daughter of Gobryas; and after his accession to the throne, four others by Atossa, daughter of Cyrus. Of the former, Artabazanes was the eldest; of those after born, Xerxes: and these two not being of the same mother, were at variance. Artabazanes *urged* that he was the eldest of all the sons, and that it was the established usage among all men that the eldest son should succeed to the sovereignty: on the other hand, Xerxes *alleged* that he was son of Atossa, daughter of Cyrus, and that it was Cyrus who had acquired freedom for the Persians. 3. When Darius had not yet declared his opinion, at this very conjuncture, Demaratus, son of Ariston, happened to come up to Susa, having been deprived of the kingly office at Sparta, and having imposed on himself a voluntary exile from Lacedaemon. This man, having heard of the difference between the sons of Darius, went to Xerxes, as report says, and advised him to say in addition to what he had already said; that "he was born to Darius after he had become king, and was possessed of the empire of the Perisans; whereas Artabazanes was born to Darius while he was yet a private person; wherefore it was not reasonable or just that any other should possess that dignity in preference to himself, since in Sparta also," Demaratus continued to suggest, "this custom prevailed, that if some children were born before their father became king, and one was born subsequently when he had now come to the throne, this last born son should succeed to the kingdom." Xerxes having availed himself to the suggestion of Demaratus, Darius, acknowledging that he said what was just, declared him king. But it appears to me that even without this suggestion Xerxes would have been made king; for Atossa had unbounded influence. 4. Darius, having appointed Xerxes to be king over the Persians, prepared to march. However after these things, and in the year after the revolt of Egypt it happened that Darius himself, while he was making preparations, died, having reigned thirty-six years in all; nor was he able to avenge himself either on the Egyptians, who had revolted, or on the Athenians. When Darius was dead, the kingdom devolved on his son Xerxes.

     5. Xerxes, however, was at first by no means inclined to make war against Greece, but he levied forces for the reduction of Egypt. But Mardonius, son of Gobryas, who was cousin to Xerxes, and son of Darius's sister, being present and having the greatest influence with him of all the Persians, constantly held the following language, saying, "Sir, it is not right that the Athenians, having already done much mischief to the Persians, should go unpunished for what they have done. However, for the present, finish the enterprise you have in hand; and when you have quelled the insolence of Egypt, lead your army against Athens; that you may acquire a good reputation among men, and any one for the future may be cautious of marching against your territory." This language was used by him for the purposes of revenge, but he frequently made the following addition to it, that "Europe was a very beautiful country,

and produced all kinds of cultivated trees, and was very fertile, and worthy to be possessed by the king alone of all mortals." 6. He spake thus, because he was desirous of new enterprises, and wished to be himself governor of Greece: in time he effected his purpose, and persuaded Xerxes to do as he advised; for other things happening favourably assisted him in persuading Xerxes. In the first place messengers coming from Thessaly on the part of the Aleuadae, invited the king, with earnest importunity, to invade Greece: these Aleuadae were kings of Thessaly. And in the next place, those of the Pisistratidae, who had gone up to Susa, holding the same language as the Aleuadae, still more eagerly pressed him, having with them Onomacritus, an Athenian, a soothsayer and dispenser of the oracles of Musaeus. For they went *to Susa,* having first reconciled their former enmity *with him.* For Onomacritus had been banished from Athens by Hipparchus, son of Pisistratus, having been detected by Lasus the Hermionian, in the very act of interpolating among the oracles of Musaeus, one importing, that the islands lying off Lemnos would disappear beneath the sea: wherefore Hipparchus banished him, although he had before been very familiar with him. But at that time having gone up with them, whenever he came into the presence of the king, as the Pisistratidae spoke of him in very high terms, he recited some of the oracles; if, however, there was amongst them any that portended misfortune to the barbarians, of these he made no mention; but selecting such as were most favourable, he said it was fated that the Hellespont should be bridged over by a Persian, describing the march. Thus he continually assailed *the king,* rehearsing oracles, as did the Pisistratidae and Aleuadae, by declaring their opinions. 7. When Xerxes was persuaded to make war against Greece, he then, in the second year after the death of Darius, first made an expedition against those who had revolted; and, having subdued them and reduced all Egypt to a worse state of servitude than it was under Darius, he committed the government to Achaemenes, his own brother, and son of Darius. Some time after, Inarus, son of Psammitichus, a Libyan, slew Achaemenes, to whom the government of Egypt was committed.

8. Xerxes, after the reduction of Egypt, when he was about to take in hand the expedition against Athens, convoked an assembly of the principal Persians, that he might both hear their opinions, and himself make known his intentions before them all. When they were assembled Xerxes addressed them as follows: (1.)"Men of Persia, I shall not be the first to introduce this custom among you, but shall adopt it, having received it from my forefathers. For, as I learn from older men, we have never remained inactive since we wrested the sovereign power from the Medes, and Cyrus overthrew Astyages: but the deity thus leads the way, and to us who follow his guidance many things result to our advantage. What deeds Cyrus, and Cambyses, and my father Darius have achieved, and what nations they have added to our empire, no one need mention to you who know them well. But I, since I have succeeded to the throne, have carefully considered this, in what way I may not fall short of my predecessors in this honour, nor acquire less additional power to the Persians.

And on mature consideration, I find that we may at once acquire an increase of glory, and a country not inferior nor poorer, but even more productive than that we now possess; and at the same time that satisfaction and vengeance will accrue to us. Wherefore I have now called you together, that I may communicate to you what I purpose to do. (2.) I intend to throw a bridge over the Hellespont, and to march an army through Europe against Greece, that I may punish the Athenians for the injuries they have done to the Persians and to my father. You have already seen Darius preparing to make war against those people; but he died, and had it not in his power to avenge himself. But I, in his cause and that of the other Persians, will not rest till I have taken and burnt Athens; for they first began by doing acts of injustice against my father and me. First of all having come to Sardis, with Aristagoras the Milesian, our servant on their arrival they burnt down both the groves and the temples. And, secondly, how they treated us on our making a descent on their territory, when Datis and Artaphernes led our forces, you all know well enough. (3.) For these reasons, therefore, I have resolved to make war upon them. And on reflection, I find the following advantages in this course: if we shall subdue them, and their neighbours, who inhabit the country of Pelops the Phrygian, we shall make the Persian territory co-extensive with the air of heaven; nor will the sun look down upon any land that borders on ours; but I, with your assistance, will make them all one territory, marching through the whole of Europe. For I am informed that such is the case; and that no city or nation of the world will remain, which will be able to come to a battle with us, when those whom I have mentioned have been brought into subjection. Thus, both those who are guilty, and those who are not guilty, must equally submit to the yoke of servitude. (4.) But you, by doing what I require, will gratify me exceedingly; when I shall have informed you of the time, it will be the duty of each of you to come promptly. And whosoever shall appear with the best-appointed troops, to him I will give such presents as are accounted most honourable in our country. But that I may not appear to follow my own counsel only, I lay the matter before you, bidding any one of you who wishes, to declare his opinion." Having said this, he ceased.

9. After him Mardonius spoke: "Sir, not only are you the most excellent of all the Persians that have yet been, but even of all that ever shall be; you also, in other respects, have in speaking touched upon the most important topics and the most exact truth, and especially will not suffer the Ionians, who dwell in Europe, to mock us, worthless as they are. For it would indeed be a great indignity, if, having subdued the Sacae, Indians, Ethiopians, and Assyrians, and other nations, many and powerful, which never did the Persians any wrong, but, in order only to enlarge our dominions, we hold them in servitude; and yet shall not avenge ourselves on the Greeks, who were the first to commit injustice. Having what to fear? what confluence of numbers? what power of wealth? (1.) We are acquainted with their manner of fighting; and we are acquainted with their power, that it is weak. We hold their children in subjection, those who dwell within our territories, and are called Ionians,

Aeolians, and Dorians. I myself have made trial of these men already, marching against them at the command of your father; and when I advanced as far as Macedonia, and was within a short distance of reaching Athens itself, no one opposed me in battle. (2.) And yet the Greeks are accustomed, as I am informed, to undertake wars without deliberation, from obstinacy and folly. For when they have declared war against one another, having found out the fairest and most level spot, they go down to it and fight; so that the conquerors depart with great loss, and of the conquered I say nothing at all, for they are utterly destroyed. Whereas, being of the same language, they ought, by the intervention of heralds and ambassadors, to adjust their differences, and in any way rather than by fighting. But if they must needs go to war with each other, they ought to find out where they are each least likely to be conquered, and there try *the issue of a battle.* The Greeks, accordingly, adopting a disadvantageous method, when I marched as far as Macedonia, never ventured so far as to come to a battle. (3.) Will any one, then, O king, have recourse to war, and oppose you, when you lead the multitudes of Asia, and all her ships? In my opinion, indeed, the Grecians will never proceed to such a degree of audacity. But if I should happen to be deceived in my opinion, and they, elated by folly, should come to battle with us, they will learn, that of all men we are the most skilled in war. Let nothing then be untried; for nothing is accomplished of its own self, but all things are usually achieved by men through endeavours." Mardonius, having thus smoothed over the opinion of Xerxes, ceased to speak.

10. The rest of the Persians continuing silent, and not daring to declare an opinion to the one proposed, Artabanus, son of Hystaspes, being uncle to Xerxes, and relying on this, spoke as follows: (1.) "O king, unless opinions opposite to each other are spoken, it is impossible to choose the better, but it becomes necessary to adopt that which has been advanced; whereas, when various opinions have been given, it is possible: just as with unalloyed gold, we cannot distinguish it by itself, but when we have rubbed it by the side of other gold, we do distinguish the better. I warned your father and my brother not to make war upon the Scythians, a people who have no city in any part of their territory; but he hoping to subdue the Scythian nomades, heeded not my advice, and having led an army against them, returned with the loss of many brave men of his army. But you, O king, are about to make war on men far superior to the Scythians; who are said to be most valiant both by sea and land; it is, therefore, right that I should inform you of the danger we have to fear. (2.) You say, that having thrown a bridge over the Hellespont, you will march an army through Europe into Greece; now, it may happen that we shall be worsted either by land or by sea, or even by both; for the people are said to be valiant; and this we may infer, since the Athenians alone destroyed so great an army that invaded the Attic territory, under Datis and Artaphernes. They were not, however, successful in both; but if they should attack us with their fleet, and having obtained a naval victory, should sail to the Hellespont, and destroy the bridge, this surely, O king, were a great danger. (3.) Nor do I found this conjecture on any wisdom of my own, but from the calamity that

once all but befel us, when your father, having joined the shores of the Thracian Bosphorus, and thrown a bridge over the Ister, crossed over to attack the Scythians; then the Scythians used every means to induce the Ionians, to whom the guard of the passage over the Ister had been intrusted, to break up the bridge: and if, at that time, Histiaeus, tyrant of Miletus, had assented to the opinion of the other tyrants, and had not opposed it, the power of the Persians would have been utterly ruined. It is dreadful even to hear it said, that the whole power of the king depended on a single man. (4.) Do not, therefore, willingly expose yourself to any such danger, when there is no necessity; but be persuaded by me; dismiss this assembly; and hereafter, whenever it shall seem fit to you, having considered with yourself, proclaim what appears to you to be most advantageous. For to deliberate well, I find is the greatest gain. For if the result prove unfortunate, the matter has, nevertheless, been well deliberated on, but our deliberation is defeated by fortune; but he who has deliberated badly, if fortune attend him, has met with a success he had no right to expect, but has, nevertheless, formed bad plans. (5.) Do you see how the deity strikes with his thunder the tallest animals, and suffers them not to be ostentatious, but the smaller ones do not at all offend him? Do you see how he ever hurls his bolts against the loftiest buildings, and trees of the like kind? For the deity is wont to cut off every thing that is too highly exalted. Thus, even a large army is often defeated by a small one, in such manner as this: when the deity, through jealousy, strikes them with terror or lightning, whereby they perish in a manner unworthy of themselves; for the deity will not suffer any one but himself to have high thoughts. (6.) Again, to hasten any matter produces failures from whence great losses are wont to follow; but in delay there are advantages, which, though not immediately apparent, yet one may discover after a time. This, then, O king, is the advice I give you. (7.) But do you, Mardonius, son of Gobryas, cease to speak vain words of the Grecians, who do not deserve to be spoken lightly of. For by calumniating the Greeks, you urge the king himself to lead an army against them; and to this end you appear to me to exert all your efforts. But may it not so be. For calumny is the worst of evils; in it there are two who commit injustice, and one who is injured: for he who calumniates another, acts unjustly by accusing one that is not present: and he acts unjustly, who is persuaded before he has learnt the exact truth; and he that is absent when the charge is made, is thus doubly injured, being calumniated by the one, and by the other deemed to be base. (8.) But if, at all events, it must needs be, that war must be made on these people, come, let the king himself remain in the abodes of the Persians; let both of us risk our children, and do you lead the expedition, having selected what men you choose, and taken with you as large a force as you think fit; and if matters succeed to the king in the manner you say, let my children be put to death, and me also with them. But if the event prove such as I foretel, then let your children suffer the same, and you also with them, if ever you return. If, however, you are unwilling to submit to these terms, and will at all events lead an army against Greece, I affirm, that some of those who are left in this country, will hear that Mardonius, having brought some great disaster upon the Persians, and being torn in pieces by dogs and birds either in the territory of the Athenians, or in that of the Lacedaemonians, if not sooner on his march, has discovered against what sort of men you now persuade the king to make war."

11. Artabanus thus spoke, but Xerxes, inflamed with anger, answered as follows: "Artabanus, you are my father's brother; this will protect you from receiving the just recompence of your foolish words. However I inflict this disgrace upon you, base and cowardly as you are, not to accompany me in my expedition against Greece, but to remain here with the women; and I, without your assistance, will accomplish all that I have said. For I should not be sprung from Darius, son of Hystaspes, son of Arsames, son of Ariaramnes, son of Teispes, son of Cyrus, son of Cambyses, son of Achaemenes, if I did not avenge myself on the Athenians, knowing full well that if we continue quiet, yet they will not, but will even invade our territories, if we may conjecture from what has been already done by them, who have both burnt Sardis, and advanced into Asia. Wherefore it is not possible for either party to retreat, but the alternative lies before us to do or suffer: so that all these dominions must fall under the power of the Grecians, or all theirs under that of the Persians; for there is no medium in this enmity. It is therefore honourable for us, who have first suffered, to take revenge, that I may also be informed of the danger to which I shall expose myself, by marching against those men, whom Pelops the Phrygian, who was a slave of my ancestors, so completely subdued, that even to this day the people themselves and their country are called after the name of the conqueror."

12. These things were said so far: But afterwards night came on, and the opinion of Artabanus occasioned uneasiness to Xerxes, and deliberating with himself during the night, he clearly discovered that it would not be to his interest to make war on Greece: having thus altered his resolution, he fell asleep; and some time in the night, he saw the following vision, as is related by the Persians. Xerxes imagined that a tall and handsome man stood by him and said: "Do you then change your mind, O Persian, *and resolve* not to lead an army against Greece, after having ordered the Persians to assemble their forces? You do not well to change your resolution, nor is there any man who will agree with you. Therefore pursue that course which you resolved upon in the day." Xerxes thought that the man, having pronounced these words, flew away. 13. When day dawned, he paid no attention to this dream, but having assembled those Persians whom he had before convened, he addressed them as follows: "Pardon me, O Persians, that I suddenly change my plans; for I have not yet attained to the highest perfection of judgment, and they who persuade me to this enterprise, are never absent from me. When therefore I heard the opinion of Artabanus, my youth immediately boiled with rage against him, so that I threw out words more unbecoming than I ought to a person of his years. But now, conscious of my error, I will follow his advice: since therefore I have changed my resolution, *and determined* not to make war

against Greece, do you remain quiet." The Persians, when they heard this, being transported with joy, did him homage. 14. When night came, the same dream, again standing by Xerxes as he slept, said: "Son of Darius, you have then openly renounced, in the presence of the Persians, the intended expedition; and make no account of my words, as if you had not heard them from any one. Be well assured, however, of this, that unless you immediately undertake this expedition, this will be the consequence to you; as you have become great and powerful in a short time, so you shall become low again in an equally short space." 15. Xerxes, being alarmed by this vision, rushed from his bed and sent a messenger to call Artabanus; and when he came, Xerxes spoke to him as follows: "Artabanus, I on the moment was not in my senses, when I used hasty words to you in return for your good advice; however, after no long time I repented and acknowledged that those measures which you suggested ought to be adopted by me. I am not, however, able to perform them, though desirous of doing so; for after I had altered my resolution, and acknowledged my error, a dream frequently presents itself to me, by no means approving of my so doing; and it has just now vanished, after threatening me. If, then, it is a deity who sends this dream, and it is his pleasure that an expedition against Greece should at all events take place, this same dream will also flit before you, and give the same injunction as to me. This I think will happen, if you should take all my apparel, and having put it on, should afterwards sit on my throne, and then go to sleep in my bed." 16. Xerxes thus addressed him; but Artabanus not obeying the first order, as he did not think himself worthy to sit on the royal throne, when he was at last compelled, did as he was desired, after he had spoken as follows. (1.) "I deem it an equal merit, O king, to form good plans, and to be willing to yield to one who gives good advice: and though both of these qualities attach to you, the converse of wicked men leads you astray; just as blasts of wind falling on the sea, which of all things is the most useful to mankind, do not suffer it to follow its proper nature. As for me, grief did not so much vex me at hearing your reproaches, as that when two opinions were proposed by the Persians, one tending to increase their arrogance, the other to check it, and to show how hurtful it is to teach the mind to be constantly seeking for more than we already possess; that, when these two opinions were proposed, you should choose that which is more dangerous both to yourself and the Persians. (2.) Now, however, after you have changed to the better resolution, you say, that since you have given up the expedition against the Greeks, a dream has come to you, sent by some god, which forbids you to abandon the enterprise. But these things, my son, are not divine, for dreams which wander among men, are such as I will explain to you, being many years older than you are. Those visions of dreams most commonly hover around men, *respecting things* which one has thought of during the day; and we, during the preceding days, have been very much busied about this expedition. (3.) If, however, this is not such as I judge, but has something divine in it, you have correctly summed up the whole in few words; then let it appear and give the same injunction to me as to you: and it ought not to appear to me any the more for my having your apparel than my own; nor the more because I go to sleep on your bed than on my own; if indeed it will appear at all. For that which has appeared to you in your sleep, whatever it be, can never arrive to such a degree of simplicity as to suppose that when it sees me, it is you, conjecturing from your apparel. But if it shall hold me in contempt and not deign to appear to me, whether I be clothed in your robes or in my own; and if it shall visit you again, this indeed would deserve consideration: for if it should repeatedly visit you, I should myself confess it to be divine. If, however, you have resolved that so it should be, and it is not possible to avert this, but I must needs sleep in your bed, well, when this has been done, let it appear also to me. But till that time I shall persist in my present opinion." 17. Artabanus, having spoken thus, and hoping to show that Xerxes had said nothing of any moment, did what was ordered: and having put on the apparel of Xerxes and sat in the royal throne, when he afterwards went to bed, the same dream which had appeared to Xerxes, came to him when he was asleep, and standing over Artabanus, spoke as follows: "Art thou, then, the man who dissuadeth Xerxes from invading Greece, as if thou wert very anxious for him? But neither hereafter nor at present shalt thou escape unpunished for endeavouring to avert what is fated to be. What Xerxes must suffer if he continues disobedient, has been declared to him himself." 18. Artabanus imagined that the dream uttered these threats, and was about to burn out his eyes with hot irons. He therefore, having uttered a loud shriek, leapt up, and seating himself by Xerxes, when he had related all the particulars of the vision in the dream, spoke to him in this manner: "I, O king, being a man who have seen already many and great powers overthrown by inferior ones, would not suffer you to yield entirely to youth; knowing how mischievous it is to desire much, calling to mind the expedition of Cyrus against the Massagetae, how it fared, and calling to mind also that of Cambyses against the Ethiopians, and having accompanied Darius in the invasion of Scythia, knowing all these things, I was of opinion, that if you remained quiet, you must be pronounced happy by all men. But since some divine impulse has sprung up, and, as it seems, some heaven-sent destruction impends over the Greeks, I myself am converted and change my opinion. Do you, then, make known to the Persians the intimation sent by the deity, and command them to follow the orders first given by you for the preparations; and act so, that, since the deity permits nothing on your part may be wanting." When he had thus spoken, both being carried away by the vision, as soon as it was day Xerxes acquainted the Persians with what had happened; and Artabanus, who before was the only man who greatly opposed the expedition, now as openly promoted it.

19. After this, when Xerxes was resolved to undertake the expedition, another vision appeared to him in his sleep, which the magi, when they heard it, interpreted to relate to the whole world, and *to signify* that all mankind should serve him. The vision was as follows: Xerxes imagined that he was crowned with the sprig of an olive-tree, and that branches from this olive covered the whole earth; and that afterwards the crown that was placed on his head disappeared. The magi having given this interpretation, every one

of the Persians, who were then assembled, departed immediately to his own government, and used all diligence to execute what had been ordered; every man hoping to obtain the proposed reward: Xerxes thus levied his army, searching out every region of the continent. . . .

138. But I return to my former subject. This expedition of the king was nominally directed against Athens, but was really sent against all Greece. The Greeks, however, though they had heard of it long beforehand, were not all affected alike. For those who had given earth and water to the Persian, felt confident that they should suffer no harm from the barbarian; but those who had refused to give them, were in great consternation, since the ships in Greece were not sufficient in number to resist the invader, and many were unwilling to engage in the war, and were much inclined to side with the Medes. 139. And here I feel constrained by necessity to declare my opinion, although it may excite the envy of most men; however, I will not refrain from expressing how the truth appears to me to be. If the Athenians, terrified with the impending danger, had abandoned their country; or not having abandoned it, but remaining in it, had given themselves up to Xerxes, no other people would have attempted to resist the king at sea. If, then, no one had opposed Xerxes by sea, the following things must have occurred on land. Although many lines of walls had been built by the Peloponnesians across the Isthmus, yet the Lacedaemonians, being abandoned by the allies, (not willingly, but by necessity, they being taken by the barbarian city by city,) would have been left alone; and being left alone, after having displayed noble deeds, would have died nobly. They would either have suffered thus, or before that, seeing the rest of the Greeks siding with the Medes, would have made terms with Xerxes; and so, in either case, Greece would have become subject to the Persians; for I am unable to discover what would have been the advantage of the walls built across the Isthmus, if the king had been master of the sea. Any one, therefore, who should say that the Athenians were the saviours of Greece, would not deviate from the truth; for to whichever side they turned, that must have preponderated. But having chosen that Greece should continue free, they were the people who roused the rest of the Greeks who did not side with the Medes, and who, next to the gods, repulsed the king. Neither did alarming oracles, that came from Delphi, and inspired them with terror, induce them to abandon Greece; but, standing their ground, they had courage to await the invader of their country. . . .

201. King Xerxes, then, encamped in the Trachinian territory of Malis, and the Greeks in the pass. This spot is called by most of the Greeks, Thermopylae, but by the inhabitants and neighbours, Pylae. Both parties, then, encamped in these places. The one was in possession of all the parts towards the north, as far as Trachis; and the others, of the parts which stretch towards the south and meridian, on this continent.

202. The following were the Greeks who awaited the Persian in this position. Of Spartans three hundred heavy-armed men; of Tegeans and Mantineans one thousand, half of each; from Orchomenus in Arcadia one hundred and twenty; and from the rest of Arcadia one thousand, there were so many Arcadians; from Corinth four hundred; from Phlius two hundred

men, and from Mycenae eighty. These came from Peloponnesus. From Boeotia, of Thespians seven hundred, and of Thebans four hundred. 203. In addition to these, the Opuntian Locrians, being invited, came with all their forces, and a thousand Phocians. For the Greeks themselves had invited them, representing by their ambassadors that "they had arrived as forerunners of the others, and that the rest of the allies might be daily expected; that the sea was protected by them, being guarded by the Athenians, the Aeginetae, and others, who were appointed to the naval service; and that they had nothing to fear, for that it was not a god who invaded Greece, but a man; and that there never was, and never would be, any mortal who had not evil mixed with *his prosperity* from his very birth; and to the greatest of them the greatest *reverses happen.* That it must, therefore, needs be, that he who is marching against us, being a mortal, will be disappointed in his expectation." They, having heard this, marched with assistance to Trachis. 204. These nations had separate generals for their several cities; but the one most admired, and who commanded the whole army, was a Lacedaemonian, Leonidas, son of Anaxandrides, son of Leon, son of Eurycratides, son of Anaxander, son of Eurycrates, son of Polydorus, son of Alcamenes, son of Teleclus, son of Archelaus, son of Agesilaus, son of Doryssus, son of Leobotes, son of Echestratus, son of Agis, son of Eurysthenes, son of Aristodemus, son of Aristomachus, son of Cleodaeus, son of Hyllus, son of Hercules; who had unexpectedly succeeded to the throne of Sparta. 205. For as he had two elder brothers, Cleomenes and Dorieus, he was far from any thought of the kingdom. However, Clomenes having died without male issue, and Dorieus being no longer alive, having ended his days in Sicily, the kingdom thus devolved upon Leonidas; both because he was older than Cleombrotus (for he was the youngest son of Anaxandrides,) and also because he had married the daughter of Cleomenes. He then marched to Thermopylae, having chosen the three hundred men allowed by law, and such as had children. On his march he took with him the Thebans, whose numbers I have already reckoned, and whom Leontiades, son of Eurymachus, commanded. For this reason Leonidas was anxious to take with him the Thebans alone of all the Greeks, because they were strongly accused of favouring the Medes: he, therefore, summoned them to the war, wishing to know whether they would send their forces with him, or would openly renounce the alliance of the Grecians. But they, though otherwise minded, sent assistance. 206. The Spartans sent these troops first with Leonidas, in order that the rest of the allies, seeing them, might take the field, and might not go over to the Medes, if they heard that they were delaying. But afterwards, for the Carnean festival was then an obstacle to them, they purposed, when they had kept the feast, to leave a garrison in Sparta, and to march immediately with their whole strength. The rest of the confederates likewise intended to act in the same manner; for the Olympic games occurred at the same period as these events. As they did not, therefore, suppose that the engagement at Thermopylae would so soon be decided, they despatched an advance-guard. Thus, then, they intended to do.

207. The Greeks at Thermopylae, when the Persian came near the pass, being alarmed, consulted about a retreat; accordingly, it seemed best to the other Peloponnesians to retire to Peioponnesus, and guard the Isthmus; but Leonidas, perceiving the Phocians and Locrians very indignant at this proposition, determined to stay there, and to despatch messengers to the cities, desiring them to come to their assistance, as being too few to repel the army of the Medes. 208. While they were deliberating on these matters, Xerxes sent a scout on horseback, to see how many they were, and what they were doing. For while he was still in Thessaly, he had heard that a small army had been assembled at that spot, and as to their leaders, that they were Lacedaemonians, and Leonidas, who was of the race of Hercules. When the horseman rode up to the camp, he reconnoitred, and saw not indeed the whole camp, for it was not possible that they should be seen who were posted within the wall, which, having rebuilt, they were now guarding: but he had a clear view of those on the outside, whose arms were piled in front of the wall. At this time the Lacedaemonians happened to be posted outside; and some of the men he saw performing gymnastic exercises, and others combing their hair. On beholding this he was astonished, and ascertained their number; and having informed himself of every thing accurately, he rode back at his leisure, for no one pursued him, and he met with general contempt. On his return he gave an account to Xerxes of all that he had seen. 209. When Xerxes heard this, he could not comprehend the truth, that the Grecians were preparing to be slain and to slay to the utmost of their power. But, as they appeared to behave in a ridiculous manner, he sent for Demaratus, son of Ariston, who was then in the camp; and when he was come into his presence, Xerxes questioned him as to each particular, wishing to understand what the Lacedaemonians were doing. Demaratus said, "You before heard me, when we were setting out against Greece, speak of these men; and when you heard, you treated me with ridicule, though I told you in what way I foresaw these matters would issue. For it is my chief aim, O king, to adhere to the truth in your presence; hear it, therefore, once more. These men have come to fight with us for the pass, and are now preparing themselves to do so. For such is their custom, when they are going to hazard their lives, then they dress their heads. But be assured, if you conquer these men, and those that remain in Sparta, there is no other nation in the world that will dare to raise their hands against you, O king. For you are now to engage with the noblest kingdom and city of all amongst the Greeks, and with the most valiant men." What was said seemed very incredible to Xerxes, and he asked again, "how, being so few in number, they could contend with his army." He answered, "O king, deal with me as with a liar, if these things do not turn out as I say."

210. By saying this he did not convince Xerxes. He therefore let four days pass, constantly expecting that they would betake themselves to flight. But on the fifth day, as they had not retreated, but appeared to him to stay through arrogance and rashness, he being enraged, sent the Medes and Cissians against them, with orders to take them alive, and bring them into his

presence. When the Medes bore down impetuously upon the Greeks, many of them fell; others followed to the charge, and were not repulsed, though they suffered greatly. But they made it evident to every one, and not least of all to the king himself, that they were indeed many men, but few soldiers. The engagement lasted through the day. 211. When the Medes were roughly handled, they thereupon retired; and the Persians whom the king called "Immortal," and whom IIydarnes commanded, taking their place, advanced to the attack; thinking that they indeed should easily settle the business. But when they engaged with the Grecians, they succeeded no better than the Medic troops, but just the same, as they fought in a narrow space, and used shorter spears than the Greeks, and were unable to avail themselves of their numbers. The Lacedaemonians fought memorably both in other respects, showing that they knew how to fight with men who knew not, and whenever they turned their backs, they retreated in close order: but the barbarians seeing them retreat, followed with a shout and clamour; then they, being overtaken, wheeled round so as to front the barbarians, and having faced about, overthrew an inconceivable number of the Persians; and then some few of the Spartans themselves fell. So that when the Persians were unable to gain any thing in their attempt on the pass, by attacking in troops and in every possible manner, they retired. 212. It is said that during these onsets of the battle, the king, who witnessed them, thrice sprang from his throne, being alarmed for his army. Thus they strove at that time. On the following day the barbarians fought with no better success; for considering that the Greeks were few in number, and expecting that they were covered with wounds, and would not be able to raise their heads against them any more, they renewed the contest. But the Greeks were marshalled in companies and according to their several nations, and each fought in turn, except only the Phocians, they were stationed at the mountain to guard the pathway. When therefore the Persians found nothing different from what they had seen on the preceding day, they retired.

213. While the king was in doubt what course to take in the present state of affairs, Ephialtes, son of Eurydemus, a Malian, obtained an audience of him, expecting that he should receive a great reward from the king, and informed him of the path which leads over the mountain to Thermopylae; and by that means caused the destruction of those Greeks who were stationed there. But afterwards, fearing the Lacedaemonians, he fled to Thessaly; and when he had fled, a price was set on his head by the Pylagori, when the Amphictyons were assembled at Pylae. But some time after, he went down to Anticyra, and was killed by Athenades, a Trachinian. This Athenades killed him for another reason, which I shall mention in a subsequent part of my history; he was however rewarded none the less by the Lacedaemonians. . . .

217. Along this path, thus situate, the Persians, having crossed the Asopus, marched all night, having on their right the mountains of the Oetaeans, and on their left those of the Trachinians; morning appeared, and they were on the summit of the mountain. At this part of the mountain, as I have already mentioned, a thousand heavy-armed Phocians kept guard, to defend

their own country, and to secure the pathway. For the lower pass was guarded by those before mentioned; and the Phocians had voluntarily promised Leonidas to guard the path across the mountain. 218. The Phocians discovered them after they had ascended, in the following manner; for the Persian ascended without being observed, as the whole mountain was covered with oaks; there was a perfect calm, and as was likely, a considerable rustling taking place from the leaves strewn under foot, the Phocians sprung up and put on their arms, and immediately the barbarians made their appearance. But when they saw men clad in armour they were astonished, for, expecting to find nothing to oppose them, they fell in with an army. Thereupon Hydarnes, fearing lest the Phocians might be Lacedaemonians, asked Ephialtes of what nation the troops were; and being accurately informed, he drew up the Persians for battle. The Phocians, when they were hit by many and thick-falling arrows, fled to the summit of the mountain, supposing that they had come expressly to attack them, and prepared to perish. Such was their determination. But the Persians, with Ephialtes and Hydarnes, took no notice of the Phocians, but marched down the mountain with all speed.

219. To those of the Greeks who were at Thermopylae, the augur Megistias, having inspected the sacrifices, first made known the death that would befal them in the morning; certain deserters afterwards came and brought intelligence of the circuit the Persians were taking; these brought the news while it was yet night, and, thirdly, the scouts running down from the heights, as soon as day dawned, *brought the same intelligence.* Upon this the Greeks held a consultation, and their opinions were divided. For some would not hear of abandoning their post, and others opposed that view. After this, when the assembly broke up, some of them departed, and being dispersed betook themselves to their several cities; but others of them prepared to remain there with Leonidas. 220. It is said that Leonidas himself sent them away, being anxious that they should not perish; but that he and the Spartans who were there could not honourably desert the post which they originally came to defend. For my own part, I am rather inclined to think, that Leonidas, when he perceived that the allies were averse and unwilling to share the danger with him, bade them withdraw; but that he considered it dishonourable for himself to depart: on the other hand, by remaining there, great renown would be left for him, and the prosperity of Sparta would not be obliterated. For it had been announced to the Spartans, by the Pythian, when they consulted the oracle concerning this war, as soon as it commenced, "that either Lacedaemon must be overthrown by the barbarians, or their king perish." This answer she gave in hexameter verses to this effect: "To you, O inhabitants of spacious Lacedaemon, either your vast, glorious city shall be destroyed by men sprung from Perseus, or, if not so, the confines of Lacedaemon mourn a king deceased of the race of Hercules. For neither shall the strength of bulls nor of lions withstand him, with force opposed to force; for he has the strength of Zeus; and I say he shall not be restrained, before he has, certainly, obtained one of these for his share." I think, therefore, that Leonidas, considering these things,

and being desirous to acquire glory for the Spartans alone, sent away the allies, rather than that those who went away differed in opinion, and went away in such an unbecoming manner. 221. The following in no small degree strengthens my conviction on this point. For not only *did he send away* the others, but it is certain, that Leonidas also sent away the augur who followed the army, Megistias the Acarnanian, who was said to have been originally descended from Melampus, the same who announced from an inspection of the victims what was about to befal them, in order that he might not perish with them. He, however, though dismissed, did not himself depart, but sent away his son, who served with him in the expedition, being his only child. 222. The allies accordingly, that were dismissed, departed, and obeyed Leonidas; but only the Thespians and the Thebans remained with the Lacedaemonians: the Thebans, indeed, remained unwillingly, and against their inclination, for Leonidas detained them, treating them as hostages; but the Thespians willingly, for they refused to go away and abandon Leonidas and those with him, but remained and died with them. Demophilus, son of Diadromas, commanded them.

223. Xerxes, after he had poured out libations at sun-rise, having waited a short time, began his attack about the time of full market; for he had been so instructed by Ephialtes; for the descent from the mountain is more direct, and the distance much shorter, than the circuit and ascent. The barbarians, therefore, with Xerxes, advanced; and the Greeks with Leonidas, marching out as if for certain death, now advanced much farther than before into the wide part of the defile. For the fortification of the wall had protected them, and they on the preceding days, having taken up their position in the narrow part, there fought. But now engaging outside the narrows, great numbers of the barbarians fell. For the officers of the companies from behind, having scourges, flogged every man, constantly urging them forward; in consequence, many of them falling into the sea, perished, and many more were trampled alive under foot by one another; and no regard was paid to any that perished. For the Greeks, knowing that death awaited them at the hands of those who were going round the mountain, being desperate, and regardless of their own lives, displayed the utmost possible valour against the barbarians. 224. Already were most of their javelins broken, and they had begun to despatch the Persians with their swords. In this part of the struggle fell Leonidas, fighting valiantly, and with him other eminent Spartans, whose names, seeing they were deserving men, I have ascertained; indeed I have ascertained the names of the whole three hundred. On the side of the Persians, also, many other eminent men fell on this occasion, and amongst them two sons of Darius, Abrocomes and Hyperanthes, born to Darius of Phrataguna, daughter of Artanes; but Artanes was brother to king Darius, and son of Hystaspes, son of Arsames. He, when he gave his daughter to Darius, gave him also all his property, as she was his only child. 225. Accordingly, two brothers of Xerxes fell at this spot, fighting for the body of Leonidas, and there was a violent struggle between the Persians and Lacedaemonians, until at last the Greeks rescued it by their valour, and four times repulsed the enemy. Thus the contest

continued until those with Ephialtes came up. When the Greeks heard that they were approaching, from this time the battle was altered. For they retreated to the narrow part of the way, and passing beyond the wall, came and took up their position on the rising ground, all in a compact body, with the exception of the Thebans: the rising ground is at the entrance where the stone lion now stands to the memory of Leonidas. On this spot, while they defended themselves with swords, such as had them still remaining, and their hands and teeth, the barbarians overwhelmed them with missiles, some of them attacking them in front, and having thrown down the wall; and others surrounding and attacking them on every side.

226. Though the Lacedaemonians and Thespians behaved in this manner, yet Dieneces, a Spartan, is said to have been the bravest man. They relate that he made the following remark, before they engaged with the Medes, having heard a Trachinian say, that when the barbarians let fly their arrows, they would obscure the sun by the multitude of their shafts, so great were their numbers: but he, not at all alarmed at this, said, holding in contempt the numbers of the Medes, that "their Trachinian friend told them every thing to their advantage, since if the Medes obscure the sun, they would then have to fight in the shade, and not in the sun." This and other sayings of the same kind they relate that Dieneces, the Lacedaemonians, left as memorials. 227. Next to him, two Lacedaemonian brothers, Alpheus and Maron, sons of Orisiphantus, are said to have distinguished themselves most; and of the Thespians, he obtained the greatest glory whose name was Dithyrambus, son of Harmatides. 228. In honour of the slain, who were buried on the spot where they fell, and of those who died before they who were dismissed by Leonidas went away, the following inscription has been engraved over them: "Four thousand from Peloponnesus once fought on this spot with three hundred myriads." This inscription was made for all; and for the Spartans in particular: "Stranger, go tell the Lacedaemonians, that we lie here, obedient to their commands." This was for the Lacedaemonians; and for the prophet, the following: "This is the monument of the illustrious Megistias, whom once the Medes, having passed the river Sperchius, slew; a prophet, who, at the time well knowing the impending fate, would not abandon the leaders of Sparta." The Amphictyons are the persons who honoured them with these inscriptions and columns, with the exception of the inscription to the prophet; that of the prophet, Megistias, Simonides, son of Leoprepes, caused to be engraved, from personal friendship. . . .

Book VIII. Orania

74. Those at the Isthmus, then, persevered with such zeal, as having now to contend for their all, and as they did not expect to distinguish themselves by their fleet; meanwhile, those at Salamis, having heard of these

things, were alarmed, not fearing so much for themselves as for the Peloponnesus. For some time one man standing by another began to talk in secret, wondering at the imprudence of Eurybiades; till at last *their discontent* broke out openly, and a council was called, and much was said on the same subject. Some said, that they ought to sail for the Peloponnesus, and hazard a battle for that, and not stay and fight for a place already taken by the enemy; but the Athenians, Aeginetae, and Megareans, that they should stay there and defend themsleves. 75. Thereupon, Themistocles, when he saw his opinion was overruled by the Peloponnesians, went secretly out of the council; and having gone out, he despatched a man in a boat to the encampment of the Medes, having instructed him what to say: his name was Sicinnus; and he was a domestic, and preceptor to the children of Themistocles; him, after these events, Themistocles got made a Thespian, when the Thespians augmented the number of their citizens, and gave him a competent fortune. He, then, arriving in the boat, spoke as follows to the generals of the barbarians: "The general of the Athenians has sent me unknown to the rest of the Greeks, (for he is in the interest of the king, and wishes that your affairs may prosper, rather than those of the Greeks,) to inform you, that the Greeks in great consternation are deliberating on flight; and you have now an opportunity of achieving the most glorious of all enterprises, if you do not suffer them to escape. For they do not agree among themselves, nor will they oppose you; but you will see those who are in your interest, and those who are not, fighting with one another." He having delivered this message to them, immediately departed. 76. As these tidings appeared to them worthy of credit, in the first place, they landed a considerable number of Persians on the little island of Psyttalea, lying between Salamis and the continent; and, in the next place, when it was midnight, they got their western wing under weigh, drawing it in a circle towards Salamis, and those who were stationed about Ceos and Cynosura got under weigh and occupied the whole passage as far as Munychia, with their ships. And for this reason they got their ships under weigh, that the Greeks might have no way to escape, but being shut up in Salamis, might suffer punishment for the conflicts at Artemisium; and they landed the Persians at the little island of Psyttalea for this reason, that, when an engagement should take place, as they expected most part of the men and wrecks would be driven thither, (for that island lay in the strait where the engagement was likely to take place,) they might save the one party, and destroy the other. But these things they did in silence, that the enemy might not know what was going on. They therefore made these preparations by night, without taking any rest.

77. I am unable to speak against the oracles as not being true, nor wish to impugn the authority of those that speak clearly, when I look on such occurrences as the following. "When they shall bridge with ships the sacred shore of Artemis with the golden sword, and sea-girt Cynosura, having with mad hope destroyed beautiful Athens, then divine Vengeance shall quench strong Presumption, son of Insolence, when thinking to subvert all things. For brass shall engage with brass, and Ares shall redden the sea with blood. Then the far-thundering son of Cronus and benign victory shall bring a day of

freedom to Greece" *Looking on* such occurrences, and regarding Bacis, who spoke thus clearly, I neither dare myself say anything in contradiction to oracles, nor allow others to do so.

78. There was great altercation between the generals at Salamis: and they did not yet know that the barbarians had surrounded them with their ships; but they supposed that they were in the same place as they had seen them stationed in during the day. 79. While the generals were disputing, Aristides, son of Lysimachus, crossed over from Aegina; he was an Athenian, but had been banished by ostracism; having heard of his manner of life, I consider him to have been the best and most upright man in Athens. This person, standing at the entrance of the council, called Themistocles out, who was not indeed his friend, but his most bitter enemy; yet, from the greatness of the impending danger, he forgot that, and called him, wishing to confer with him; for he had already heard that those from Peloponnesus were anxious to get the ships under weigh for the Isthmus. When Themistocles came out to him, Aristides spoke as follows: "It is right that we should strive, both on other occasions, and particularly on this, which of us shall do the greatest service to our country. I assure you, that to say little or much to the Peloponnesians about sailing from hence, is the same thing; for I, an eye-witness, tell you, now, even if they would, neither the Corinthians, nor Eurybiades himself, will be able to sail away; for we are on all sides enclosed by the enemy. Go in therefore, and acquaint them with this." 80. He answered as follows: "You both give very useful advice, and have brought good news; for you are come yourself as an eye-witness of what I wished should happen. Know, then, that what has been done by the Medes, proceeds from me. For it was necessary, since the Greeks would not willingly come to an engagement, that they should be compelled to it against their will. But do you, since you come bringing good news, announce it to them yourself, for if I tell them, I shall appear to speak from my own invention, and shall not persuade them, as if the barbarians were doing no such thing. But do you go in, and inform them how the case is: and when you have informed them, if they are persuaded, so much the better; but if they attach no credit to what you say, it will be the same to us: for they can no longer escape by flight, if, as you say, we are surrounded on all sides." 81. Aristides, going in, gave this account, saving that he came from Aegina, and with difficulty sailed through unperceived by those that were stationed round; for that the whole Grecian fleet was surrounded by the ships of Xerxes. He advised them, therefore, to prepare themselves for their defence. And he, having said this, withdrew; a dispute, however, again arose, for the greater part of the generals gave no credit to the report. 82. While they were still in doubt, there arrived a trireme of Tenians that had deserted, which Panaetius, son of Socimenes, commanded, and which brought an account of the whole truth. For that action the name of the Tenians was engraved on the tripod at Delphi, among those who had defeated the barbarian. With this ship that came over at Salamis, and with the Lemnian before, off Artemisium, the Grecian fleet was made up to the full number of three hundred and eighty ships; for before it wanted two of that number.

83. When the account given by the Tenians was credited by the Greeks, they prepared for an engagement. Day dawned, and when they had mustered the marines, Themistocles, above all the others, harangued them most eloquently. His speech was entirely taken up in contrasting better things with worse, exhorting them to choose the best of all those things which depended on the nature and condition of man. Having finished his speech, he ordered them to go on board their ships: they accordingly were going on board, when the trireme from Aegina, which had gone to fetch the Aeacidae, returned. Thereupon the Greeks got all their ships under weigh. 84. When they were under weigh, the barbarians immediately fell upon them. Now all the other Greeks began to back water and made for the shore; but Aminias of Pallene, an Athenian, being carried onwards, attacked a ship; and his ship becoming entangled with the other, and the crew not being able to clear, the rest thereupon coming to the assistance of Aminias, engaged. Thus the Athenians say the battle commenced; but the Aeginetae affirm, that the ship which went to Aegina to fetch the Aeacidea, was the first to begin. This is also said, that a phantom of a woman appeared to them, and that on her appearance she cheered them on, so that the whole fleet of the Greeks heard her, after she had first reproached them in these words: "Dastards, how long will you back water?" 85. Opposite the Athenians the Phoenicians were drawn up, for they occupied the wing towards Eleusis and westward; opposite the Lacedaemonians, the Ionians occupied the wing towards the east and the Piraeus. Of these some few behaved ill on purpose, in compliance with the injunctions of Themistocles; but most of them, not so. I am able to mention the names of several captains of triremes who took Grecian ships; but I shall make no use of them except of Theomestor, son of Androdamas, and Phylacus, son of Histiaeus, both Samians. I mention these two only for this reason, because Theomestor, on account of this exploit, was made tyrant of Samos by the appointment of the Persians; and Phylacus was inscribed as a benefactor of the king, and a large tract of land was given him. The benefactors of the king are called in the Persian language, Orosangae. Such was the case with regard to these men. 86. The greater part of the ships were run down at Salamis; some being destroyed by the Athenians, others by the Aeginetae. For as the Greeks fought in good order, in line, but the barbarians were neither properly formed nor did any thing with judgment, such an event as did happen, was likely to occur. However, they were and proved themselves to be far braver on this day than off Euboea, every one exerting himself vigorously, and dreading Xerxes; for each thought that he himself was observed by the king.

87. As regards the rest, of some of them I am unable to say with certainty how each of the barbarians or Greeks fought; but with respect to Artemisia, the following incident occurred, by which she obtained still greater credit with the king. For when the king's forces were in great confusion, at that moment the ship of Artemisia was chased by an Attic ship, and she not being able to escape, for before her were other friendly ships, and her own happened to be nearest the enemy, she resolved to do that, which succeeded in the attempt. For being pursued by the Athenian, she bore down upon a friendly

ship, manned by Calyndians, and with Damasithymus himself, king of the Calyndians, on board; whether she had any quarrel with him while they were at the Hellespont, I am unable to say, or whether she did it on purpose, or whether the ship of the Calyndians happened by chance to be in her way; however, she ran it down, and sunk it, and by good fortune gained a double advantage to herself. For the captain of the Attic ship, when he saw her bearing down on a ship of the barbarians, concluding Artemisia's ship to be either a Grecian, or one that had deserted from the enemy and was assisting them, turned aside and attacked others. 88. In the first place, this was the result to her, that she escaped and did not perish; and in the next, it fell out that she having done an injury, in consequence of it, became still more in favour with Xerxes. For it is said, that Xerxes looking on observed her ship making the attack, and that some near him said: "Sire, do you see Artemisia, how well she fights, and has sunk one of the enemy's ships?" Whereupon he asked, if it was in truth the exploit of Artemisia: they answered, "that they knew the ensign of her ship perfectly well;" but they thought that it was an enemy that was sunk. For, as has been mentioned, other things turned out fortunately for her, and this in particular, that no one of the crew of the Calyndian ship was saved so as to accuse her. And it is related that Xerxes said in answer to their remarks: "My men have become women, and my women, men." They relate that Xerxes said this.

89. In this battle perished the admiral, Ariabignes, son of Darius, and brother of Xerxes, and many other illustrious men of the Persians and Medes, and the other allies; but only some few of the Greeks: for as they knew how to swim, they whose ships were destroyed, and who did not perish in actual conflict, swam safe to Salamis; whereas many of the barbarians, not knowing how to swim, perished in the sea. When the foremost ships were put to flight, then the greatest numbers were destroyed; for those who were stationed behind, endeavouring to pass on with their ships to the front, that they, too, might give the king some proof of their courage, fell foul of their own flying ships. 90. The following event also occurred in this confusion. Some Phoenicians, whose ships were destroyed, going to the king, accused the Ionians, that their ships had perished by their means, for that they had betrayed him. It, however, turned out that the Ionian captains were not put to death, but that those Phoenicians who accused them, received the following reward. For while they were yet speaking, a Samothracian ship bore down on an Athenian ship; the Athenian was sunk, and an Aeginetan ship, coming up, sunk the ship of the Samothracians. But the Samothracians being javelin-men, by hurling their javelins, drove the marines from the ship that had sunk them, and boarded and got possession of it. This action saved the Ionians: for when Xerxes saw them perform so great an exploit, he turned round to the Phoenicians, as being above measure grieved, and ready to blame all, and ordered their heads to be struck off, that they who had proved themselves cowards, might no more accuse those who were braver. (For whenever Xerxes saw any one of his men performing a gallant action in the sea-fight, being seated at the foot of the mountain opposite Salamis, which is called Aegaleos, he inquired

the name of the person who did it, and his secretaries wrote down the family and country of the captain of the trireme.) Moreover, Ariaramnes, a Persian, who was a friend *to the Ionians,* and happened to be present, contributed to the ruin of the Phoenicians. They accordingly betook themselves to the Phoenicians.

91. The barbarians being turned to flight, and sailing away towards Phalerus, the Aeginetae waylaying them in the strait, performed actions worthy of record. For the Athenians in the rout ran down both those ships that resisted and those that fled; and the Aeginetae, those that sailed away from the battle: so that when any escaped the Athenians, being borne violently on, they fell into the hands of the Aeginetae. 92. At this time there happened to meet together the ship of Themistocles, giving chace to one of the enemy, and that of Polycritus, son of Crius, an Aeginetan, bearing down upon a Sidonian ship, the same that had taken the Aeginetan ship, which was keeping watch off Sciathus, and on board of which sailed Pytheas, son of Ischenous, whom, though covered with wounds, the Persians kept in the ship from admiration of his valour. The Sidonian ship that carried him about, was taken with the Persians on board, so that Pytheas, by this means, returned safe to Aegina. But when Polycritus saw the Athenian ship, he knew it, seeing the admiral's ensign; and shouting to Themistocles, he railed at him, upbraiding him with the charge of Medism brought against the Aeginetae. Polycritus, accordingly, as he was attacking the ship, threw out these reproaches against Themistocles. But the barbarians, whose ships survived, fled and arrived at Phalerus, under the protection of the land-forces.

93. In this engagement of the Greeks, the Aeginetae obtained the greatest renown; and next, the Athenians:—of particular persons, Polycritus of Aegina, and Athenians, Eumenes the Anagyrasian, with Aminias a Pallenian, who gave chace to Artemisia; and if he had known that Artemisia sailed in that ship, he would not have given over the pursuit, till he had either taken her, or been himself taken. For such had been the order given to the Athenian captains; and besides, a reward of ten thousand drachmas was offered to whoever should take her alive; for they considered it a great indignity that a woman should make war against Athens. She, however, as has been before mentioned, made her escape; and the others, whose ships survived, lay at Phalerus. 94. The Athenians say, that Adimantus, the Corinthian admiral, immediately from the commencement, when the ships engaged, being dismayed and excessively frightened, hoisted sail and fled; and that the Corinthians, seeing their admiral's ship flying, likewise bore away; and when in their flight, they arrived off the temple of Minerva Sciras, on the coast of Salamis, a light bark fell in with them by the guidance of heaven; that no one appeared to have sent it, and that it came up to the Corinthians, who knew nothing relating to the fleet. From this circumstance they conjectured the circumstance to be divine; for that when those on board the bark neared the ships, they spoke as follows: "Adimantus, having drawn off your ships, you have hurried away in flight, betraying the Greeks: they, however, are victorious, as far as they could have desired to conquer their enemies." Having said this, as Adimantus

did not credit them, they again spoke as follows: that "they were ready to be taken as hostages, and be put to death, if the Greeks were not found to be victorious:" upon which, having put about ship, he and the rest returned to the fleet, when the work was done. Such a story is told of them by the Athenians; the Corinthians, however, do not admit its truth, but affirm that they were among the foremost in the engagement; and the rest of Greece bears testimony in their favour 95. Aristides, son of Lysimachus, an Athenian, of whom I made mention a little before as a most upright man, in this confusion that took place about Salamis, did as follows: taking with him a considerable number of heavy-armed men, who were stationed along the shore of the Salaminian territory, and were Athenians by race, he landed them on the island of Psyttalea, and they put to the sword all the Persians who were on that little island.

    96. When the sea-fight was ended, the Greeks, having hauled on shore at Salamis all the wrecks that still happened to be there, held themselves ready for another battle, expecting the king would still make use of the ships that survived. But a west wind carrying away many of the wrecks, drove them on the shore of Attica, which is called Colias, so as to fulfil both all the other oracles delivered by Bacis and Musaeus concerning this sea-fight, and also that relating to the wrecks which were drifted on this shore, which many years before had been delivered by Lysistratus, an Athenian augur, but had not been understood by any of the Greeks: "The Colian women shall broil their meat with oars." This was to happen after the departure of the king.

    97. Xerxes, when he saw the defeat he had sustained, fearing lest some of the Ionians might suggest to the Greeks, or lest they themselves might resolve to sail to the Hellespont, for the purpose of breaking up the bridges, and lest he, being shut up in Europe, might be in danger of perishing, meditated flight. But wishing that his intention should not be known either to the Greeks or his own people, he attempted to throw a mound across to Salamis; and he fastened together Phoenician merchantmen, that they might serve instead of a raft and a wall; and he made preparation for war, as if about to fight another battle at sea. All the others who saw him thus occupied, were firmly convinced that he had seriously determined to stay and continue the war; but none of these things escaped the notice of Mardonius, who was well acquainted with his design. At the same time that Xerxes was doing this, he despatched a messenger to the Persians, to inform them of the misfortune that had befallen him. 98. There is nothing mortal that reaches its destination more rapidly than these couriers: it has been thus planned by the Persians. They say that as many days as are occupied in the whole journey, so many horses and men are posted at regular intervals, a horse and a man being stationed at each day's journey: neither snow, nor rain, nor heat, nor night, prevents them from performing their appointed stage as quick as possible. The first courier delivers his orders to the second, the second to the third, and so it passes throughout, being delivered from one to the other, just like the torch-bearing among the Greeks, which they perform in honour of Hephaestus. This mode of travelling by horses the Persians call angareïon. 99. The first message that reached Susa,

with the news that Xerxes was in possession of Athens, caused so great joy
among the Persians who had been left behind, that they strewed all the roads
with myrtle, burnt perfumes, and gave themselves up to sacrifices and festivity.
But the second messenger arriving threw them into such consternation, that
they all rent their garments, and uttered unbounded shouts and lamentations,
laying the blame on Mardonius. The Persians acted thus, not so much being
grieved for the ships, as fearing for Xerxes himself. And this continued with
the Persians during all the time that elapsed until Xerxes himself arrived and
stopped them *from doing so.* . . .

Thucydides: The Greeks at War among Themselves

Book I

Thucydides, an Athenian, wrote the history of the war between the
Peloponnesians and the Athenians, how they warred against each other; having begun from its very outset, with the expectation that it would prove a great
one, and more worthy of relation than all that had been before it; inferring so
much, as well from the fact that both sides were at the height of all kinds of
preparation for it, as also because he saw the rest of Greece joining with the
one side or the other, some immediately, and some intending so to do. For this
was certainly the greatest movement that ever happened among the Greeks,
and some part of the barbarians, and extending, as one may say, even to most
nations of the world. For the events that preceded this, and those again that
are yet more ancient, it was impossible, through length of time, to ascertain
with certainty; but from such evidence as I am led to trust, on looking back
as far as possible, I do not think they were great, either with respect to the wars
or otherwise.

2. For it is evident, that what is now called Hellas, was not of old
inhabited in a settled manner; but that formerly there were frequent removals,
and that each tribe readily left the place of their abode, being forced by such
as were from time to time more numerous. For as there was no traffic, and they
did not mix with one another without fear, either by sea or land; and they each
so used what they had as but barely to live on it, without having any superfluity

Thucydides, *The History of the Peloponnesian War,* Henry Dale, trans. (New York: Harper
& Brothers, 1896), pp. 1-15, 39-53, 110-123, 129-131, 178-189, 367-376.

of riches, or planting their land (because it was uncertain when another should invade them, and carry all away, especially as they had not the defense of walls); and as they thought that they might any where obtain their necessary daily sustenance, they made little difficulty in removing: and for this cause they were not strong, either in greatness of cities, or other resources. And the best of the land was always the most subject to these changes of inhabitants; as that which is now called Thessaly, and Boeotia, and the greatest part of the Peloponnese (except Arcadia), and of the rest of Greece whatsoever was most fertile. For through the goodness of the land, both the power of some particular men growing greater caused factions among them, whereby they were ruined; and withal they were more exposed to the plots of strangers. Attica, at any rate, having through the poverty of the soil been for the longest period free from factions, was always inhabited by the same people. And this which follows is not the least evidence of my assertion, that it was owing to its migrations that Greece did not equally increase in other parts. For such as by war or sedition were driven out of the rest of Greece, the most powerful of them retired to Athens, as to a place of security; and becoming citizens at a very early period, made the city still greater in the number of inhabitants; so that afterward they even sent out colonies into Ionia, as Attica itself was not able to contain them. 3. And to me the weakness of ancient times is not a little demonstrated by this too. Before the Trojan war, Greece appears to have done nothing in common; and, as it seems to me, the whole of it had not as yet even this name; nay, before the time of Hellen, the son of Deucalion, it does not appear that this appellation existed at all; but that in their different tribes, and the Pelasgian to the greatest extent, they furnished from themselves the name [of their people]. But when Hellen and his sons had grown strong in Phthiotis, and men invited them for their aid into the other cities; from associating with them, separate communities were now more commonly called Hellenes: and yet not for a long time after could that name prevail among them all. And Homer proves this most fully; for, though born long after the Trojan war, he has nowhere called them all by that name, nor indeed any others but those that came with Achilles out of Phthiotis; who were the very original Hellenes; but in his poems he mentions Danaans, Argives, and Achaeans. Nor again does he speak of barbarians; because neither were the Hellenes, in my opinion, as yet distinguished by one common term in opposition to that. The several Hellenic communities, then, who in the different cities understood each other's language, and were afterward all so called, did nothing in a body before the Trojan war, through want of strength and mutual intercourse. Nay, even for this expedition they united [only] because they now made more use of the sea. 4. For Minos was the most ancient of all with whom we are acquainted by report, that acquired a navy: and he made himself master of the greater part of what is now the Grecian sea; and both ruled over the islands called Cyclades, and was the first that colonized most of them, having expelled the Carians, and established his own sons in them as governors; and, as was natural, he swept piracy from the sea as much as he could, for the better coming in to him of his revenues. 5. For the Grecians in old time, and of the barbarians both those on the continent who lived near the sea, and all who inhabited islands, after they began to cross over more commonly to one another in ships, turned to piracy, under the conduct of their most powerful men, with a view both to their own gain, and to maintenance for the needy; and falling upon towns that were unfortified, and inhabited like villages, they rifled them, and made most of their livelihood by this means; as this employment did not yet involve any disgrace, but rather brought with it even somewhat of glory. This is shown by some that dwell on the continent even at the present day, with whom it is an honor to perform this cleverly; and by the ancient poets who introduce men asking the question of such as sail to their coasts, in all cases alike, whether they are pirates: as though neither those of whom they inquire, disowned the employment; nor those who were interested in knowing, reproached them with it. They also robbed one another on the continent; and to this day many parts of Greece live after the old fashion; as the Locri Ozolae, the Aetolians and Acarnanians, and those in that part of the continent. And the fashion of wearing arms has continued among these continental states from their old trade of piracy. 6. For the whole of Greece used to wear arms, owing to their habitations being unprotected, and their communication with each other insecure; and they passed their ordinary life with weapons, like the barbarians. And those parts of Greece which still live in this way, are a proof of the same mode of life having also formerly extended to all. Now the Athenians were the first who laid down their armor, and by a more easy style of life changed to greater luxury. And the elders of their rich men no long time ago ceased wearing from delicacy linen tunics, and binding up a knot of the hair on their heads with a tie of golden grasshoppers. Whence also this fashion prevailed for a long time with the elders of the Ionians, from their affinity to them. But on the contrary a moderate style of dressing, and according to the present mode, was first used by the Lacedaemonians; and in other respects their wealthier men most conformed themselves in their living to the common people. And they were the first who stripped themselves, and undressing in public, smeared themselves with grease, in their gymnastic exercises. And formerly even at the Olympic games the combatants contended with girdles round their middle; and it is not many years since it ceased to be so. Nay even now among some of the barbarians, and especially those of Asia, prizes for boxing and wrestling are given, and they wear girdles when they contend for them. And in many other respects also one might show that the ancient Greeks lived in a manner similar to the barbarians of the present age.

7. Of the cities, again, such as were founded most recently, and when there were now greater facilities of navigation, having greater abundance of wealth, they were built with walls on the very shores; and occupied isthmuses, with a view both to commerce and to security against their several neighbors: whereas the old ones, owing to the long continuance of piracy, were built further off from the sea, both those in the islands and those on the mainlands; (for they used to plunder one another, and all the rest who lived

by the sea without being seamen); and even to the present day they are built inland.

8. And the islanders especially were pirates, being Carians and Phoenicians. For it was these that had colonized most of the islands. And this is a proof of it:—When Delos was purified by the Athenians in the course of this war, and all the sepulchers of those who had died in the island were taken up, above half were found to be Carians; being known by the fashion of the arms buried with them, and by the manner in which they still bury. But when the navy of Minos was established, there were greater facilities of sailing to each other. For the malefactors in the islands were expelled by him, at the same time that he was colonizing most of them. And the men on the sea-coast, now making greater acquisition of wealth, led a more settled life; and some of them even surrounded themselves with walls, on the strength of growing richer than they had before been. For through desire of gain, the lower orders submitted to be slaves to their betters; and the more powerful, having a superabundance of money, brought the smaller cities into subjection. And being now more in this state of things, some time after they made the expedition against Troy.

9. And Agamemnon appears to me to have assembled the armament because he surpassed the men of that day in power, and not so much because he took the suitors of Helen bound by their oaths to Tyndarus. It is said too by those of the Peloponnesians who have received the most certain accounts by tradition from their forefathers, that Pelops first acquired power by the abundance of riches with which he came from Asia to men who were in needy circumstances; and although a new-comer, yet gave his name to the country; and that afterward still greater power fell to the lot of his descendants, as Eurystheus was killed in Attica by the Heraclidae, and Atreus was his mother's brother, and Eurystheus, when going on the expedition, intrusted Mycenae and the government to Atreus, on the ground of their connection; (he happened to be flying from his father on account of the death of Chrysippus): and when Eurystheus did not return again, they say that at the wish of the Mycenaeans themselves, through their fear of the Heraclidae, and also because he appeared to be powerful, and had courted the commons, Atreus received the kingdom of the Mycenaeans and all that Eurystheus ruled over; and that so the descendants of Pelops became greater than those of Perseus. And I think that Agamemnon, from having received this inheritance, and from being strong in his navy also at the same time to a greater extent than others, assembled and made the expedition not so much by favor as by fear. For he appears to have both come himself with most ships, and to have furnished them for the Arcadians besides; as Homer has also shown, if he is sufficient authority for any one, and also, in [his account of] the transmission of the scepter, he has mentioned that he "O'er numerous islands and all Argos ruled." Now, as he lived on the mainland, he would not have been master of islands, except those that were adjacent (and those would not be numerous), if he had not also had some naval force. And we must conjecture by this expedition, what was the character of those before it.

10. And as to Mycenae having been a small place, or if any town in those times appear now to be inconsiderable, this would be no certain proof to rest upon, for disbelieving that the armament was as large as the poets have said, and as report prevails. For if the city of the Lacedaemonians were laid desolate, and the temples and foundations of the public buildings were left, I think that when a long time had passed by, posterity would have great disbelief of their power in proportion to their fame. (And yet they occupy two of the five divisions of the Peloponnese, and take the lead of the whole of it, and of their allies out of it in great numbers. Still, as the city is neither built closely, nor has sumptuous temples and public buildings, but is built in villages, after the old fashion of Greece, it would have an inferior appearance.) Whereas if the Athenians were to suffer the same fate, I think their power would be conjectured, from the appearance of the city to the eye, to have been double what it is. It is not therefore right to be incredulous, nor to look at the appearance of cities rather than their power; but to think that that expedition was greater indeed than any that were before it, but inferior to those of the present day; if on this point again we must believe the poetry of Homer, which it is natural that he, as a poet, set off on the side of exaggeration; but, nevertheless, even on this view it appears inferior. For he has made it to consist of twelve hundred ships, those of the Boeotians carrying 120 men, and those of Philoctetes 50; meaning to show, as I think, the largest and the least; at any rate he has made no mention of the size of any others in the catalogue of the ships. And that they all were themselves rowers and fighting men, he has shown in the case of the ships of Philoctetes. For he has represented all the men at the oar as bowmen. And it is not probable that many supernumeraries would sail with them, except the kings and highest officers; especially as they were going to cross the open sea with munitions of war; and, on the other hand, had not their vessels decked, but equipped, after the old fashion, more like privateers. Looking then at the mean of the largest and the smallest ships, they do not appear to have gone in any great number, considering that they were sent by the whole of Greece in common.

11. And the reason was not so much scarcity of men as want of money. For owing to difficulty of subsistence, they took their army the smaller, and such only as they hoped would live on the country itself while carrying on the war; and when on their arrival they were superior in battle (and that they were so is evident, for they would not else have built the fortifications for their camp), they appear not even then to have employed all their force, but to have turned to the cultivation of the Chersonese, and to piracy, for want of food. And in this way the Trojans, owing to their being scattered, the more easily held out by open force those ten years; being a match for those who successively were left behind. But if they had gone with abundance of food, and in a body had continuously carried through the war, without foraging and agriculture, they would easily have conquered them in battle, and taken the place; since even though not united, but only with the part that was successively present, they held out against them. Now by pressing the siege, [I say],

they would have taken Troy both in less time and with less trouble; but through want of money both the undertakings before this were weak, and this itself, though more famous than the former, is shown by facts to have been inferior to its fame, and to the present report of it, which has prevailed by means of the poets.

12. For even after the Trojan war Greece was still moving about, and settling itself; so that it could not increase its power by remaining at rest. For the return of the Greeks from Troy, having taken place so late, caused many revolutions; and factions, generally speaking, arose in the states; in consequence of which men were expelled, and founded cities. For those who are now called Boeotians, being driven out of Arne by the Thessalians in the sixtieth year after the taking of Troy, settled in what is now called Boeotia, but was before called the Cadmean country. (Though there was a division of them in this country before, some of whom also joined the expedition against Troy.) And the Dorians in the eightieth year took possession of the Peloponnese with the Heraclidae. And Greece having with difficulty, after a long time, enjoyed settled peace, and being no longer subject to migrations, began to send out colonies; and the Athenians colonized Ionia, and most of the islands; and the Peloponnesians, the greater part of Italy and Sicily, and some places in the rest of Greece. But all these places were founded after the Trojan war.

13. Now when Greece was becoming more powerful, and acquiring possession of money still more than before, tyrannies, generally speaking, were established in the cities, from the revenues becoming greater; whereas before there had been hereditary kingly governments with definite privileges; and Greece began to fit out navies, and they paid more attention to the sea. Now the Corinthians are said first to have managed naval matters most nearly to the present fashion, and triremes to have been built at Corinth first in Greece. And Aminocles, a Corinthian shipwright, appears to have built four ships for the Samians also. Now it is about three hundred years to the end of this war from the time that Aminocles went to the Samians; and the most ancient sea-fight with which we are acquainted was fought between the Corinthians and the Corcyraeans. And from that too it is about two hundred and sixty years to the same period. For the Corinthians, having their city situated on the isthmus, had always possessed an emporium; as the Greeks of old, both those within the Peloponnese and those without, had intercourse with each other by land more than by sea, through *their* country: and they were very rich, as is shown even by the old poets; for they gave the title of "wealthy" to the place. And when the Greeks began to make more voyages, having got their ships they put down piracy; and rendered their city rich in income of money, as they afforded an emporium both ways. And the Ionians afterward had a large navy in the time of Cyrus, the first king of the Persians, and Cambyses his son; and while at war with Cyrus, commanded the sea along their coast for some time. Polyerates also, tyrant of Samos, in the time of Cambyses, having a strong fleet, both made some other of the islands subject to him, and took Rhenea and dedicated it to the Delian Apollo. And the

Phocaeans, while founding Massalia, conquered the Carthaginians in a sea-fight.

14. These were the strongest of their navies. But even these, though many generations after the Trojan war, appear to have used but few triremes, and to have been still fitted out with fifty-oared vessels, and long boats, as that fleet was. And it was but a short time before the Median war, and the death of Darius, who was king of the Persians after Cambyses, that triremes were possessed in any number by the tyrants of Sicily and the Corcyraeans. For these were the last navies worth mentioning established in Greece before the expedition of Xerxes: as the Aeginetans and Athenians, and whoever else had any, possessed but small ones, and of those the greater part fifty-oared vessels; and it was only lately that Themistocles persuaded the Athenians, when at war with the Aeginetans, and when the barbarian was also expected, to build those very ships with which they fought him by sea; and these were not yet decked throughout.

15. Of such a [deficient] character then were the navies of the Greeks, both the ancient ones and those which were built afterward. And yet those who paid attention to them obtained the greatest power, both by income of money and dominion over others: for they sailed against the islands, and subdued them; especially those who had not a sufficient extent of country. But as for war by land, from which any *power* was acquired, there was none. Such as did arise, were all against their several neighbors; and the Greeks did not go out in any foreign expeditions far from their country for the subjugation of others. For they had not ranged themselves with the chief states as subjects; nor, on the other hand, did they of their own accord, on fair and equal terms, make common expeditions; but it was rather neighboring states that separately waged war upon each other. But it was for the war carried on at an early period between the Chalcidians and Eretrians, that the rest of Greece also was most generally divided in alliance with one side or the other.

16. Now to others there arose in other ways obstacles to their increase; and in the case of the Ionians, when their power had advanced to a high pitch, Cyrus and the Persian kingdom, having subdued Croesus and all within the Halys to the sea, marched against them, and reduced to bondage their cities on the mainland, as Darius afterward did even the islands, conquering them by means of the fleet of the Phoenicians.

17. As for the tyrants, such as there were in the Grecian cities, since they provided only for what concerned themselves, with a view to the safety of their own persons, and the aggrandizement of their own family, they governed their cities with caution, as far as they possibly could; and nothing memorable was achieved by them; [indeed nothing], except it might be against their own several border states. [I speak of those in old Greece], for those in *Sicily* advanced to a very great degree of power. Thus on all sides Greece for a long time was kept in check; so that it both performed nothing illustrious in common, and was less daring as regards individual states.

18. But after the tyrants of the Athenians and those in the rest of Greece (which even at an earlier period was for a long time subject to tyrants), the most and last, excepting those in Sicily, had been deposed by the Lacedaemonians; (for Lacedaemon, after the settlement of the Dorians, who now inhabit it, though torn by factions for the longest time of any country that we are acquainted with, yet from the earliest period enjoyed good laws, and was always free from tyrants; for it is about four hundred years, or a little more, to the end of this war, that the Lacedaemonians have been in possession of the same form of government; and being for this reason powerful, they settled matters in the other states also;) after, I say, the deposition of the tyrants in the rest of Greece, not many years subsequently the battle of Marathon was fought between the Medes and Athenians. And in the tenth year after it, the barbarians came again with the great armament against Greece to enslave it. And when great danger was impending, the Lacedaemonians took the lead of the confederate Greeks, as being the most powerful; and the Athenians, on the approach of the Medes, determined to leave their city, and having broken up their establishments, went on board their ships, and became a naval people. And having together repulsed the barbarian, no long time after, both those Greeks who had revolted from the king, and those who had joined in the war [against him], were divided between the Athenians and Lacedaemonians. For these states respectively appeared the most powerful; for the one was strong by land, and the other by sea. And for a short time the confederacy held together; but afterward the Lacedaemonians and Athenians, having quarreled, waged war against each other with their allies: and of the rest of the Greeks, whoever in any quarter were at variance, now betook themselves to these. So that, from the Persian war all the time to this, making peace at one time, and at another war, either with each other or with their own revolting allies, they prepared themselves well in military matters, and became more experienced from going through their training in scenes of danger.

19. Now the Lacedaemonians did not treat as tributaries the allies whom they led, but only took care that they should be governed by an oligarchy, in accordance with their own interest; whereas the Athenians had in course of time taken ships from the states [in *their* league], except the Chians and Lesbians, and had commanded all to pay a tribute in money. And their own separate resources for this war were greater than when before they had been in their fullest bloom with their entire alliance.

20. Such then I found to be the early state of things, though it is difficult to trust every proof of it in succession. For men receive alike without examination from each other the reports of past events, even though they may have happened in their own country. For instance, the mass of the Athenians think that Hipparchus was tyrant when he was slain by Harmodius and Aristogiton; and do not know that Hippias held the government as being the eldest of the sons of Pisistratus, and Hipparchus and Thessalus were his brothers. But Harmodius and Aristogiton having suspected that on that day,

and at the very moment, some information had been given to Hippias by their accomplices, abstained from attacking him, as being forewarned; but as they wished before they were seized to do something even at all hazards, having fallen in with Hipparchus near the Leocorium, as it is called, while arranging the Panathenaic procession, they slew him. And there are many other things also, even at the present day, and not such as are thrown into oblivion by time, of which the rest of the Greeks too have not correct notions; as, that the kings of the Lacedaemonians do not vote with one vote each, but with two; and that they have a Pitanensian Lochus; which never yet existed. With so little pains is the investigation of truth pursued by most men; and they rather turn to views already formed.

21. If, however, from the proofs which have been mentioned any one should suppose that things were, on the whole, such as I have described them; instead of rather believing what either poets have sung of them, setting them off in terms of exaggeration, or historians have composed, in language more attractive to the ear than truthful, their subjects admitting of no proof, and most of them, through length of time, having come to be regarded as fabulous—and if he should consider that, allowing for their antiquity, they have been sufficiently ascertained from the most certain data; he would not be mistaken in his opinion. And though men always think the war of their own times to be the greatest while they are engaged in it, but when they have ceased from it, regard earlier events with more admiration; yet, to such as look at it from the facts themselves, this war will evidently appear to be greater than those.

22. And as for what they severally advanced in speaking, either when about to go to war, or when already in it, it was hard to remember the exact words of what was said; both for myself, with regard to what I heard in person, and for those who reported it to me from any other quarters: but as I thought that they would severally have spoken most to the purpose on the subjects from time to time before them, while I adhered as closely as possible to the general sense of what was really said, so have I recorded it. But with regard to the *facts* of what was done in the war, I did not presume to state them on hearsay from any chance informant, nor as I thought probable myself; but those at which I was personally present, and, when informed by others, only after investigating them accurately in every particular, as far as was possible. And it was with labor that they were ascertained; because those who were present in the several affairs did not give the same account of the same things, but as each was well inclined to either party, or remembered [the circumstances.] Now, for hearing it recited, perhaps the unfabulous character of my work will appear less agreeable: but as many as shall wish to see the truth of what both *has* happened, and *will* hereafter happen again, according to human nature—the same or pretty nearly so—for such to think it useful will be sufficient. And it is composed as a possession forever, rather than as a prize-task to listen to at the present moment.

23. Now, of former achievements, the greatest that was performed was the Median; and yet that had its decision quickly, in two battles by sea and two by land. But of this war both the duration was very long, and sufferings befell Greece in the course of it, such of it as were never matched in the same time. For neither were so many cities ever taken and laid desolate, some by barbarians, and some by the parties themselves opposed in the war; (some, too, changed their inhabitants when taken;) nor was there so much banishing of men and bloodshed, partly in the war itself, and partly through sedition. And things which were before spoken of from hearsay, but scantily confirmed by fact, were rendered not incredible; both about earthquakes, which at once extended over the greatest part of the world, and most violent at the same time, and eclipses of the sun, which happened more frequently than was on record of former times; and great droughts in some parts, and from them famines also; and what hurt them most, and destroyed a considerable part—the plague. For all these things fell upon them at once along with this war: which the Athenians and Peloponnesians began by breaking the thirty years' truce after the taking of Euboea. As for the reason why they broke it, I have first narrated their grounds of complaint and their differences, that no one might ever have to inquire from what origin so great a war broke out among the Greeks. For the truest reason, though least brought forward in words, I consider to have been, that the Athenians, by becoming great, and causing alarm to the Lacedaemonians, compelled them to proceed to hostilities. But the following were the grounds of complaints openly alleged on either side, from which they broke the truce, and set to the war. . . .

66. The Athenians then and Peloponnesians had had these previous grounds of complaint against each other; the Corinthians, because Potidaea, which was a colony of their own, and men of Corinth and from the Peloponnese in it, were being besieged; the Athenians against the Peloponnesians, because they had caused the revolt of a city which was their ally and tributary, and had come and openly fought with them in conjunction with the Potidaeans. The war however had not yet positively broken out, but at present there was a suspension of hostilities; for the Corinthians had done these things on their own responsibility alone.

67. When, however, Potidaea was being besieged, they did not remain quiet, as they had men in it, and were alarmed for the place. And immediately they summoned the allies to Lacedaemon, and came and cried out against the Athenians, as having broken the treaty, and as injuring the Peloponnese. And the Aeginetans, though they did not openly send embassadors, for fear of the Athenians, yet in secret most of all urged on the war in conjunction with them, saying that they were not independent according to the treaty. So the Lacedaemonians, after summoning any one of the allies besides, who said that in any other respect he had been injured by the Athenians, held their ordinary assembly, and told them to speak. And others came forward and severally made their complaints, and especially the Megareans, who urged no

few other grounds of quarrel, but most of all their being excluded from the ports in the Athenian dominions, and from the Attic market, contrary to the treaty. And the Corinthians came forward last, after permitting the others first to exasperate the Lacedaemonians; and they spoke after them as follows.

68. "The trustiness of your policy and intercourse among yourselves, Lacedaemonians, renders you the more distrustful with regard to others, if we say any thing [against them]; and from this you have a character for sober-mindedness, but betray too great ignorance with regard to foreign affairs. For though we often forewarned you what injuries we were going to receive from the Athenians, you did not gain information respecting what we told you from time to time, but rather suspected the speakers of speaking for their own private interests. And for this reason it was not before we suffered, but when we are in the very act of suffering, that you have summoned the allies here; among whom *we* may speak with the greatest propriety, inasmuch as we have also the greatest complaints to make, being insulted by the Athenians, and neglected by you. And if they were an obscure people any where who were injuring Greece, you might have required additional warning, as not being acquainted with them; but as it is, why need we speak at any great length, when you see that some of us are already enslaved, and that they are plotting against others, and especially against our allies, and have been for a long time prepared beforehand, in case they should ever go to war. For they would not else have stolen Corcyra from us, and kept it in spite of us, and besieged Potidaea; of which places, the one is the most convenient for their deriving the full benefit from their possession Thraceward, and the other would have supplied the largest navy to the Peloponnesians.

69. "And for these things it is you who are to blame, by having at first permitted them to fortify their city after the Median war, and subsequently to build the long walls; and by continually up to the present time depriving of liberty, not only those who had been enslaved by them, but your own allies also now. For it is not he who has enslaved them, but he who has the power to stop it, but overlooks it, that more truly does this; especially if he enjoys the reputation for virtue as being the liberator of Greece. But with difficulty have we assembled now, and not even now for any clearly defined object. For we ought to be considering no longer whether we are injured, but in what way we shall defend ourselves. For the aggressors come with their plans already formed against us who have not made up our minds; at once, and not putting it off. And we know in what way, and how gradually, the Athenians encroach upon their neighbors. And while they think that they are not observed through your want of perception, they feel less confident; but when they know that you are aware of their designs, but overlook them, they will press on you with all their power. For you alone of the Greeks, Lacedaemonians, remain quiet, defending yourselves against any one, not by exertion of your power, but by mere demonstration of it; and you alone put down the power of your enemies, not when beginning, but when growing twice as great as it was. And yet you used to have the name of cautious; but in your case the

name, it seems, was more than the reality. For we ourselves know that the Mede came from the ends of the earth to the Peloponnese, before your forces went out to meet him as they should have done; and now the Athenians, who are not far removed, as he was, but close at hand, you overlook; and instead of attacking them, prefer to defend yourselves against their attack, and to reduce yourselves to mere chances in struggling with them when in a much more powerful condition: though you know that even the barbarian was chiefly wrecked upon himself; and that with regard to these very Athenians, we have often ere this escaped more by their errors than by assistance from you. For indeed hopes of you have before now in some instances even ruined some, while unprepared through trusting you. And let none of you think that this is spoken for enmity, rather than for expostulation; for expostulation is due to friends who are in error, but accusation to enemies who have committed injustice.

70. "At the same time we consider that we, if any, have a right to administer rebuke to our neighbors, especially as the differences [between you and them] are great; of which you do not seem to us to have any perception, nor to have ever yet considered with what kind of people you will have to struggle in the Athenians, and how very, nay, how entirely different from yourselves. They, for instance, are innovating, and quick to plan and accomplish by action what they have designed; while you are disposed to keep what you have, and form no new design, and by action not even to carry out what is necessary. Again, they are bold even beyond their power, and adventurous beyond their judgment, and sanguine in dangers; while your character is to undertake things beneath your power, and not to trust even the sure grounds of your judgment, and to think that you will never escape from your dangers. Moreover, they are unhesitating, in opposition to you who are dilatory; and fond of going from home, in opposition to you who are most fond of staying at home: for they think that by their absence they may acquire something; whereas you think that by attempting [more] you would do harm to what you have. When they conquer their enemies, they carry out their advantage to the utmost; and when conquered, they fall back the least. Further, they use their bodies as least belonging to them, for the good of their country; but their mind, as being most peculiarly their own, for achieving something on her account. And what they have planned but not carried out, they think that in this they lose something already their own; what they have attempted and gained, that in this they have achieved but little in comparison with what they mean to do. Then, if they fail in an attempt at any thing, by forming fresh hopes in its stead, they supply the deficiency: for they are the only people that succeed to the full extent of their hope in what they have planned, because they quickly undertake what they have resolved. And in this way they labor, with toils and dangers, all their life long; and least enjoy what they have, because they are always getting, and think a feast to be nothing else but to gain their ends, and inactive quiet to be no less a calamity than laborious occupation. So that if any one should sum up their character, by saying that they are made neither to be quiet themselves, nor let the rest of the world be so, he would speak correctly.

71. "And yet when such is the character of this state that is opposed to you, Lacedaemonians, you go on delaying, and think that peace is not most lasting in the case of those men, who with their resources do what is right, while as regards their feelings, they are known to be determined not to put up with it, if they are injured; but you practice fair dealing on the principle of neither annoying others, nor being hurt yourselves in self-defense. Scarcely, however, could you have succeeded in this, though you had lived by a state of congenial views: while as it is, your ways, as we just now showed you, are old-fashioned compared with them. But, as in the case of art, improvements must ever prevail; and though for a state that enjoys quiet, unchanged institutions are best; yet, for those who are compelled to apply to many things, many a new device is also necessary. And for this reason the institutions of the Athenians, from their great experience, have been remodeled to a greater extent than yours. At this point then let your dilatoriness cease: and now assist us, and especially the Potidaeans, as you undertook, by making with all speed an incursion into Attica; that you may not give up men who are your friends and kinsmen to their bitterest enemies, and turn the rest of us in despair to some other alliance. And in that we should do nothing unjust, in the sight either of the gods who received our oaths or of the men who witness [our conduct]: for the breakers of a treaty are not those who from destitution apply to others, but those who do not assist their confederates. If, however, you will be zealous, we will stand by you; for neither should we act rightly in changing, nor should we find others more congenial. Wherefore deliberate well, and endeavor to keep a supremacy in the Peloponnese no less than your fathers bequeathed to you."

72. To this effect spoke the Corinthians. And the Athenians, happening before this to have an embassy at Lacedaemon, and hearing what was said, thought that they ought to come before the Lacedaemonians, not to make any defense on the subject of the charges which the states brought against them, but to prove, on a general view of the question, that they ought not to deliberate in a hurry, but take more time to consider it. They wished also to show how powerful their city was; and to remind the older men of what they knew, and to relate to the younger what they were unacquainted with; thinking that in consequence of what they said, they would be more disposed to remain quiet than to go to war. So they came to the Lacedaemonians, and said that *they* also, [as the Corinthians had done], wished to speak to their people, if nothing prevented. They told them to come forward; and the Athenians came forward, and spoke as follows.

73. "Our embassy was not sent for the purpose of controversy with your allies, but on the business on which the state sent us. Perceiving, however, that there is no small outcry against us, we have come forward, not to answer the charges of the states (for our words would not be addressed to you as judges, either of us or of them), but to prevent your adopting bad counsel through being easily persuaded by the allies on matters of great importance; and at the same time with a wish to show, on a view of the general argument

as it affects us, that we do not improperly hold what we possess, and that our state is worthy of consideration. Now as to things of very ancient date, why need we mention them? since hearsay must attest them, rather than the eyes of those who will be our auditors. But the Median war, and the deeds with which you yourselves are acquainted, we must speak of; though it will be rather irksome to us to be forever bringing them forward: for when we performed them, the danger was run for a benefit, of the reality of which you had your share; and let us not be deprived of the whole credit, if it is of any service to us. Our words, however, will be spoken, not so much for the purpose of exculpation, as of testimony, and of showing with what kind of a state you will have to contend, if you do not take good counsel. For we say that at Marathon we alone stood in the van of danger against the barbarian; and that when he came a second time, though we were not able to defend ourselves by land, we went on board our ships with all our people, and joined in the sea-fight at Salamis; which prevented his sailing against and ravaging the Peloponnese, city by city, while you would have been unable to assist one another against his numerous ships. And he himself gave the greatest proof of this; for when conquered by sea, thinking that his power was no longer what it had been, he retreated as quickly as he could with the greater part of his army.

74. "Such now having been the result, and it having been clearly shown that it was on the fleet of the Greeks that their cause depended, we contributed the three most useful things toward it; viz., the greatest number of ships, the most able man as a general, and the most unshrinking zeal. Toward the four hundred ships we contributed not less than two parts; and Themistocles as commander, who was chiefly instrumental of their fighting in the Strait, which most clearly saved their cause; and you yourselves for this reason honored him most, for a stranger, of all that have ever gone to you. And a zeal by far the most daring we exhibited, inasmuch as when no one came to assist us by land, the rest as far as us being already enslaved, we determined, though we had left our city, and sacrificed our property, not even in those circumstances to abandon the common cause of the remaining allies, nor to become useless to them by dispersing; but to go on board our ships, and face the danger; and not to be angry because you had not previously assisted us. So then we assert that we ourselves no less conferred a benefit upon you, than we obtained one. For *you,* setting out from cities that were inhabited, and with a view to enjoying them in future, came to our assistance [only] after you were afraid for yourselves, and not so much for us (at any rate, when we were still in safety, you did not come to us); but *we,* setting out from a country which was no more, and running the risk for what existed only in scanty hope, bore our full share in the deliverance both of you and of ourselves. But if we had before joined the Mede through fear for our country, like others, or had afterward had no heart to go on board our ships, considering ourselves as ruined men; there would have been no longer any need of your fighting by sea without a sufficient number of ships, but things would have quietly progressed for him just as 'he wished.

75. "Do we not then deserve, Lacedaemonians, both for our zeal at that time, and the intelligence of our counsel, not to lie under such excessive odium with the Greeks, at least for the empire we possess? For this very empire we gained, not by acting with violence, but through your having been unwilling to stand by them to finish the business with the barbarian and through the allies having come to us, and of their own accord begged us to become their leaders: and from this very fact we were compelled at first to advance it to its present height, principally from motives of fear, then of honor also, and afterward of advantage too. And it no longer appeared to be safe, when we were hated by the generality, and when some who had already revolted had been subdued, and you were no longer friends with us, as you had been, but suspicious of us, and at variance with us, to run the risk of giving it up; for those who revolted would have gone over to you. And all may without odium secure their own interests with regard to the greatest perils.

76. "You, at least, Lacedaemonians, have settled to your own advantage the government of the states in the Peloponnese over which you have a supremacy; and if at that time you had remained through the whole business, and been disliked in your command, as we were, we know full well that you would have become no less severe to the allies, and would have been compelled either to rule with a strong hand, or yourselves be exposed to danger. So neither have *we* done any thing marvelous, or contrary to the disposition of man, in having accepted an empire that was offered to us, and not giving it up, influenced as we are by the strongest motives, honor, and fear, and profit; and when, again, we had not been the first to set such a precedent, but it had always been a settled rule that the weaker should be constrained by the stronger; and when at the same time we thought ourselves worthy of it, and were thought so by you, until, from calculations of expediency, you now avail yourselves of the appeal to justice; which no one ever yet brought forward when he had a chance of gaining any thing by might, and abstained from taking the advantage. Nay, all are worthy of praise, who, after acting according to human nature in ruling others, have been more just than their actual power enabled them to be. At any rate we imagine that if some others had possessed our means, they would have best shown whether we are at all moderate or not: though to us there has unfairly resulted from our good nature disrepute rather than commendation.

77. "For from putting up with less than we might have had in contract-suits with the allies, and from having made our decisions in our own courts on the footing of equal laws, we are thought to be litigious. And none of them considers why this reproach is not brought against those who have empire in any other quarter also, and are less moderate toward their subjects than we have been: for those who can act with violence have no need besides to act with justice. But they, from being accustomed to have intercourse with us on a fair footing, if contrary to their notions of right they have been worsted in any thing, either by a legal judgment or by the power of our empire, even in any degree whatever; they feel no gratitude for not being deprived of the

greater part [of their possessions], but are more indignant for what is lost, than if from the first we had laid aside law, and openly taken advantage of them. In that case not even they themselves would have denied that it was right for the weaker to yield to the stronger. But when injured, it seems, men are more angry than when treated with violence: for the one case is regarded as an advantage taken by their equal; the other, as compulsion by their superior. At least they endured much harder treatment than this at the hand of the Medes; whereas *our* rule is thought to be severe; and naturally so; for their present condition is always irksome to subjects. You, at any rate, should you subdue us and possess an empire, would quickly lose the good-will which you have enjoyed through their fear of us; if you have the same views now as you gave symptoms of then, when you led them against the Mede for a short time. For you have institutions by yourselves, distinct from the rest of the world; and, moreover, each individual of you, on going abroad, neither acts according to these, nor to those which the rest of Greece recognizes.

78. "Deliberate therefore slowly, as on no trifling matters; and do not, though being influenced by other people's views and accusations, bring on yourselves trouble of your own: but consider beforehand, previously to your being engaged in it, how far beyond calculation is war; for when long protracted, it generally becomes in the end to depend on chances; from which we are equally removed, and run the risk in uncertainty as to which way it will turn out. And in going to war men generally turn to deeds first, which they ought to do afterward; and when they are in distress, then they have recourse to words. We, however, being neither ourselves yet involved in such an error, nor seeing you in it, charge you, while good council is still eligible to both sides, not to break treaty nor offend against your oaths, but to let our differences be judicially settled according to agreement. Else we will call to witness the gods who received our oaths, and endeavor to requite you for commencing hostilities, in such a way as you may set the example."

79. Thus spoke the Athenians. After the Lacedaemonians had heard from the allies their charges against the Athenians, and from the Athenians what they had to say, they made them all withdraw, and consulted by themselves on the question before them. And the opinions of the majority went the same way; viz, that the Athenians were already guilty of injustice, and that they ought to go to war with all speed. But Archidamus their king, a man who was considered both intelligent and prudent, came forward and spoke as follows.

80. "I have both myself already had experience in many wars, Lacedaemonians, and see that those of you who are of the same age [have had it also]; so that one would neither desire the business from inexperience, as might be the case with most men, nor from thinking it a good and safe one. But this war, about which you are now consulting, you would find likely to be none of the least, if any one should soberly consider it. For against the Peloponnesians and our neighbors our strength is of the same description, and we can quickly reach our destination in each case. But against men who live

in a country far away, and besides are most skillful by sea, and most excellently provided with every thing else, with riches, both private and public, and ships, and horses, and heavy-armed, and a crowd of irregulars, such as there is not in any one Grecian town beside, and moreover, have many allies under payment of tribute; how can it be right to declare war rashly against these men? and in what do we trust, that we should hurry on to it unprepared? Is it in our ships? Nay, we are inferior to them: but if we shall practice and prepare against them, time will pass in the interval. Well then, is it in our money? Nay, but we are still more deficient in this, and neither have it in the public treasury, nor readily contribute it from our private funds.

81. "Perhaps some one might feel confident because we excel them in heavy-armed troops, and in numbers, so that we might invade and ravage their land. But they have other land in abundance over which they rule, and will import what they want by sea. If, again, we shall attempt to make their allies revolt from them, we shall have to assist these also with ships, as they are generally islanders. What then will be the character of our war? For if we do not either conquer them by sea, or take away the revenues with which they maintain their fleet, we shall receive the greater damage; and at such a time it will no longer even be honorable to make peace; especially if we are thought to have begun the quarrel more than they. For let us now not be buoyed up with *this* hope, at any rate, that the war will soon be ended, if we ravage their land. Rather do I fear that we should bequeath it even to our children: so probable is it that the Athenians would neither be enslaved in spirit to their land, nor, like inexperienced men, be panic-stricken by the war.

82. "I do not, however, on the other hand, tell you to permit them without noticing it, to harm our allies, and not to detect them in plotting against us; but I tell you not to take up arms at present, but to send and remonstrate; neither showing too violent signs of war, nor yet that we will put up with their conduct; and in the mean time to complete our own preparations also, both by bringing over allies, whether Greeks or barbarians, from whatever source we shall receive additional strength, either in ships or in money; (for all who, like us, are plotted against by the Athenians, may without odium save themselves by accepting the aid not only of Greeks, but of barbarians also); and at the same time let us bring out our own resources. And if they listen at all to our embassadors, this is the best conclusion; but if not, after an interval of two or three years, we shall then go against them, if we think fit, in a better state of defense. And perhaps when they then saw our preparation, and our language speaking in accordance with it, they might be more disposed to yield, while they had their land as yet unravaged, and were deliberating about good things still enjoyed by them, and not yet sacrificed. For in their land consider that you have nothing else but a hostage; and the more so, the better it is cultivated. You should therefore spare it as long as possible, and not, through having reduced them to desperation, find them the more difficult to subdue. For if we are hurried on by the complaints of our allies, and ravage

it while we are unprepared, see that we do not come off in a manner more disgraceful and perplexing to the Peloponnese [than we should wish]. For complaints, both of states and individuals, it is impossible to settle: but when all together have, for their own separate interests, undertaken a war, of which it is impossible to know how it will go on, it is not easy to effect a creditable arrangement.

83. "And let no one think it shows a want of courage for many not to advance at once against one state. For they too have no fewer allies who pay them tribute; and war is not so much a thing of arms as of money, by means of which arms are of service; especially in the case of continental against maritime powers. Let us first then provide ourselves with this, and not be excited beforehand by the speeches of the allies; but as we shall have the greater part of the responsibility for the consequences either way, so also let us quietly take a view of them beforehand.

84. "And as for the slowness and dilatoriness which they most blame in us, be not ashamed of them. For by hurrying [to begin the war] you would be the more slow in finishing it, because you took it in hand when unprepared: and at the same time we always enjoy a city that is free and most glorious; and it is a wise moderation that can best constitute this. For owing to it we alone do not grow insolent in success, and yield less than others to misfortunes. We are not excited by the pleasure afforded by those who with praise stimulate us to dangers contrary to our conviction; and if any one provoke us with accusation, we are not the more prevailed on through being thus annoyed. We are both warlike and wise through our orderly temper: warlike, because shame partakes very largely of moderation, and courage of shame; and wise, because we are brought up with no little learning to despise the laws, and with too severe a self-control to disobey them; and are not over-clever in useless things, so that while in word we might ably find fault with our enemies' resources, we should not go against them so well in deed; but are taught to think that our neighbor's plans, and the chances which befall in war, are very similar, as things not admitting of nice distinction in language. But we always provide *in deed* against our adversaries with the expectation of their planning well; and must not rest our hopes on the probability of their blundering, but on the belief of our own taking cautious forethought. Again, we should not think that one man differs much from another, but that he is the best who is educated in the most necessary things.

85. "These practices then, which our fathers bequeathed to us, and which we have always retained with benefit, let us not give up, nor determine hurriedly, in the short space of a day, about many lives, and riches, and states, and honors, but let us do it calmly; as *we* may do more than others, on account of our power. And send to the Athenians respecting Potidaea, and send respecting those things in which the allies say they are injured; especially as they are ready to submit to judicial decision; and against the party which offers that, it is not right to proceed as against a guilty one. But prepare for war at the

same time. For in this you will determine both what is best, and what is most formidable to your adversaries." Archidamus spoke to this effect; but Sthenelaidas, who was one of the ephors at that time, came forward last, and spoke before the Lacedaemonians as follows.

86. "As for the long speech of the Athenians, I do not understand it; for though they praised themselves a great deal, in no part did they deny that they are injuring our allies and the Peloponnese. And yet if they were good men then against the Medes, but are bad ones now against us, they deserve double punishment for having become bad instead of good. But *we* are the same both then and now; and shall not, if we are wise, overlook our allies' being injured, nor delay to assist them; for there is no longer delay in their being ill-treated. Others have in abundance riches, and ships, and horses; but *we* have good allies, whom we must not give up to the Athenians, nor decide the question with suits and words, while it is not also in word that we are injured; but we must assist them with speed and with all our might. And let no one tell me that it is proper for us to deliberate who are being wronged. It is for those who are about to commit the wrong that it is much more proper to deliberate for a long time. Vote then, Lacedaemonians, for war, as is worthy of Sparta; and neither permit the Athenians to become greater, nor let us betray our allies; but with the help of the gods let us proceed against those who are wronging them."

87. Having spoken to this effect he himself, as ephor, put the question to the assembly of the Lacedaemonians. As they decide by acclamation and not by vote, he said that he did not distinguish on which side the acclamation was greater; but wishing to instigate them the more to war by their openly expressing their views, he said, "Whoever of you, Lacedaemonians, thinks the treaty to have been broken, and the Athenians to have been guilty, let him rise and go yonder" (pointing out a certain place to them); "and whoever does not think so, let him go to the other side." They arose and divided, and there was a large majority who thought that the treaty had been broken. And having summoned the allies, they told them that their own opinion was that the Athenians were in the wrong; but that they wished to summon all the allies also, and to put it to the vote; that after general consultation they might declare war, if they thought fit. They then, after having settled this, returned home; as did the embassadors of the Athenians afterward, when they had dispatched the business they had gone on. This decision of the assembly, that the treaty had been broken, was made in the fourteenth year of the continuance of the thirty years' truce, which had been concluded after the war with Euboea.

88. Now the Lacedaemonians voted that the treaty had been broken, and that war should be declared, not so much because they were convinced by the arguments of the allies, as because they were afraid that the Athenians might attain to greater power, seeing that most parts of Greece were already under their hands. . . .

34. In the course of this winter the Athenians, in accordance with the custom of their forefathers, buried at the public expense those who had first fallen in the war, after the following manner. Having erected a tent, they lay out the bones of the dead three days before, and each one brings to his own relative whatever [funeral offering] he pleases. When the funeral procession takes place, cars convey coffins of cypress wood, one for each tribe; in which are laid the bones of every man, according to the tribe to which he belonged; and one empty bier is carried, spread in honor of the missing, whose bodies could not be found to be taken up. Whoever wishes, both of citizens and strangers, joins in the procession; and their female relatives attend at the burial to make the wailings. They lay them then in the public sepulcher, which is in the fairest suburb of the city, and in which they always bury those who have fallen in the wars (except, at least, those who fell at Marathon; but to them, as they considered their valor distinguished above that of all others, they gave a burial on the very spot). After they had laid them in the ground, a man chosen by the state—one who in point of intellect is considered talented, and in dignity is pre-eminent—speaks over them such a panegyric as may be appropriate; after which they all retire. In this way they bury them: and through the whole of the war, whenever they had occasion, they observed the established custom. Over these who were first buried at any rate, Pericles son of Xanthippus was chosen to speak. And when the time for doing so came, advancing from the sepulcher on to a platform, which had been raised to some height, that he might be heard over as great a part of the crowd as possible, he spoke to the following effect:

35. "The greater part of those who ere now have spoken in this place, have been accustomed to praise the man who introduced this oration into the law; considering it a right thing that it should be delivered over those who are buried after falling in battle. To me, however, it would have appeared sufficient, that when men had shown themselves brave by deeds, their honors also should be displayed by deeds—as you now see in the case of this burial, prepared at the public expense—and not that the virtues of many should be periled in one individual, for credit to be given him according as he expresses himself well or ill. For it is difficult to speak with propriety on a subject on which even the impression of one's truthfulness is with difficulty established. For the hearer who is acquainted [with the facts], and kindly disposed [toward those who performed them], might perhaps think them somewhat imperfectly set forth, compared with what he both wishes and knows; while he who is unacquainted with them might think that some points were even exaggerated, being led to this conclusion by envy, should he hear any thing surpassing his own natural powers. For praises spoken of others are only endured so far as each one thinks that he is himself also capable of doing any of the things he hears; but that which exceeds their own capacity men at once envy and

disbelieve. Since, however, our ancestors judged this to be a right custom, I too, in obedience to the law, must endeavor to meet the wishes and views of every one, as far as possible.

36. "I will begin then with our ancestors first: for it is just, and becoming too at the same time, that on such an occasion the honor of being thus mentioned should be paid them. For always inhabiting the country without change, through a long succession of posterity, by their valor they transmitted it free to this very time. Justly then may they claim to be commended; and more justly still may our own fathers. For in addition to what they inherited, they acquired the great empire which we possess, and by painful exertions bequeathed it to us of the present day: though to most part of it have additions been made by ourselves here, who are still, generally speaking in the vigor of life; and we have furnished our city with every thing, so as to be most self-sufficient both for peace and for war. Now with regard to our military achievements, by which each possession was gained, whether in any case it were ourselves, or our fathers, that repelled with spirit hostilities brought against us by barbarian or Greek; as I do not wish to enlarge on the subject before you who are well acquainted with it, I will pass them over. But by what mode of life we attained to our power, and by what form of government and owing to what habits it became so great, I will explain these points first, and then proceed to the eulogy of these men; as I consider that on the present occasion they will not be inappropriately mentioned, and that it is profitable for the whole assembly, both citizens and strangers, to listen to them.

37. "For we enjoy a form of government which does not copy the laws of our neighbors; but we are ourselves rather a pattern to others than imitators of them. In name, from its not being administered for the benefit of the few but of the many, it is called a democracy; but with regard to its laws, all enjoy equality, as concerns their private differences; while with regard to public rank, according as each man has reputation for any thing, he is preferred for public honors, not so much from consideration of party, as of merit; nor, again, on the ground of poverty, while he is able to do the state any good service, is he prevented by the obscurity of his position. We are liberal then in our public administration; and with regard to mutual jealousy of our daily pursuits, we are not angry with our neighbor, if he does any thing to please himself; nor wear on our countenance offensive looks, which though harmless, are yet unpleasant. While, however, in private matters we live together agreeably, in public matters, under the influence of fear, we most carefully abstain from transgression, through our obedience to those who are from time to time in office, and to the laws; especially such of them as are enacted for the benefit of the injured, and such as, though unwritten, bring acknowledged disgrace [on those who break them].

38. "Moreover, we have provided for our spirits the most numerous recreations from labors, by celebrating games and sacrifices through the whole year, and by maintaining elegant private establishments, of which the daily gratification drives away sadness. Owing to the greatness too of our city,

every thing from every land is imported into it; and it is our lot to reap with no more peculiar enjoyment the good things which are produced here, than those of the rest of the world likewise.

39. "In the studies of war also we differ from our enemies in the following respects. We throw our city open to all, and never, by the expulsion of strangers, exclude any one from either learning or observing things, by seeing which unconcealed any of our enemies might gain an advantage; for we trust not so much to preparations and stratagems, as to our own valor for daring deeds. Again, as to our modes of education, *they* aim at the acquisition of a manly character, by laborious training from their very youth; while *we,* though living at our ease, no less boldly advance to meet equal dangers. As a proof of this, the Lacedaemonians never march against our country singly, but with all [their confederates] together: while we, generally speaking, have no difficulty in conquering in battle upon hostile ground those who are standing up in defense of their own. And no enemy ever yet encountered our whole united force, through our attending at the same time to our navy, and sending our troops by land on so many different services: but wherever they have engaged with any part of it, if they conquer only some of us, they boast that we were all routed by them; and if they are conquered, they say it was by all that they were beaten. And yet if with careless ease rather than with laborious practice, and with a courage which is the result not so much of laws as of natural disposition, we are willing to face danger, we have the advantage of not suffering beforehand from coming troubles, and of proving ourselves, when we are involved in them, no less bold than those who are always toiling; so that our country is worthy of admiration in these respects, and in others besides.

40. "For we study taste with economy, and philosophy without effeminacy; and employ wealth rather for opportunity of action than for boastfulness of talking; while poverty is nothing disgraceful for a man to confess, but not to escape it by exertion is more disgraceful. Again, the same men can attend at the same time to domestic as well as to public affairs; and others, who are engaged with business, can still form a sufficient judgment on political questions. For we are the only people that consider the man who takes no part in these things, not as unofficious, but as useless; and we ourselves judge rightly of measures, at any rate, if we do not originate them; while we do not regard words as any hinderance to deeds, but rather [consider it a hinderance] not to have been previously instructed by word, before undertaking in deed what we have to do. For we have this characteristic also in a remarkable degree, that we are at the same time most daring and most calculating in what we take in hand; whereas to other men it is ignorance that brings daring, while calculation brings fear. These, however, would deservedly be deemed most courageous, who know most fully what is terrible and what is pleasant, and yet do not on this account shrink from dangers. As regards beneficence also we differ from the generality of men; for we make friends, not by receiving, but by conferring kindness. Now he who has conferred the favor is the firmer friend, in order

that he may keep alive the obligation by good will toward the man on whom he has conferred it; whereas he who owes it in return feels less keenly, knowing that it is not as a favor, but as a debt, that he will repay the kindness. Nay, we are the only men who fearlessly benefit any one, not so much from calculations of expediency, as with the confidence of liberality.

41. "In short, I say that both the whole city is a school for Greece, and that, in my opinion, the same individual would among us prove himself qualified for the most varied kinds of action, and with the most graceful versatility. And that this is not mere vaunting language for the occasion, so much as actual truth, the very power of the state, which we have won by such habits, affords a proof. For it is the only country at the present time that, when brought to the test, proves superior to its fame; and the only one that neither gives to the enemy who has attacked us any cause for indignation at being worsted by such opponents, nor to him who is subject to us room for finding fault, as not being ruled by men who are worthy of empire. But we shall be admired both by present and future generations as having exhibited our power with great proofs, and by no means without evidence; and as having no further need, either of Homer to praise us, or any one else who might charm for the moment by his verses, while the truth of the facts would mar the idea formed of them; but as having compelled every sea and land to become accessible to our daring, and every where established everlasting records, whether of evil or of good. It was for such a country then that these men, nobly resolving not to have it taken from them, fell fighting; and every one of their survivors may well be willing to suffer in its behalf.

42. "For this reason, indeed, it is that I have enlarged on the characteristics of the state; both to prove that the struggle is not for the same object in our case as in that of men who have none of these advantages in an equal degree; and at the same time clearly to establish by proofs [the truth of] the eulogy of those men over whom I am now speaking. And now the chief points of it have been mentioned; for with regard to the things for which I have commended the city, it was the virtues of these men, and such as these, that adorned her with them; and few of the Greeks are there whose fame, like these men's, would appear but the just counterpoise of their deeds. Again, the closing scene of these men appears to me to supply an illustration of human worth, whether as affording us the first information respecting it, or its final confirmation. For even in the case of men who have been in other respects of an inferior character, it is but fair for them to hold forth as a screen their military courage in their country's behalf; for, having wiped out their evil by their good, they did more service collectively, than harm by their individual offenses. But of these men there was none that either was made a coward by his wealth, from preferring the continued enjoyment of it; or shrank from danger through a hope suggested by poverty, namely, that he might yet escape it, and grow rich; but conceiving that vengeance on their foes was more to be desired than these objects, and at the same time regarding this as the most glorious of hazards, they wished by risking it to be avenged on their enemies,

and so to aim at procuring those advantages; committing to hope the uncertainty of success, but resolving to trust to action, with regard to what was visible to themselves; and in that action, being minded rather to resist and die, than by surrendering to escape, they fled from the shame of [a discreditable] report, while they endured the brunt of the battle with their bodies; and after the shortest crisis, when at the very height of their fortune, were taken away from their glory rather than their fear.

43. "Such did these men prove themselves, as became the character of their country. For you that remain, you must pray that you may have a more successful resolution, but must determine not to have one less bold against your enemies; not in word alone considering the benefit [of such a spirit] (on which one might descant to you at great length—though you know it yourselves quite as well—telling you how many advantages are contained in repelling your foes); but rather day by day beholding the power of the city as it appears in fact, and growing enamored of it, and reflecting, when you think it great, that it was by being bold, and knowing their duty, and being alive to shame in action, that men acquired these things; and because, if they ever failed in their attempt at any thing, they did not on that account think it right to deprive their country also of their valor, but conferred upon her a most glorious joint-offering. For while collectively they gave her their lives, individually they received that renown which never grows old, and the most distinguished tomb they could have; not so much that in which they are laid, as that in which their glory is left behind them, to be everlastingly recorded on every occasion for doing so, either by word or deed, that may from time to time present itself. For of illustrious men the whole earth is the sepulcher; and not only does the inscription upon columns in their own land point it out, but in that also which is not their own there dwells with every one an unwritten memorial of the heart, rather than of a material monument. Vieing then with these men in your turn, and deeming happiness to consist in freedom, and freedom in valor, do not think lightly of the hazards of war. For it is not the unfortunate [and those] who have no hope of any good, that would with most reason be unsparing of their lives; but those who, while they live, still incur the risk of a change to the opposite condition, and to whom the difference would be the greatest, should they meet with any reverse. For more grievous, to a man of high spirit at least, is the misery which accompanies cowardice, than the unfelt death which comes upon him at once, in the time of his strength and of his hope for the common welfare.

44. "Wherefore to the parents of the dead—as many of them as are here among you—I will not offer condolence, so much as consolation. For they know that they have been brought up subject to manifold misfortunes; but that happy is *their* lot who have gained the most glorious—death, as these have,—sorrow, as you have; and to whom life has been so exactly measured, that they were both happy in it, and died in [that happiness]. Difficult, indeed, I know it is to persuade you of this, with regard to those of whom you will often be reminded by the good fortune of others, in which you yourselves also

once rejoiced; and sorrow is felt, not for the blessings of which one is bereft without full experience of them, but of that which one loses after becoming accustomed to it. But you must bear up in the hope of other children, those of you whose age yet allows you to have them. For to yourselves individually those who are subsequently born will be a reason for your forgetting those who are no more; and to the state it will be beneficial in two ways, by its not being depopulated, and by the enjoyment of security; for it is not possible that those should offer any fair and just advice, who do not incur equal risk with their neighbors by having children at stake. Those of you, however, who are past that age, must consider that the longer period of your life during which you have been prosperous is so much gain, and that what remains will be but a short one; and you must cheer yourselves with the fair fame of these [your lost ones]. For the love of honor is the only feeling that never grows old; and in the helplessness of age it is not the acquisition of gain, as some assert, that gives greatest pleasure, but the enjoyment of honor.

45. "For those of you, on the other hand, who are sons or brothers of the dead, great, I see, will be the struggle of competition. For every one is accustomed to praise the man who is no more; and scarcely, though even for an excess of worth, would you be esteemed, I do not say equal to them, but only slightly inferior. For the living are exposed to envy in their rivalry; but those who are in no one's way are honored with a good will free from all opposition. If, again, I must say any thing on the subject of woman's excellence also, with reference to those of you who will now be in widowhood, I will express it all in a brief exhortation. Great will be your glory in not falling short of the natural character that belongs to you; and great is hers, who is least talked of among the men, either for good or evil.

46. "I have now expressed *in word,* as the law required, what I had to say befitting the occasion; and, *in deed,* those who are here interred, have already received part of their honors; while, for the remaining part, the state will bring up their sons at the public expense, from this time to their manhood; thus offering both to these and to their posterity a beneficial reward for such contests; for where the greatest prizes for virtue are given, there also the most virtuous men are found among the citizens. And now, having finished your lamentations for your several relatives, depart."

47. Such was the funeral that took place this winter, at the close of which the first year of this war ended. At the very beginning of the next summer the Peloponnesians and their allies, with two thirds of their forces, as on the first occasion, invaded Attica, under the command of Archidamus, the son of Zeuxidamus, king of the Lacedaemonians; and after encamping, they laid waste the country. When they had not yet been many days in Attica, the plague first began to show itself among the Athenians; though it was said to have previously lighted on many places, about Lemnos and elsewhere. Such a pestilence, however, and loss of life as this was nowhere remembered to have happened. For neither were physicians of any avail at first, treating it as they did, in ignorance of its nature—nay, they themselves died most of all, inas-

much as they most visited the sick—nor any other art of man. And as to the supplications that they offered in their temples or the divinations, and similar means, that they had recourse to, they were all unavailing; and at last they ceased from them, being overcome by the pressure of the calamity.

48. It is said to have first begun in the part of Aethiopia above Egypt, and then to have come down into Egypt, and Libya, and the greatest part of the king's territory. On the city of Athens it fell suddenly, and first attacked the men in the Piraeus; so that it was even reported by them that the Peloponnesians had thrown poison into the cisterns; for as yet there were no fountains there. Afterward it reached the upper city also; and then they died much more generally. Now let every one, whether physician or unprofessional man, speak on the subject according to his views; from what source it was likely to have arisen, and the causes which he thinks were sufficient to have produced so great a change [from health to universal sickness]. I, however, shall only describe what was its character; and explain those symptoms by reference to which one might best be enabled to recognize it through this previous acquaintance, if it should ever break out again; for I was both attacked by it myself, and had personal observation of others who were suffering with it.

49. That year then, as was generally allowed, happened to be of all years the most free from disease, so far as regards other disorders; and if any one *had* any previous sickness, all terminated in this. Others, without any ostensible cause, but suddenly, while in the enjoyment of health, were seized at first with violent heats in the head, and redness and inflammation of the eyes; and the internal parts, both the throat and the tongue, immediately assumed a bloody tinge, and emitted an unnatural and fetid breath. Next after these symptoms, sneezing and hoarseness came on; and in a short time the pain descended to the chest, with a violent cough. When it settled in the stomach, it caused vomiting; and all the discharges of bile that have been mentioned by physicians succeeded, and those accompanied with great suffering. An ineffectual retching also followed in most cases, producing a violent spasm, which in some cases ceased soon afterward, in others much later. Externally the body was not very hot to the touch, nor was it pale; but reddish, livid, and broken out in small pimples and sores. But the internal parts were burnt to such a degree that they could not bear clothing or linen of the very lightest kind to be laid upon them, nor to be any thing else but stark naked; but would most gladly have thrown themselves into cold water if they could. Indeed many of those who were not taken care of did so, plunging into cisterns in the agony of their unquenchable thirst: and it was all the same whether they drank much or little. Moreover, the misery of restlessness and wakefulness continually oppressed them. The body did not waste away so long as the disease was at its height, but resisted it beyond all expectation: so that they either died in most cases on the ninth or the seventh day, through the internal burning, while they had still some degree of strength; or if they escaped [that stage of the disorder], then, after it had further descended into the bowels, and violent ulceration was

produced in them, and intense diarrhoea had come on, the greater part were afterward carried off through the weakness occasioned by it. For the disease, which was originally seated in the head, beginning from above, passed throughout the whole body: and if any one survived its most fatal consequences, yet it marked him by laying hold of his extremities; for it settled on the pudenda, and fingers, and toes, and many escaped with the loss of these, while some also lost their eyes. Others, again, were seized on their first recovery with forgetfulness of every thing alike, and did not know either themselves or their friends.

50. For the character of the disorder surpassed description; and while in other respects also it attacked every one in a degree more grievous than human nature could endure, in the following way, especially, it proved itself to be something different from any of the diseases familiar to man. All the birds and beasts that prey on human bodies, either did not come near them, though there were many lying unburied, or died after they had tasted them. As a proof of this, there was a marked disappearance of birds of this kind, and they were not seen either engaged in this way, or in any other; while the dogs, from their domestic habits, more clearly afforded opportunity of marking the result I have mentioned.

51. The disease, then, to pass over many various points of peculiarity, as it happened to be different in one case from another, was in its general nature such as I have described. And no other of those to which they were accustomed afflicted them besides this at that time; or whatever there was, it ended in this. And [of those who were seized by it] some died in neglect, others in the midst of every attention. And there was no one settled remedy, so to speak, by applying which they were to give them relief; for what did good to one, did harm to another. And no constitution showed itself fortified against it, in point either of strength or weakness; but it seized on all alike, even those that were treated with all possible regard to diet. But the most dreadful part of the whole calamity was the dejection felt whenever any one found himself sickening (for by immediately falling into a feeling of despair, they abandoned themselves much more certainly to the disease, and did not resist it), and the fact of their being charged with infection from attending on one another, and so dying like sheep. And it was this that caused the greatest mortality among them; for if through fear they were unwilling to visit each other, they perished from being deserted, and many houses were emptied for want of some one to attend to the sufferers; or if they did visit them, they met their death, and especially such as made any pretensions to goodness; for through a feeling of shame they were unsparing to themselves, in going into their friends' houses [when deserted by all others]; since even the members of the family were at length worn out by the very moanings of the dying, and were overcome by their excessive misery. Still more, however, than even these, did such as had escaped from the disorder show pity for the dying and the suffering, both from their previous knowledge of what it was, and from their being now in no fear of it themselves; for it never seized the same person twice, so as to prove actually

fatal. And such persons were felicitated by others; and themselves, in the excess of their present joy, entertained for the future also, to a certain degree, a vain hope that they would never now be carried off even by any other disease.

52. In addition to the original calamity, what oppressed them still more was the crowding into the city from the country, especially the new comers. For as they had no houses, but lived in stifling cabins at the hot season of the year, the mortality among them spread without restraint; bodies lying on one another in the death-agony, and half-dead creatures rolling about the streets and round all the fountains, in their longing for water. The sacred places also in which they had quartered themselves, were full of the corpses of those that died there in them: for in the surpassing violence of the calamity, men not knowing what was to become of them, came to disregard every thing, both sacred and profane, alike. And all the laws were violated which they before observed respecting burials; and they buried them as each one could. And many from want of proper means, in consequence of so many of their friends having already died, had recourse to shameless modes of sepulture; for on the piles prepared for others, some, anticipating those who had raised them, would lay their own dead relative and set fire to them; and others, while the body of a stranger was burning, would throw on the top of it the one they were carrying, and go away.

53. In other respects also the plague was the origin of lawless conduct in the city, to a greater extent [than it had before existed]. For deeds which formerly men hid from view, so as not to do them just as they pleased, they now more readily ventured on; since they saw the change so sudden in the case of those who were prosperous and quickly perished, and of those who before had had nothing, and at once came into possession of the property of the dead. So they resolved to take their enjoyment quickly, and with a sole view to gratification; regarding their lives and their riches alike as things of a day. As for taking trouble about what was thought honorable, no one was forward to do it; deeming it uncertain whether, before he had attained to it, he would not be cut off; but every thing that was immediately pleasant, and that which was conducive to it by any means whatever, this was laid down to be both honorable and expedient. And fear of gods, or law of men, there was none to stop them; for with regard to the former they esteemed it all the same whether they worshiped them or not, from seeing all alike perishing; and with regard to their offenses [against the latter], no one expected to live till judgment should be passed on him, and so to pay the penalty of them; but they thought a far heavier sentence was impending in that which had already been passed upon them; and that before it fell on them, it was right to have some enjoyment of life.

54. Such was the calamity which the Athenians had met with, and by which they were afflicted, their men dying within the city, and their land being wasted without. In their misery they remembered this verse among other things, as was natural they should; the old men saying that it had been uttered long ago:

A Dorian war shall come, and plague with it.

Now there was a dispute among them, [and some asserted] that it was not "a plague" [*loimos*] that had been mentioned in the verse by the men of former times, but "a famine," [*limos*]: the opinion, however, at the present time naturally prevailed that "a plague" had been mentioned: for men adapted their recollections to what they were suffering. But, I suppose, in case of another Dorian war ever befalling them after this, and a famine happening to exist, in all probability they will recite the verse accordingly. Those who were acquainted with it recollected also the oracle given to the Lacedaemonians when on their inquiring of the god whether they should go to war, he answered, "that if they carried it on with all their might, they would gain the victory; and that he would himself take part with them in it." With regard to the oracle then, they supposed that what was happening answered to it. For the disease had begun immediately after the Lacedaemonians had made their incursion; and it did not go into the Peloponnese, worth even speaking of, but ravaged Athens most of all, and next to it the most populous of the other towns. Such were the circumstances that occurred in connection with the plague. . . .

    65. . . . Pericles endeavored both to divert the Athenians from their anger toward himself, and to lead away their thoughts from their present hardships. And in a public point of view they were persuaded by his speech, and were no longer for sending to the Lacedaemonians, but were more resolute for the war; though in their private feelings they were distressed by their sufferings; the commons, because, having set out with less resources, they had been deprived of even those; the higher orders, because they had lost fine possessions in the country, both in buildings and expensive establishments, and, what was the greatest evil of all, had war instead of peace. They did not, however, cease from their public displeasure toward him, till they had fined him in a sum of money. But no long time after, as the multitude is wont to act, they again elected him general, and committed every thing to him; for on the points in which each man was vexed about his domestic affairs, they now felt less keenly; but with regard to what the whole state needed, they thought that he was most valuable. For as long as he was at the head of the state in time of peace, he governed it with moderation, and kept it in safety, and it was at its height of greatness in his time; and when the war broke out, he appears to have foreknown its power in this respect also. He survived its commencement two years and six months; and when he was dead, his foresight with regard to its course was appreciated to a still greater degree. For he said that if they kept quiet, and attended to their navy, and did not gain additional dominion during the war, nor expose the city to hazard, they would have the advantage in the struggle. But they did the very contrary of all this, and in other things which seemed to have nothing to do with the war, through their private ambition and private gain, they adopted evil measures both toward themselves and their allies; which, if successful, conduced to the honor and

benefit of individuals; but if they failed, proved detrimental to the state with regard to the war. And the reason was, that he, being powerful by means of his high rank and talents, and manifestly proof against bribery, controlled the multitude with an independent spirit, and was not led by them so much as he himself led them; for he did not say any thing to humor them, for the acquisition of power by improper means; but was able on the strength of his character to contradict them even at the risk of their displeasure. Whenever, for instance, he perceived them unseasonably and insolently confident, by his language, he would dash them down to alarm; and, on the other hand, when they were unreasonably alarmed, he would raise them again to confidence. And so, though in name it was a democracy, in fact it was a government administered by the first man. Whereas those who came after, being more on a level with each other, and each grasping to become first, had recourse to devoting [not only their speeches, but] even their *measures,* to the humors of the people. In consequence of this both many other blunders were committed, as was likely in a great and sovereign state, and especially the expedition to Sicily; which was not so much an error of judgment with respect to the people they went against, as that those who had sent them out, by not afterward voting supplies required by the armament, but proceeding with their private criminations, to gain the leadership of the commons, both blunted the spirit of measures in the camp, and for the first time were embroiled with one another in the affairs of the city. But even when they had suffered in Sicily the loss of other forces, and of the greater part of their fleet, and were now involved in sedition at home, they nevertheless held out three years, both against their former enemies, and those from Sicily with them, and moreover against the greater part of their allies who had revolted, and Cyrus, the king's son, who afterward joined them, and who supplied the Peloponnesians with money for their fleet: nor did they succumb, before they were overthrown and ruined by themselves, through their private quarrels. Such a superabundance of means had Pericles at that time, by which he himself foresaw that with the greatest ease he could gain the advantage in the war over the Peloponnesians by themselves. . . .

Book III

36. On the arrival of the men with Salaethus, the Athenians immediately put the latter to death, though he held out certain promises, and among others, that he would obtain the retreat of the Peloponnesians from Plataea (for it was still being besieged): but respecting the former they deliberated what to do; and in their anger they determined to put to death, not only these that were there, but all the Mytilenaeans also that were of age; and to make slaves of the women and children. For they both urged against them [the aggravated character of] their revolt in other respects, namely, that they had executed it without being subject to their dominion, like the rest; and the fact of the

Peloponnesian ships having dared to venture over to Ionia to assist them, contributed also no little to their wrath; for they thought it was with no short premeditation that they had revolted. They sent therefore a trireme to Paches with intelligence of their resolution, and commanded him to dispatch the Mytilenaeans as quickly as possible. The next day they felt immediately a degree of repentance, and reflected that the resolution they had passed was a cruel and sweeping one, to put a whole city to the sword, instead of those who were guilty. When the Mytilenaean embassadors who were present, and those of the Athenians who co-operated with them, perceived this, they got the authorities to put the question again to the vote; and the more easily prevailed on them to do it, because they also saw plainly that the majority of the citizens wished some one to give them another opportunity of deliberating. An assembly therefore being immediately summoned, different opinions were expressed on both sides; and Cleon, son of Cleaenetus, who had carried the former resolution, to put them to death, being on other subjects also the most violent of the citizens, and by far the most influential with the commons, at that time came forward again, and spoke as follows:

37. "On many other occasions before this have I been convinced that a democracy is incapable of maintaining dominion over others, and I am so more than ever from your present change of purpose respecting the Mytilenaeans. For owing to your daily freedom from fear, and plotting against each other, you entertain the same views toward your allies also. And you do not reflect, in whatever case you may either have made a mistake through being persuaded by their words, or may have given way to pity, that you show such weakness to your own peril, and at the same time to gain no gratitude from your allies; not considering that it is a tyrannical dominion which you hold, and over men who are plotting against you, and involuntarily subject to you; and who obey you not from any favors you confer on them to your own hurt, but from the fact of your being superior to them through your power, rather than their good feeling. But of all things it is the most fearful, if nothing of what we have resolved is to be steadfast; and if we are not convinced that a state with inferior laws which are unchanged is better than one with good ones which are not authoritative; that homely wit with moderation is more useful than cleverness with intemperance; and that the duller class of men, compared with the more talented, generally speaking, manage public affairs better. For the latter wish to appear wiser than the laws, and to overrule what is ever spoken for the public good—thinking that they could not show their wisdom in more important matters—and by such means they generally ruin their country. But the former, distrusting their own talent, deign to be less learned than the laws, and less able than to find fault with the words of one who has spoken well; and being judges on fair terms, rather than rivals for a prize, they are more commonly right in their views. So then ought *we* also to do, and not to advise your people contrary to our real opinion, urged on by cleverness and rivalry of talent.

38. "I, then, continue of the same opinion; and am astonished at those who have proposed to discuss a second time the case of the Mytilenaeans,

and caused in it a delay of time, which is all for the advantage of the guilty (for so the sufferer proceeds against the offender with his anger less keen; whereas when retribution treads most closely on the heels of suffering, it best matches it in wreaking vengeance). I wonder, too, who will be the man to maintain the opposite opinion, and to pretend to show that the injuries done by the Mytilenaeans are beneficial to us, and that our misfortunes are losses to our allies. It is evident that either trusting to his eloquence he would strive to prove, in opposition to us, that what we consider most certain has not been ascertained; or, urged on by the hope of gain, will endeavor to lead us away by an elaborate display of specious language. But in such contests as these the state gives the prizes to others, and takes only the dangers itself. And it is you who are to blame for it, through unwisely instituting those contests; inasmuch as you are accustomed to attend to speeches like spectators [in a theater], and to facts like mere listeners [to what others tell you]; with regard to things future, judging of their possibility from those who have spoken cleverly about them; and with regard to things which have already occurred, not taking what has been done as more credible from your having seen it, than what has been only heard from those who in words have delivered a clever invective. And so you are the best men to be imposed on with novelty of argument, and to be unwilling to follow up what has been approved by you; being slaves to every new paradox, and despisers of what is ordinary. Each of you wishes, above all, to be able to speak himself; but if that is not possible, in rivalry of those who so speak, you strive not to appear to have followed his sentiments at second-hand; but when he has said any thing cleverly, you would fain appear to have anticipated its expression by your applause, and are eager to catch beforehand what is said, and at the same time slow to foresee the consequences of it. Thus you look, so to speak, for something different from the circumstances in which we are actually living; while you have not a sufficient understanding of even that which is before you. In a word, you are overpowered by the pleasures of the ear, and are like men sitting to be amused by rhetoricians rather than deliberating upon state affairs.

39. "Wishing then to call you off from this course, I declare to you that the Mytilenaeans have injured you more than any one state ever did. For I can make allowance for men who have revolted because they could not endure your government, or because they were compelled by their enemies. But for those who inhabited an island with fortifications, and had only to fear our enemies by sea, on which element, too, they were themselves not un-protected against them by a fleet of triremes, and who lived independent, and were honored in the highest degree by us, and then treated us in this way; what else did those men do than deliberately devise our ruin, and rise up against us, rather than revolt from us (revolt, at least, is the part of those who are subject to some violent treatment), and seek to ruin us by siding with our bitterest enemies? Yet surely that is more intolerable than if they waged war against you by themselves for the acquisition of power. Again, neither were the calami-ties of their neighbors, who had already revolted from us and been subdued, a warning to them; nor did the good fortune they enjoyed make them loathe

to come into trouble; but being over-confident with regard to the future, and having formed hopes beyond their power, though less than their desire, they declared war, having determined to prefer might to right; for at a time when they thought they should overcome us, they attacked us, though they were not being wronged. But success is wont to make those states insolent to which it comes most unexpected and with the shortest notice; whereas the good fortune which is according to men's calculation is generally more steady than when it comes beyond their expectation; and, so to say, they more easily drive off adversity than they preserve prosperity. The Mytilenaeans, then, ought all along to have been honored by us on the same footing as the rest, and in that case they would not have come to such a pitch of insolence; for in other instances, as well as theirs, man is naturally inclined to despise those who court him, and to respect those who do not stoop to him. But let them even now be punished as their crime deserves; and let not the guilt attach to the aristocracy, while you acquit the commons. For at any rate they all alike attacked *you*; since they might have come over to us, and so have been now in possession of their city again. Thinking, however, the chance they ran with the aristocracy to be the safer, they joined them in revolting. And now consider; if you attach the same penalties to those of the allies who were compelled by their enemies to revolt, and to those who did it voluntarily, which of them, think you, will not revolt on any slight pretext, when he either gains his liberation, if he succeed, or incurs no extreme suffering, if he fail? And so we shall presently have to risk both our money and our lives against each separate state. And if we are successful, by taking possession of a ruined city, you will hereafter be deprived of all future revenue from it—in which our strength consists; while if we fail, we shall have fresh enemies in addition to those we have already; and during the time that we ought to be opposing our present foes, we shall be engaged in hostilities with our own allies.

40. "You ought not therefore to hold out any hope, either relying on oratory or purchased with money, of their receiving allowance for having erred through human infirmity. For they did not involuntarily hurt you, but wittingly plotted against you; and it is only what is involuntary that can claim allowance. I, then, both on that first occasion [so advised you], and now contend that you should not rescind your former resolutions, nor err through three things, the most inexpedient for empire, namely, pity, delight in oratory, and lenity. For pity is properly felt toward those of a kindred temper, and not toward those who will not feel it in return, but are of necessity our enemies forever. And the orators who delight us with their language will have a field in other subjects of less importance, instead of one in which the state, after being a little pleased, will pay a great penalty; while they themselves from their good speaking will receive good treatment in return. And lenity is shown to those who will be well-disposed in future, rather than to those who remain just what they were, and not at all less hostile. To sum up in one word, if you are persuaded by me, you will do what is just toward the Mytilenaeans, and at the same time expedient; but if you decide otherwise, you will not oblige *them,* but

will rather pass sentence upon *yourselves*. For if they were right in revolting, you can not properly maintain your empire. If, however, you determine to do so, even though it is not proper, you must also, overlooking what is right, punish these men from regard to expediency, or else give up your empire, and act the honest man without danger. Resolve, then, to requite them with the same penalty; and not to show yourselves, in escaping their design, more insensible than those who formed them against you; considering what they would probably have done, if they had prevailed over you; especially as they were the first to begin the wrong. For it is those who do ill to any one without reason, that persecute him most bitterly, nay, even to the death, from suspicion of the danger of their enemy's being spared; since he who has suffered evil without any necessity, [but by provoking it himself], is more bitter, if he escape, than one who was an enemy on equal terms. Be not therefore traitors to your own cause; but bringing yourselves in feeling as near as possible to the actual state of suffering, and reflecting how you would in that case have valued their subjection above every thing, now pay them back in return, not indulging in weakness at the present moment, nor forgetting the danger which once hung over you. Punish these men, I say, as they deserve; and give a striking example to the rest of your allies, that whoever revolts will pay the penalty for it with his life. For if they know this, you will less frequently have to neglect your enemies, while you are fighting with your own confederates."

41. To this effect spoke Cleon. After him Diodotus son of Eucrates, who in the former assembly spoke most strongly against putting the Mytilenaeans to death, came forward then also, and said as follows.

42. "I neither blame those who have a second time proposed the discussion of the case of the Mytilenaeans, nor commend those who object to repeated deliberation on the most important subjects; but I think that the two things most opposed to good counsel are haste and passion, one of which is generally the companion of folly, and the other of coarseness and narrowness of mind. And whoever contends that words are not to be the exponents of measures, is either wanting in understanding, or self-interested: wanting in understanding, if he thinks it possible to express himself in any other way on what is future and not certain; self-interested, if, when wishing to persuade to something base, he thinks that he could not speak to his credit on a discreditable subject, but that by clever calumniation he might confound both his opponents and audience. But most cruel of all are those who charge us besides with a display [of rhetoric] for pecuniary motives. For if they only imputed ignorance, he who failed in carrying his point would retire with a character for want of understanding, rather than of honesty: but when a charge of dishonesty is brought against him, if successful, he is suspected; and if unsuccessful, together with his inability, he is also thought dishonest. And the state is not benefited by such a system; for through fear it is deprived of its counselors. Most prosperous indeed would it be, if such of its citizens were incapable of speaking; for then they would be less often persuaded to do wrong. But the good citizen ought to show himself the better speaker not by terrifying his

opponent, but by meeting him on equal terms; and the state that acts wisely should not, indeed, confer honor on the man who most frequently gives good advice, but neither should it detract from what he enjoys already; and so far from punishing him who is wrong in his judgment, it should not even degrade him. For so the successful counselor would be least tempted to speak any thing contrary to his real opinion, in order to gratify his hearers; and the unsuccessful one would be least anxious, by the same means of gratification, to bring over the multitude to *his* side also.

43. "But we do the contrary of this; and moreover, if any one be suspected of speaking with a view to his own advantage, though at the same time what is best, through grudging him the gain of which we have but an uncertain idea, we deprive the state of its certain benefit. And thus good advice, given in a straightforward manner, has come to be no less suspected than bad; so that it is equally necessary for one who wishes to carry the most dreadful measures to win over the multitude by trickery, and for one who speaks on the better side to gain credit by falsehood. And the state alone it is impossible, owing to these over-wise notions, to serve in an open manner and without deceiving it; for he who openly confers any good upon it is suspected of getting secretly, in some way or other, an advantage in return. Now on subjects of the greatest importance, and with such an estimate of our conduct, we [orators] ought to speak with more extensive forethought than you who take but an off-hand view of measures; especially as we are responsible for the advice we give, whereas you are irresponsible for listening to it. For if he who offered counsel, and he who followed it, suffered alike, you would judge more prudently. But as it is, through whatever passion you may at any time have met with disasters, you punish the single judgment of the man who persuaded you, and not your own, for having so numerously joined in the blunder.

44. "I came forward, however, neither to speak against any one in defense of the Mytilenaeans, nor to accuse any one. For the question we have to decide is not, if we take a wise view of it, respecting their guilt, but respecting our taking good counsel. For though I should prove them to be utterly guilty, I will not for that reason also bid you to put them to death, unless it were expedient: and though they might claim some allowance [I would not bid you make it], unless it should appear good for the state. But I am of opinion that we are deliberating for the future, rather than the present; and as to what Cleon most positively asserts, that it will be advantageous to us in future, with a view to less frequent revolts, if we hold out death as the penalty; I too as positively contradict him, with regard to what is good for the future, and maintain the opposite opinion. And I beg you not to reject the utility of my advice for the plausibility of his. For his words might perhaps attract you, through being more just with regard to your present displeasure against the Mytilenaeans: but we are not holding a judicial inquiry in their case, that we should want what is just; but are deliberating respecting them, how they may be of service to us.

45. "Now the penalty of death has been enacted in states for many offenses, and those not equal to this, but less heinous; and yet, urged on by

hope, men venture to commit them; and no one ever yet came into danger with a conviction of his own mind that he would not succeed in his attempt. What city, too, when bent on revolt, ever attempted it with deficient resources—according to its own idea—either internal, or by means of alliance with others? Indeed all men, both in a private and public capacity, are naturally disposed to do wrong, and there is no law that will keep them from it; at least men have gone through all kinds of punishments in their enactments, to try if by any means they might be less injured by evil-doers, and it is probable that in early times the punishments for the greatest offenses were more lenient; but as they are disregarded, they generally, in the course of time, extend to death; and still even this is disregarded. Either, then, some fear more dreadful than this must be discovered, or this, at any rate, does not restrain men: but poverty inspiring boldness through necessity, and larger means inspiring ambition through insolence and pride, and the other conditions of life through some human passion or other, according as they are severally enslaved by some fatal and overpowering one, lead men on to dangers. Moreover, hope and desire for every thing, the one taking the lead, and the other following; and the one devising the attempt, while the other suggests the facility of succeeding in it; cause the most numerous disasters; and though unseen, they are more influential than the dangers that are seen. Fortune, too, aids them no less in urging men on; for by sometimes siding with them unexpectedly, she induces them to run the risk even with inferior means; especially in the case of states, inasmuch as the venture is for the greatest objects, namely, freedom, or empire over others; and as each individual, when acting in concert with all, unreasonably carries his ideas to an extravagant length concerning them. In short, it is impossible [to remedy the evil], and the man is very simple who thinks, that when human nature is eagerly set on doing a thing, he has any means of diverting it, either by the rigor of laws, or any other kind of terror.

46. "We must not, then, either take bad counsel through trusting to the punishment of death as a thing to be relied on, or leave to those who have revolted no hope of being allowed to change their minds, and wipe out their offense in as short a time as possible. For consider that at present, if any city, even after revolting, find that it will not succeed, it would come to terms while it has still means of refunding the expenses, and of paying tribute in future. But in the other case, which of them, think you, would not make better preparations for the attempt than they do now, and hold out against its besiegers to the utmost, if it is all one whether it surrender slowly or quickly? And how can it fail to be injurious for us to be put to expense by sitting down before it, because it will not surrender; and if we take the city, to recover it in a ruined condition, and be deprived of the revenue from it in future? For our strength against the enemy lies in this. So then we must not hurt ourselves, by being strict judges of the offenders, but rather see how, by punishing them moderately, we may be able in future to avail ourselves of the cities with unimpaired means on the score of money; and we must resolve to derive our protection, not from severity of laws, but from attention to deeds. The very

contrary of which we do at present; and if we have subdued any power that was [once] free, and, when harshly governed, naturally revolted for its independence, we fancy that we are bound to avenge ourselves with severity. But in dealing with freemen, we must not *punish* them rigorously when they revolt, but *watch* them rigorously *before* they revolt, and prevent their even coming to the thought of it: and when we have got the mastery of them, we should attach the guilt to as few as possible.

47. "Now consider what an error you would commit in this also, if persuaded by Cleon. For at present the commons in all the states are well disposed toward you, and either do not revolt with the aristocratical party, or if compelled to do so, are straightway hostile to those who made them; and you have the mass of the city opposed to you on your side, when you proceed to war. But if you butcher the commons of Mytilene, who took no part in the revolt, and when they had got possession of arms, voluntarily gave up the city; in the first place you will act unjustly by slaying your benefactors; and in the next you will produce for the higher classes of men a result which they most desire; for when they lead their cities to revolt, they will immediately have the commons on their side, because you had shown them beforehand that the same penalty is appointed for those who are guilty and those who are not. On the contrary, even if they *were* guilty, you ought to pretend not to notice it; that the only class still allied with us may not become hostile to us. And this I consider far more beneficial toward retaining our empire—that we should voluntarily be treated with injustice—than that with justice we should put to the sword those whom we ought not. And so the identity of the justice and expediency of the punishment, which Cleon asserts, is found impossible to exist therein.

48. "Being convinced then that this is the better course, and not allowing too much weight either to pity or to lenity (for neither do *I* [any more than Cleon], wish you to be influenced by these), but judging from the advice itself which is given you, be persuaded by me to try calmly those of the Mytilenaeans whom Paches sent off as guilty, and to allow the rest to live where they are. For this is both profitable for the future, and terrible to your enemies at the present moment; since whoever takes good advice against his adversaries is stronger than one who recklessly proceeds against them with violence of action."

49. To this effect spoke Diodotus. These being the views that were expressed in most direct opposition to one another, the Athenians, notwithstanding [their wish to reconsider the question], came to a conflict of opinion respecting them, and were nearly matched in the voting, though that of Diodotus prevailed. And they immediately dispatched another trireme with all speed, that they might not find the city destroyed through the previous arrival of the first; which had the start by a day and a night. The Mytilenaean embassadors having provided for the vessel wine and barley-cakes, and promising great rewards if they should arrive first, there was such haste in their course, that at the same time as they rowed they ate cakes kneaded with oil

and wine; and some slept in turns, while others rowed. And as there happened to be no wind against them, and the former vessel did not sail in any haste on so horrible a business, while this hurried on in the manner described; though the other arrived so much first that Paches had read the decree, and was on the point of executing the sentence, the second came to land after it, and prevented the butchery. Into such imminent peril did Mytilene come.

50. The other party, whom Paches had sent off as the chief authors of the revolt, the Athenians put to death, according to the advice of Cleon, amounting to rather more than one thousand. They also dismantled the walls of the Mytilenaeans, and seized their ships. After this, they did not impose any tribute on the Lesbians, but having divided the land, excepting that of the Methymnaeans, into three thousand portions, they set apart three hundred of them as consecrated to the gods, and to the rest sent out as shareholders those of their own citizens to whose lot they had fallen; with whom the Lesbians having agreed to pay in money two minae a year for each portion, farmed the land themselves. The Athenians also took possession of the towns on the continent of which the Mytilenaeans were masters, and they were afterward subject to Athens. Such then was the issue of affairs as regarded Lesbos. . . .

Book V

84. The next summer, Alcibiades sailed to Argos with twenty ships, and seized three hundred men, who were still thought to be suspicious characters, and to favor the cause of the Lacedaemonians; and these the Athenians deposited in the neighboring islands within their dominions. The Athenians also undertook an expedition against the island of Melos, with thirty ships of their own, six of the Chians, two of the Lesbians, sixteen hundred of their own heavy-armed, three hundred bowmen, twenty mounted archers, and about five thousand five hundred heavy-armed of the allies and the islanders. Now the Melians are a colony of the Lacedaemonians, and would not submit to the Athenians, like the rest of the islanders, but at first remained quiet as neutrals, and then, when the Athenians tried to compel them by devastating their land, went openly to war with them. The generals therefore, Cleomedes son of Lycomedes, and Tisias son of Tisimachus, having gone and encamped in their territory with this armament, before injuring any part of the land, first sent embassadors to hold a conference with them. These the Melians did not introduce to their popular assembly, but desired them to state the objects of their mission before the magistrates and the few. The embassadors of the Athenians then spoke as follows:

85. *Ath.* "Since our words are not to be addressed to your populace, in order that the many may not be deceived, forsooth, by hearing at once in one continuous oration persuasive and irrefutable arguments (for we know that this is the meaning of your introducing us to the few), do ye who are seated here in congress pursue a still more cautious method. For do not ye, either,

make one continuous speech on the several topics, but immediately taking us up at whatever does not appear to be advanced in accordance with your interest, decide that question. And first tell us if you are pleased with what we propose." The commissioners of the Melians made this reply:

86. *Mel.* "The fairness of thus calmly instructing each other is open to no objection: but your preparations for war, which are already here, and not merely coming, appear to be at variance with it. For we see that you are come to be yourselves judges of what will be said; and that the issue of the conference will in all probability bring us war, if we are stronger in the justice of our cause, and therefore refuse to submit; or slavery, if we are convinced by you."

87. *Ath.* "If now you have met to argue upon suspicions of the future, or to do any thing else but to consult for your country with a view to its preservation, according to what is present and before your eyes, we will stop; but if for this object we will speak."

88. *Mel.* "It is but natural and pardonable for men so circum-stanced to have recourse to many things, both in thinking and speaking. However, this our meeting *is* held with a view to our preservation; and let the discussion proceed, if you please, in the way which you propose.

89. *Ath.* "We then shall not ourselves advance fair pretenses, either of our justly enjoying empire in consequence of having overthrown the Mede, or of now coming against you because we are being injured—and so make a long speech which would not be believed; nor do we wish you to think of persuading us by saying, either that you did not join the standard of the Lacedaemonians, though you were their colony; or that you have done us no wrong. But we advise you, according to the real sentiments of us both, to think of getting what you can; since you know, and are speaking to those who know, that, in the language of men, what is right is estimated by equality of power to compel; but what is possible is that which the stronger practice, and to which the weak submit."

90. *Mel.* "So far then as our opinion goes, it is for our advantage (for we must, since you have so prescribed, speak of what is expedient, to the neglect of what is right) that you should not take away what is a common benefit; but that for every one who at any time is in danger, what is reasonable should also be considered right; and that if he can gain assent to something which falls short of strict justice, he should have the benefit of it. And this is not less for your interest; inasmuch, as you would afford to others, should you fail, a pattern for inflicting the heaviest vengeance upon you."

91. *Ath.* "Nay, for our part, we are not disheartened about the end of our empire, even should it be brought to an end. For it is not those who rule over others, like the Lacedaemonians, that are to be feared by the van-quished. Nor is it with the Lacedaemonians that we have to struggle, but with the possibility of our subjects in any quarter by themselves attacking and overpowering those who have had rule over them. So on this point let the danger be left to us. But that we are come here for the benefit of our empire,

and that we shall also speak on the present occasion for the preservation of your country, on these points we will give you proofs; since we wish to maintain our own sovereignty over you without trouble, and to have you preserved for the advantage of us both."

92. *Mel.* "And how then could it prove advantageous for us to serve, as it is for you to govern?"

93. *Ath.* "Because you would have the benefit of submitting before you suffered the last extremities; while we should be gainers by not destroying you."

94. *Mel.* "But would you not accept our proposals, on condition of our remaining quiet, and being friends instead of enemies, but in alliance with neither side?"

95. *Ath.* "No; for your enmity is not so hurtful to us, as your friendship is to our subjects an evident proof of our weakness, but your hatred, of our power."

96. *Mel.* "And do your subjects then take such a view of equity, as to put on the same footing those who are not at all connected with you, and those who, being in most cases your colonists, and in some cases having revolted from you, have been reduced to subjection?"

97. *Ath.* "Why, for an argument resting on justice they think that neither of us are at a loss; but that on the ground of their power they escape, and we, through fear, abstain from attacking them. So that, besides our ruling over more subjects, you would also through your subjection confer security upon us; especially by the fact that you who are islanders, and weaker too than some others, did not escape our dominion, who have the command of the sea."

98. *Mel.* "And do you consider that there is no security in that other case? (For here again, as you have excluded us from appeals to justice, and urge us to yield to considerations of your advantage, we too must explain what is expedient for us, and so endeavor to persuade you, if the same happen to be for your interest also.) For how can you avoid making enemies of all that are at present neutral, when, on looking to the present case, they reckon that some time or other you will proceed against them also? And by that course what do you do, but aggrandize your present enemies, and bring those upon you against their will who would never else be likely to become hostile to you?"

99. *Ath.* "Why, we do not consider those who live any where on the mainland, and who in consequence of their liberty will long delay taking precautions against us, to be so formidable to us as those who are islanders any where without being under our rule, like you, and those who by the severity of our rule are now exasperated against us. For it is these who would most give way to recklessness, and bring both themselves and us into danger that was evident beforehand."

100. *Mel.* "Surely then, if you run such a risk not to be deprived of your empire, and those who are already in subjection, to be released from it; for us who are still free it were great baseness and cowardice not to have recourse to every thing before we submit to it."

101. *Ath.* "No; not at least if you take a sensible view of the case. For you are not on equal terms contending for honor, to avoid incurring disgrace; but you are rather deliberating for your preservation, to avoid resisting those who are far stronger than yourselves."

102. *Mel.* "But we know that warlike measures sometimes come to more impartial results than might have been expected from the different numbers on each side. And in our case to yield is immediate despair; but by making an effort there is yet hope of our keeping ourselves up."

103. *Ath.* "Hope, which is the solace of danger, when entertained by those who have abundant means, though it may injure, yet does not ruin them. But in the case of those who risk all they have on a throw (for it is naturally an extravagant passion), it is only found out at the time of their ruin, and leaves no room for guarding against it in future, when it is found out. Do not you then, weak as you are, and hanging on one single turn of the scale, be desirous of this fate, nor of resembling the greater part of mankind, who, when they might have been saved by human means, after visible hopes have failed them in their distress, betake themselves to such as are invisible, namely, prophecy, and oracles, and all such things as bring men to ruin, together with the hopes resting upon them."

104. *Mel.* "Difficult indeed even we, be well assured, consider it to contend against your power and fortune, unless we are able to do it on equal terms. However, we trust that in point of fortune we shall, by the favor of the gods, not be worsted, because we are standing up in a righteous cause against unjust opponents; and that our deficiency in power will be made up by our Lacedaemonian allies; who are under a necessity of succoring us, if for no other reason, yet on account of our connection with them, and for very shame."

105. *Ath.* "As regards then the favor of heaven, we trust that we too shall not fall short of it: since we are not requiring or doing any thing beyond the opinion of men, with respect to the gods, or their determination, with respect to themselves. For of the gods we hold as a matter of opinion, and of men we know as a certainty, that, in obedience to an irresistible instinct, they always maintain dominion, wherever they are the stronger. And we neither enacted this law, nor were the first to carry it out when enacted; but having received it when already in force, and being about to leave it after us to be in force forever, we only avail ourselves of it; knowing that both you and others, if raised to the same power, would do the same. And so, with regard to the gods, we are with good reason fearless of defeat. But with regard to your opinion respecting the Lacedaemonians, according to which you trust, that from a sense of shame, forsooth, they will assist you; though we bless your simplicity, we do not admire your folly. For with respect to themselves, and the institutions of their country, the Lacedaemonians do indeed to a very great extent practice virtue; but with respect to others, though we might descant at length on their conduct toward them, speaking most concisely we should declare, that of all the men we are acquainted with, they most evidently consider what is agreeable to be honorable, and what is expedient to be just.

And yet such a view of things is not in favor of your present unreasonable hopes of safety."

106. *Mel.* "But it is on this very ground that we now rely on their sense of interest, and believe that they will not betray us Melians, who are their colonists, and so lose the confidence of those Greeks who wish them well, while they help those who are hostile to them."

107. *Ath.* "Then you do not think that interest is connected with security, whereas justice and honor are practiced with danger; a course on which the Lacedaemonians, generally speaking, least of all men venture."

108. *Mel.* "Nay, but we are of opinion that they would even incur dangers for our sake, more than usual, and would regard them as less hazardous than in the case of others; inasmuch as we lie near the Peloponnese, for the execution of their measures; while in feeling we are, through our kindred with them, more to be trusted than another party would be."

109. *Ath.* "Ay, but to men going to take part in a quarrel safety does not appear to consist in the good feeling of those who call them to their aid, but in the fact of their being far superior in power for action; and the Lacedaemonians look to this even more than the rest of the world. At any rate, through their mistrusting their own resources, it is only in concert with many allies that they attack those who are near to them; so that it is not likely they will cross over to an *island,* while we are masters of the sea."

110. *Mel.* "But they would have others to send; and the Cretan sea is of wide extent, and to intercept a party in crossing it is more difficult for those who command it, than to escape is for those who wish to elude observation. Besides, if they should be disappointed in this, they would proceed against your territory, and to the remainder of your allies, such as Brasidas did not reach; and you will have to exert yourselves, not so much for territory which does not belong to you, as for your own confederacy and country."

111. *Ath.* "On this point you, as well as others, may learn by actual experience, and not remain ignorant, that from no single siege did the Athenians ever yet retreat through fear of others. But it strikes us that though you said you would consult for the safety of your country, you have in all this long discussion advanced nothing which men might trust to for thinking that they would be saved; but your strongest points depend on hope and futurity, while your present resources are too scanty, compared with those at present opposed to you, to give you a chance of escape. And so you afford proof of great folly in your views, if you do not even yet, after allowing us to retire, adopt some counsel more prudent than this. For you surely will not betake yourselves to that shame, which in dangers that are disgraceful, because foreseen, destroys men more than any thing else. For in the case of many men, though they foresee all the time what they are running into, the thing which is called disgrace, by the influence of a seducing name, allures them on, enslaved as they are to the word, in fact to fall wilfully into irretrievable disasters, and to incur a shame more shameful as the attendant on folly than on fortune. Against this then you, if you take good advice, will be on your

guard, and will not consider it discreditable to submit to the most powerful state, when it offers you fair terms, namely, that you should become tributary allies, with the enjoyment of your own country; and when a choice of war or safety is given you, to avoid choosing through animosity what is worse for you. For whatever men do not yield to their equals, while they keep on good terms with their superiors, and are moderate to their inferiors, they would be most successful. Consider then, even after we have retired; and reflect again and again, that it is for your country that you are consulting, which you can do but for one country, and for once, whether it prove successful or unsuccessful."

112. So the Athenians retired from the conference; and the Melians, having been left to themselves, as they still thought pretty nearly the same as they had maintained in the discussion, gave the following answer: "We neither think differently from what we did at first, Athenians, nor will we in a short space of time rob of its liberty a city which has now been inhabited seven hundred years; but trusting to the fortune which, by the favor of heaven, has hitherto preserved it, and to the help of man, especially of the Lacedaemonians, we will endeavor to save ourselves. But we propose to you that we should be your friends, and the enemies of neither party; and that you should retire from our country after making such a treaty as may appear suitable for both sides."

113. Such then was the answer which the Melians gave. The Athenians, now departing from the conference, said: "Well then you are the only men who by these counsels, as appears to us, consider what is future as more certain than what is seen, and regard what is out of sight as already occurring, because you wish it; and having staked and relied most on [such things as] Lacedaemonians, and fortune, and hopes, you will also be most disappointed."

114. So the Athenian embassadors returned to their forces: and their generals, since the Melians did not listen at all to their proposals, immediately proceeded to apply themselves to war; and having divided the work between the different states, inclosed the Melians with lines on all sides. Afterwards, the Athenians left a part of their own troops and the allies, to keep guard both by land and sea, and returned with the main body of the forces. Those who were left behind remained and besieged the place.

115. About the same time an Argive force invaded the Phliasian territory, and being intercepted by an ambuscade of the Phliasians and their allies, were cut off to the number of eighty. And now the Athenians at Pylus took great spoils from the Lacedaemonians; in consequence of which the Lacedaemonians, though even then they did not renounce the treaty, and go to war with them, proclaimed that any of their people who pleased might plunder the Athenians. Moreover, the Corinthians proceeded to hostilities with the Athenians for some private quarrels of their own; but the rest of the Peloponnesians remained quiet. The Melians, too, attacked by night the part of the Athenian lines opposite the market-place, and slew some of the men; and having carried in corn, and as many useful things as they could, returned

and kept quiet; while the Athenians made better provision for the guard in future. And so the summer ended.

116.   The following winter, the Lacedaemonians intended to march against the Argive territory, but returned on finding, when at the frontier, that the sacrifices for crossing it were not favorable. Owing to this intention on their part, the Argives, suspecting a certain party in their city, seized some of them, while others escaped them. About the same time, the Melians again took a part of the Athenian lines in another direction, the garrison not being numerous. A fresh force having afterwards come from Athens in consequence of these occurrences, under the command of Philocrates son of Demeas, and the inhabitants being now vigorously blockaded, after there had also been some treachery practiced by their own men, they surrendered at discretion to the Athenians; who put to death all the Melian adults they took, and made slaves of the children and women. As for the country, they afterward sent out five hundred colonists, and inhabited it themselves.

2

The Greek
Dramatists:
Justice –
The Blood Feud
or Social Order?

The Oresteian Trilogy, consisting of the plays *Agamemnon, The Libation-Bearers,* and *The Eumenides,* was presented in 458 B.C. at the theatre of Dionysus in Athens, and it won first prize in the dramatic competition. Aeschylus (525–456) was an Athenian who participated in his fellow citizens' armed struggle against the invading Persians and was devoted to the new Athenian democracy. The festival of Dionysus included a contest in tragedy as one of its chief features, and the theatre at Athens became an integral part of that intense Athenian combination of political and religious life, the life of the *polis.*

With their early origin in ritual religious expression, the tragedies were intended not to entertain but to instruct the assembled populace and to move it emotionally. The subject matter of the plays was invariably the legends and myths of the Hellenic peoples, well-known in story and song. These stories were the raw material the playwright used to confront his audience with the dilemmas, crises, and conflicts of human life. These tragedies were ritual in nature, showing the suffering and enlightenment of heroic figures from the past as they came into conflict with the laws of the gods and the requirements of their own personal and human situations and of social life. The tragedies are, thus, an excellent source for the highest concerns of the assembled Athenian citizenry in the fifth century, the height of its glory and power.

The Oresteia tells the story of the family of Atreus which was cursed by the gods for its violation of the laws of morality and filial piety; the tragedy introduces the concept of redemption (justice) through suffering. Agamemnon, King of Argos, returns from the Trojan War to be murdered by his wife, Clytemnestra, and her lover, Aegisthus, himself a member of a rival branch of the same accursed family. Clytemnestra's hatred for Agamemnon stemmed from his ritual sacrifice of their daughter, Iphigenia, in order to expedite the beginning of the Trojan War. In *The Libation-Bearers,* Agamemnon's son Orestes avenges his murdered father at the command of the god Apollo by killing his adulterous mother and her lover. In *The Eumenides,* Orestes is pursued for his crime by the Furies, and a unique solution is proposed to the problem of vengeance and justice, in search of a social order more stable than one based on the traditional blood feud.

The first play of the trilogy, the *Agamemnon,* follows. If every Athenian generation reinterpreted these ancient myths in the light of present experience and need, then it should be clear that the Athenian experience of the fifth century—the defeat of the Persians and democratic Athens' leadership of the other Greek cities—suggested new solutions to the age-old problem of justice.

Excerpts of the remainder of the Oresteia follow *Agamemnon.* Orestes' murderous deed satisfied Apollo, the god of light, but defied the older gods of the earth and of the generative process, represented by the Furies, who held the crime of matricide, the murder of one's mother, in horror. This struggle between the demands of the higher and lower gods was resolved by Aeschylus through a trial before a new high court in Athens presided over by the patroness of the city, Athena. What follows the *Agamemnon* is the final portion of *The Eumenides,* in which the laws of the Athenian *polis,* and not the blood feud, are made the embodiment of justice and religious piety. Thus a jury of mere mortals, citizens of Athens, judges the affairs of gods and men. Man truly rules his own destiny—a novel idea indeed. This integration of political and religious obligation in the deification of the *polis* was a pillar of the outlook of classical man. When the various city–states gave way to vast empires under Alexander the Great, Caesar Augustus and the other Roman emperors, deification of the person of the emperor constituted this unity of the political and the religious life of classical man—an identification against which Christianity arose and which it finally overthrew.

Aeschylus:
Agamemnon

Dramatis Personae

Watchman
Chorus of Argive Elders
Clytemnestra
Herald
Agamemnon
Cassandra
Aegisthus

Scene: Argos
Watchman [... *reclining on the flat roof of the palace*]:

I pray the gods deliverance from these toils,
Release from year-long watch, which, couch'd aloft
On these Atreidan roofs, dog-like, I keep,
Marking the stars which nightly congregate;
And those bright potentates who bring to mortals
Winter and summer, signal in the sky,
What time they wane I note, their risings too.
And for the beacon's token now I watch,
The blaze of fire, bearing from Troy a tale,
Tidings of capture; for so proudly hopes
A woman's heart, with manly counsel fraught.
Dew-drenched and restless is my nightly couch,
By dreams unvisited, for at my side,
Fear stands, in place of sleep, nor suffers me
Soundly, in slumberous rest, my lids to close.
Then when I think to chant a strain, or hum,
(Such against sleep my tuneful counter-charm,)
Moaning, I wail the sorrows of this house,
Not wisely governed as in days of old.
But may glad respite from these toils be mine,
When fire, joy's herald, through the darkness gleams.

[*He suddenly beholds the beacon-light and starts to his feet.*]

Hail lamp of night, forth shining like the day,

Of many a festive dance in Argos' land,
Through joy at this event, the harbinger.

Hurrah! Hurrah! To Agamemnon's queen,
Thus with shrill cry I give th' appointed sign,
That from her couch up-rising with all speed,
She in the palace jubilant may lift
The joyous shout, to gratulate this torch,
If Ilion's citadel in truth is ta'en,
As, shining forth, this beacon-fire proclaims.

The joyous prelude I myself will dance,
For to my lords good fortune I shall score,
Now that this torch hath cast me triple six.
Well! be it mine, when comes this mansion's lord,
In this my hand his much-loved hand to hold!

The rest I speak not; o'er my tongue hath passed
An ox with heavy tread: the house itself,
Had it a voice, would tell the tale full clear;
And I, with those who know, am fain to speak,
With others, who know nothing, I forget.

[Enter Chorus of Argive Elders.]

> *Chorus.*
> Lo the tenth year rolls apace
> Since Priam's mighty challenger,
> Lord Menelas and Atreus' heir,
> Stalwart Atridae,—by heaven's grace
> Twin-throned, twin-sceptered,—from this land
> A thousand sail, with Argives manned,
> Unmoor'd,—a martial armament,
> Warriors on just reprisal bent,
> Fierce battle clanging from their breast,
> Like vultures of their young bereaved,
> Who, for their nestlings sorely grieved,
> Wheel, eddying high above their nest,
> By oarage of strong pennons driven,
> Missing the eyrie-watching care
> Of callow fledglings; but from heaven,

Reprinted from Anna Swanwick, trans., *The Dramas of Aeschylus* (London: George Bell & Sons, 1886), pp. 3-74.

Some guilt-avenging deity,
Or all-retrieving Zeus, doth lend
An ear attentive to the cry
Of birds, shrill-wailing, sore-distrest,
And doth upon the guilty send
Erinys, late-avenging pest.

So for the dame, by many wooed.
Doth mighty Zeus, who shields the guest,
'Gainst Paris send th' Atridan brood;
Struggles limb-wearing, knees earth-pressed
The spear-shaft, rudely snapt in twain
In war's initial battle,—these
For Danaoi as for Trojans he decrees.
As matters stand, they stand; the yet to be
Must issue as ordained by destiny.
Nor altar fires, nor lustral rain
Poured forth, nor tear-drops shed in vain,
The wrath relentless can appease
     Of violated sanctities.
But we, unhonoured, weak of frame,
Excluded from that proud array,
Tarry at home, and, age-oppressed,
On staves our child-like strength we lean;
In tender years and age, the same,
Life's current feebly sways the breast;
His station Ares holds no more;
Decrepid Eld, with leafage hoar,
No stronger than a child for war,
Treadeth his triple-footed way,
Like dream in daylight seen.

[*Enter* Clytemnestra]

But Clytemnestra, thou,
Tyndareus' daughter, Argos queen,
What hath befallen? What hast heard?
Confiding in what tidings now
Sendest thou round the altar-kindling word?
Of all the gods who guard the state,
Supernal, or of realms below,
In heaven, or in the mart who wait,
     With gifts the altars glow.

Now here, now yonder, doth a torch arise,
Streaming aloft to reach the skies,
Charmed with pure unguent's soothing spell,
Guileless and suasive, from the royal cell.

What here 'tis lawful to declare,
What may be told proclaim;
Be healer of this care
Which now a lowering form doth wear,
Till fawning Hope, from out the flame
Of sacrifice, with gentle smile
Doth sateless grief's soul-gnawing pang beguile.

[*While* Clytemnestra *offers sacrifice, the following Ode is
      sung by the Chorus from the altar of Zeus.*]

The way-side omen mine it is to sing,
The leaders' prosperous might fore-shadowing,
For still my age, unquenched its natal power,
Doth suasive song inspire, a heaven-sent dower,
How the rapacious bird, the feathered king,
      Sends forth against the Teucrid land,
      With spear and with avenging hand,
      Achaia's double-thronèd Might,
Accordant chiefs of Hellas' martial flower.
Toward spear-poising hand, the palace near,
On lofty station, manifest to sight,
The bird-kings to the navy-kings appear,
One black, and one with hinder plumage white;
A hare with embryo young, in evil hour,
Amerced of future courses, they devour.
      Chant the dirge, uplift the wail!
      But may the right prevail!

Then the sagacious army-seer, aware
How diverse-minded the Atridan kings,
In the hare-renders sees the martial pair,
And thus, the augury expounding, sings;—
"Priam's stronghold in time this martial raid
      Captures, but first the city's store,
      The people's wealth, shall fate destroy;
      Now from no god may jealous ire
O'ercloud the mighty curb forged against Troy,

Marshalled for battle; for the holy Maid
Is angered at the house, since of her sire
The wingèd hounds the wretched trembler tare,
Mother and young unborn, her special care;
Therefore doth she the eagles' meal abhor.
      Chant the dirge, uplift the wail!
      But may the right prevail!

For she, the beauteous goddess, loves
The tender whelps, new-dropped, of creatures rude,
Sparing the udder-loving brood
Of every beast through field or wood that roves,—
Hence with Apollo pleads the seer that he
From these events fair omens will fulfil,
      Judging the way-side augury,
Partly auspicious, partly fraught with ill.
Oh! God of healing! thee I supplicate,
Let not the Huntress on the Danaï bring
Dire ship-detaining blasts and adverse skies,
      Preluding other sacrifice,
      Lawless, unfestive, natal spring
      Of feudful jar and mortal hate,
      By husband-fear unawed;
For child-avenging wrath, with fear and fraud,
Dread palace-warden, doth untiring wait."

      Such woes, with high successes blent,
By Fate on the twain royal houses sent,
Did Calchas from the way-side auguries
Bodeful proclaim:—Then consonant with these,
      Chant the dirge, uplift the wail!
      But may the right prevail!

      Zeus, whoe'er he be, this name
      If it pleaseth him to claim,
      This to him will I address;
      Weighing all, no power I know
Save only Zeus, if I aside would throw
In sooth as vain this burthen of distress.
      Nor doth he so great of yore,
      With all-defying boldness rife,
      Longer avail; his reign is o'er.
      The next, thrice vanquished in the strife,
      Hath also passed; but who the victor-strain
To Zeus uplifts, true wisdom shall obtain.

To sober thought Zeus paves the way,
    And wisdom links with pain.
In sleep the anguish of remembered ill
Drops on the troubled heart; against their will
Rebellious men are tutored to be wise;
A grace I ween of the divinities,
Who mortals from their holy seats arraign.

    E'en so the elder of the twain,
    Achaia's fleet who swayed,
No seer upbraiding, bowed, with grief suppressed,
His soul to fortune's stroke; what time the host,
In front of Chalcis, tossing off the coast
Of wave-vexed Aulis, lingered, sore-distressed,
While store-exhausting gales their progress stayed.

Blasts, dire delay and faminine in their train,
And evil-anchorage, from Strymon sweep,—
Ruin to mortals; with malignant power,
    Ruthless to ships and cordage, they
    Doubling the sojourn on the deep
       Wither the Argive flower.
But to the chiefs of that array,
When, than the bitter storm, the seer
A cure shrieked forth, weighted with deadlier bane,—
In name of Artemis,—the Atridan twain,
Smiting on earth their sceptres, strove in vain
       To quell the rising tear.

Then thus aloud the elder chieftain cried:—
"Grievous, in sooth, the doom to disobey,
But grievous too if I my child must slay,
    My home's fair ornament, my pride,
    Defiling these paternal hands,
      E'en at the altar's side,
With virgin-slaughter's gory tide.
What course exempt from evil? Say,
The fleet can I desert, the leaguèd bands
Failing? With hot desire to crave the spell
Of virgin blood, the storm that shall allay,
    Is just. May all be well!"

Then harnessed in Necessity's stern yoke
An impious change-wind in his bosom woke,
Profane, unhallowed, with dire evil fraught,

His soul perverting to all daring thought.
For frenzy, that from primal guilt doth spring,
Emboldens mortals, prompting deeds of ill;
Thus, armed a woman to avenge, the king
In sacrifice his daughter dared to kill;
The fleet's initial rite accomplishing.
Her prayers, her cries of "Father," her young life
Were nought to those stern umpires, breathing strife:
So, after prayer, her sire the servants bade,
Stooping, with steelèd hearts, to lift the maid
Robe-tangled, kid-like, as for sacrifice,
High o'er the altar; them he also bade,
Guarding her lovely mouth, her bodeful cries,
Stern curse entailing on their houses twain,
With voiceless muzzles forceful to restrain.

Then letting fall her veil of saffron dye,
She smote, with piteous arrow from her eye,
Each murderer; while, passing fair,
Like to a pictured image, voiceless there,
Strove she to speak; for oft in other days,
She in her father's hospitable halls,
With her chaste voice had carolled forth his praise,
    What time the walls
   Rang to the Paean's sound,
Gracing her sire, with third libation crowned.

What next befel I know not, nor relate;
Not unfulfill'd were Calchas' words of fate.
For justice doth for sufferers ordain
To purchase wisdom at the cost of pain.
Why seek to read the future? Let it go!
Since dawns the issue clear with dawning day,
What boots it to forestal our date of woe?
    Come weal at last!
So prays, these mischiefs past,
Of Apia's land this one sole guard and stay.

Hail Clytemnestra! Hither am I come
Thy majesty revering. For 'tis meet
When the male throne is empty, that we pay
To our high captain's consort honour due.
If thou hast heard auspicious news, or not,
That with joy-vouching hope thou lightest up

The altar fires, I, as a friend, would know,—
Yet shall thy silence nought unkind be deemed.

       Clytemnestra.
Joy's harbinger, be radiant Morning born
From kindly mother Night! So runs the saw.
But thou of joy beyond all hope shalt hear,
For Priam's city have the Argives won.

       Chorus.
How queen! through unbelief I miss thy word.

       Clytemnestra.
Troy is in Argive hands; now speak I plain?

       Chorus.
Joy, stealing o'er my heart, calls forth the tear.

       Clytemnestra.
'Tis true, thine eye thy loyalty bewrays.

       Chorus.
Of these great tidings what the certain proof?

       Clytemnestra.
Warrant I have;—how not? or Heaven deceives me.

       Chorus.
Trusting the suasive augury of dreams?

       Clytemnestra.
The fancies of the sleep-bound soul I heed not.

       Chorus.
But hath some wingless rumour buoy'd thee up?

       Clytemnestra.
Thou chidest me as were I a young girl.

       Chorus.
But since what time was Priam's city spoiled?

       Clytemnestra.
This very night now bringing forth the day.

Chorus.
What messenger could travel with such speed?

Clytemnestra.
Hephaestos, a bright flash from Ida sending.
Hither through swift relays of courier-flame,
Beacon transmitted beacon. Ida first
To the Hermaean rock on Lemnos' Isle;
Thence Athos' summit, dedicate to Zeus,
The third in order, caught the mighty glow.
Upsoaring, bridging in its might the sea,
With gathered strength, the onward speeding torch,
In golden splendour, like another sun,
Its message to Makistos' watch-tower sends,
Who, nor delaying, nor by Sleep o'erpowered,
The courier's duty faithfully discharged.
The torch, far-gleaming to Euripos' stream,
Gives signal to Messapios' sentinels.
Firing of withered heath a giant pile,
With answering blaze, they pass the message on.
The stalwart flame, unwearied and undimm'd,
Like a bright moon, o'erleaps Asopos' plain,
And wakens, on Cithaeron's lofty crag,
Another speeder of the fiery post.
The warder hailing the far-journeying fire,
Kindles a beacon of surpassing glow;
Bounded the radiance o'er Gorgopis' lake,
And reaching Aegiplanctos' mountain peak
Urged on without delay the fiery chain.
With vigour unimpaired they onward send,
Kindled anew, a mighty beard of flame,
That, flaring from afar, the headland crossed
O'erlooking Saron's gulf. Down shotting then,
The blaze, alighting on Arachnae's height,
The city's nearest watch-tower, reached its goal;
Thence to the roof of Atreus' son this light
Darted,—true scion of Idaian fire.
Thus in succession, flame awakening flame
Fulfilled the order of the fiery course:
The first and last are victors in the race.
Such is the proof, the warrant that I give
Of tidings sent me by my Lord from Troy.

Chorus.
The gods, O queen, will I invoke hereafter.
But now I fain would marvel at thy words,
Heard more at large so thou wouldst speak again.

Clytemnestra.

Troy on this very day th' Achaians hold.
I ween ill-blending clamour fills the town:
Pour in one vessel vinegar and oil,
They will not livingly consort, I trow;
So now from captives and from captors rise
Two voices, telling of their two-fold fate.
For *those* flung prostrate on the lifeless forms
Of husbands and of brothers, children too,
Prone on their aged sires, lamenting wail;
While *these,* night-stragglers after toilsome fight,
Keen for all viands that the city yields,
Upon no order standing, but as each
Hath snatched the lot of fortune, take their fill.
At length from frost and skiey dews set free,
They dwell in Ilion's spear-won halls, and sleep
The live-long night, unsentinelled like gods.
If now the tutelary powers they fear,
Who hold the conquered land, and spare their shrines,
Captors, they shall not captured be in turn.
But may no greedy passion seize the host
To plunder things unlawful, smit with gain.
A safe return has yet to be secured,
And half the double course is yet to run.
But guilty to the gods if come the host,
Wakeful may rise the sorrows of the slain
For vengeance, though no sudden ill befal.
These words from me, a woman thou hast heard;
But may the good in overpoise prevail!
For I of many blessings choose this joy.

Chorus.

Like prudent man well hast thou spoken, lady.—
But I, on hearing of thy certain proofs,
Forthwith prepare me to salute the gods,
For no unworthy meed requites our toil.

[*Exit* Clytemnestra

Hail, sovereign Zeus, and friendly Night,
Mistress of mighty glories, hail!
Thou who o'er Troia's tower-crowned height,
A snare so closely meshed hast flung,
That none, or fully grown or young,
Thraldom's huge drag-net may avail
To overleap. Vast ruin captures all.
Great guardian of the guest,
    Thee I adore;—

Wrought were those deeds at thy behest:
    The bow thou didst of yore
    'Gainst Alexander strain,
That nor the destined hour before,
Nor shooting o'er the stars, in vain
    The shaft might fall.

'Tis Zeus who smote them, this we may aver,
    For easy 'tis to trace;
    The end he shaped as he decreed.
    Yet gods supernal, some declare,
    To sinful mortals give no heed
    Who trample under foot the grace
Of sacred things. But such are reprobate;—
Kindred they claim with those, in heaven's despite,
Who rebel war breathe forth, transgressing right.
Wealth in excess breeds mischief, and o'erturns
    The balance of the constant mind;
    No bulwark 'gainst destructive fate
    In riches shall that mortal find
Who Justice' mighty altar rudely spurns.

Frenzy's unhappy suasion, fraught with bane
    To hapless children, sways the will;
    Against the mischief cure is vain;
    Not hidden is the flagrant ill;—
    Baleful it bursts upon the sight;
    Like spurious coin, his metal base
    Use and the touchstone bring to light,
Who, boy-like, to a wingèd bird gives chase,
And whelms his native soil in hopeless night.
His orisons the heavenly powers disclaim,
    But sweep to doom the sinful wight
    Practised in guile;—thus Paris came
    To Atreus' halls;—the friendly board
He shamed, the consort luring from her lord.
Bequeathing to her people deadly stour
Of shielded hosts, of spears, and ships' array,
And Ilion's ruin bearing as her dower,
She through the portal swiftly took her way,
Daring what none may dare;—with many a wail,
The palace seers peal'd forth the tale.

"Woe for the house, the house and chieftains, woe!
Woe for the couch, the trace of her once true!"

Wronged, yet without reproach, in speechless woe
There stands he, yearning still her form to view
Lost o'er the far sea-wave: his dreamy pain
Conjures her phantom in his home to reign.
　　He loathes the sculptor's plastic skill
　　　　Which living grace belies;
　　　Not Aphroditè's self can still
　　　　The hunger of his eyes.

And dreamy fancies, coinage of the brain,
Come o'er the troubled heart with vain delight;
For vain the rapture, the illusion vain,
When forms beloved in visions of the night;
With changeful aspect, mock our grasp, and sweep
On noiseless wing adown the paths of sleep.
Such sorrows o'er the hearth brood evermore,
And woes o'ertowering these. The warrior train
Comrades in danger, steered from Hellas' shore,
Leaving in Hellas' homes heart-withering pain;
Full many sorrows rankle at the core.
　　Those whom he sent each holds in ken,
　　　　But to their homes return
　　　Armour and in the funeral urn,
　　　　Ashes instead of men.
For Ares, bartering for gold
The flesh of men, the scales doth hold
　　In battle of the spear.
From Ilion, back to sorrowing friends,
Rich dust, fire-purified, he sends,
　　Wash'd with full many a tear.
No living warriors greet them, but instead
Urns filled with ashes smoothly spread.
Groaning, each hero's praise they tell;
How *this* excelled in martial strife;
And *that* in fields of carnage fell,
Right nobly for another's wife.
Breathing such murmurs, jealous hate
Doth on the Atridan champions wait.
Achaians, cast in fairest mould,
Ensepulchred 'neath Ilion's wall,
The foughten shore now firmly hold,
　　The hostile sod their pall.

Direful the people's voice, to hate
Attuned, which worketh soon or late

As ban of public doom.
Now o'er my spirit anxious fear
Broodeth, lest tidings I should hear
　　That night still shrouds in gloom;
For blind to deeds of blood the gods are not.
　　In Time the swarthy brood of Night
　　With slow eclipse reverse his lot,
　　Who Fortune reareth in despite
　　Of Justice. Reft of succour lies
　　The wretch once prone. Excessive praise
　　Is bodeful ever; 'gainst men's eyes
　　Zeus hurls his blinding rays.
　　But may ungrudged success be mine!
　　No city-spoiler let me be!
　　Nor, subject to another, pine
　　　　Myself in slavery.

Borne by the joy-announcing flame
Swift through the town thy tidings fly;
But whether true who may proclaim,
　　Or not a heavenly lie?
For who so childish, so distraught,
To warm his spirit at the beacon's glow,
　　When other news, with evil fraught,
　　　　His joy may change to woe?
'Tis woman's way the boon, ere seen, to prize;
Too credulous, her fancy open lies
To rumour's rapid inroad, but the fame
Published by women quickly dies.

Chorus Leader.
Soon shall we know whether the signal fires,
The swift relays of courier-light be true,
Or whether, dreamlike, they beguiled our minds
With grateful splendour;—Yonder, from the coast,
A herald comes, shaded with laurel boughs;
While Clay's twin-brother, thirsty Dust, attests
That neither voiceless, nor of mountain wood
Kindling the blaze, will he report in smoke;
No,—either will his voice announce more joy,
Or,—but ill-omened words I deprecate.
Be omens fair with fair assurance crown'd!
May he who 'gainst the state breathes other prayer,
First reap the fruit of his malignant thought.

[*Enter Herald.*]

Herald.
Oh soil of Argos, oh my native land,
In light of this tenth year to thee I come;
While many a hope hath snapt, this one still holds,
For ne'er I counted, dying here, to share
Belovèd sepulture in Argive soil.
Now hail, O earth, bright sunlight hail, and Zeus,
Supreme o'er Argos.

[*Here the Herald salutes the statues of the gods in the
orchestra.*]

Thou too, Pythian king,
With thy fell darts assailing us no more;
Let it suffice that on Scamander's banks
Thy mien was hostile;—now, Apollo, lord,
Be thou the Saviour,—be the Healer thou!
Ye Gods of Council, all I now invoke,
Thee, my protector Hermes, Herald dear,
Whom Heralds venerate,—and Heroes, ye
Who sent us forth, now kindly welcome back
The Argive host, poor remnant of the spear.

[*He turns to the stage.*]

Hail royal palace! roofs belovèd, hail!
Ye seats august, ye powers that front the sun,
If e'er of yore, now, with those cheerful eyes
Receive in state the monarch absent long,
For he returns bringing in darkness light
Common to you and all assembled here,
King Agamemnon. Welcome, as beseems,
Him who with mattock of avenging Zeus
Hath Ilion razed, her under-soil uptorn.
Quenched are the fanes, the altars of the gods,
And of the land entire the seed is crushed.
Such yoke round Troy hath Atreus' elder son
Fastened: and lo! blest by the gods, he comes
Of living men most worthy of renown.
Nor Paris now nor his associate town
Their deed may vaunt as greater than their woe
Cast in a suit for rapine and for theft,

His surety forfeit, he to utter doom
Hath mowed his natal home. Thus Priam's sons
With twofold forfeit have atoned their crime.

> *Chorus.*
Hail, herald of Achaia's Host!

> *Herald.*
All hail!
So please the gods, I grudge not now to die.

> *Chorus.*
Love for thy father-land thy heart hath wrung!

> *Herald.*
So wrung that from mine eyes fall tears of joy.

> *Chorus.*
Sweet the heart-sickness that o'ercame you thus.

> *Herald.*
The key I lack which may thy words unlock.

> *Chorus.*
Smit with desire for those who longed for you.

> *Herald.*
Hath Argos yearned then for the yearning host?

> *Chorus.*
Ay, so that oft from darken'd soul I groaned.

> *Herald.*
Whence this sad gloom, abhorrent to the host?

> *Chorus.*
Silence I long have held bale's safest cure.

> *Herald.*
How! Aught didst fear in absence of thy lords?

> *Chorus.*
To die was oft my wish as whilom thine.

> *Herald.*
Well ended, all is well. But, in long years,
Some chances, one might say, fell happily,

While others adverse were. For who, save gods,
Lives through the whole of life by grief unscathed?
For should I tell of toils, of lodgment rude,
Infrequent landings, vexed by dangerous surf,
What portion of the day exempt from groans?
Still more abhorrent was our life ashore;—
For close to hostile walls our beds were strewn;
Dank vapours fell from heaven, while from the earth
Drizzled the meadow dews,—our raiment's canker,
Matting, like savage beast's, our shaggy hair.
Or spake I of bird-killing winter's cold,
Unbearable, from snows of Ida born;
Or summer's heat, when, stretched on noonday couch,
By breeze unruffled, slept the waveless sea?
But why lament these hardships? Past the toil!
Past now and gone,—past also for the dead,
Who ne'er will trouble them again to rise.
Why call the spectral army-roll? and why,
Living, bemoan reverses? Nay, I claim
With many a farewell to salute mischance.
For us, the remnant of the Argive host,
Joy triumphs, nor can Sorrow tilt the scale.
Winging o'er land and sea our homeward flight.
We to the sun-light well may make this boast,
"The Argive host, captors at length of Troy,
These spoils, an off'ring to Achaia's gods,
Hang up, bright glory of their ancient shrines."
Whoso these tidings hears must needs extol
The city and the leaders of the host;
Also the consummating grace of Zeus
Due honour shall attain. My tale is told.

　　　Chorus.
Ungrudged surrender yield I to thy words.
Age still is young enough for grateful lore.
But Atreus' halls and Clytemnestra most
These news concern; me also they enrich.

　　[*Enter* Clytemnestra.]

　　　Clytemnestra.
The shout of jubilee erewhile I raised,
When first by night the fiery herald came,
Telling if Ilion captured and o'erthrown.
Then some one spake and taunting asked, "Dost think,
Trusting the beacon-light, that Troy is sacked?
'Tis woman's way to be elate of heart."

By such bold utt'rance was my wit misprised:
Yet still I sacrificed: and through the town
With woman's note they tuned the joyous trill,
Paeans uplifting in the gods' abodes,
The while they lulled the fragrant incense-flames.
And now, what need that thou shouldst tell me more?
I from the king himself the tale shall hear.
With honour due, my venerated lord
To welcome home, myself will hasten: for—
What sight for woman sweeter than the day
Which to her spouse, Heaven-shielded from the fight,
Throws wide the gates? Then hither bid my lord,
Beloved of Argos, to return with speed.
Arriving, may he find a faithful wife,
Such as he left her, watch-dog of his house,
To him devoted, hostile to his foes,
In all points like herself, no single seal
Through these long years invaded by her hand.
Pleasure, or blameful word from other man,
Foreign to me as dyer's hue to brass.
A boast like this, fraught as it is with truth,
The lip misseems not of a high-born dame.

[*Exit* Clytemnestra

      Chorus.
Behold! The queen herself hath tutored thee;
Decorous words her clear interpreters.
But tell me, Herald, touching Menelas,
Doth he in safety homeward with the host
Hither return, prince to his country dear?

      Herald.
False news were I to tell, in flatt'ring terms,
Not long would friends enjoy the fair deceit.

      Chorus.
Oh, could'st thou speak auspicious words yet true!
That here they sundered are is all too plain.

      Herald.
The man is vanished from th' Achaian host;
Himself and galley. No untruth I tell.

      Chorus.
Steering ahead from Troy? or hath a storm,
A common terror, snatched him from the host?

Herald.
Like skilful archer thou hast hit the mark;
And hast in brief a mighty woe declared.

Chorus.
Say, doth the voice of other mariners
Report of him as living, or as dead?

Herald.
Not one so knoweth as to speak his doom,
Save the bright Sun, feeder of teeming earth.

Chorus.
How! Burst the tempest on the naval host
Through anger of the gods? say, what the end?

Herald.
Auspicious day with ill-announcing tongue
Beseems not to defile. In weal and woe
Diverse the honour due unto the gods.
When messenger, sad-visaged, tidings dire
Of routed armies to the city bears,
A common wound inflicting on the state,
While many men from many homes are banned,
Smit by the twofold scourge which Ares loves,
Twin-speared Calamity, a gory pair;—
Whoso is laden with such woes as these
The paean of the Furies well may raise.
But coming to a town in jubilee,
Glad messenger of safety and success,
How shall I tidings mingle fair and foul,
The tale unfolding of the storm that smote
The Achaian host, not without wrath of Heaven?
For fire and ocean, bitter foes of yore,
Sware true alliance and redeemed their pledge,
Whelming Achaia's luckless armament.
Then in the night foul-surging mischiefs rose:
Beneath the Thracian blasts ship against ship
Dashed wildly; they, sore-butted by the storm,
With furious wind and stress of pelting rain,
Vanished from sight, 'neath whirl of shepherd dire.
And when uprose the sun's fair light, behold,
The Aegean sea with flowerage overstrewn,—
Corpses of Grecian men and wrecks of ships.
Us, and our vessel with undamaged hull,
Some god, I ween, (not mortal was the power,)

Ruling the helm, hath saved, by stealth or prayer.
But Saviour Fortune lighting on our ship,
At moorage she nor felt the billows' strain,
Nor drave against the iron-girded coast.
Then safe at last, from watery Hades snatch'd,
In genial daylight, still mistrusting chance,
With anxious thought o'er this new grief we brooded,—
Our host sore wearied, and in evil plight.
And doubtless now, if any still survive,
They speak of us as dead. Why should they not?
As we imagine a like fate for them.
But may the best befal! For Menelas,
Foremost and chief, expect him to arrive;
If any sunbeam knows of him as safe,
Rejoicing in the light, (through the device
Of Zeus, not willing yet the race to whelm,)
Good hope there is that he may yet return.
Hearing this tale, know, thou the truth hast heard.

>   *Chorus.*
>   Who, oh who, with truest aim,
>   Did the battle-wedded dame,
>   Prize of conflict, Helen name?
> Was it not one, unseen, in happy hour,
> Guiding his tongue with Fate-presaging power?
> Helen, the captor;—titled fittingly,—
> Captor of ships, of men, of cities, she
>   From dainty curtained bower hath fled,
>   By Titan zephyr borne along;
>   Straight in her quarrel mustered strong
>   The shielded hunters' mighty throng,
>   Marshalled for battle;—forth they sped,
>   Swift on their track whose viewless oar
> Harbour had found on Simois' leafy shore.

>   Wrath, with direful issue fraught,
>   Thus to hapless Ilion brought
>   Dear alliance, dearly bought:
> Requiter of the outraged festal board,
> And of high Zeus, the hearth's presiding Lord;
> Late vengeance wreaking on the guilty throng,
> Who carol jubilant the bridal song,
> Which, fate-impelled, the bridegroom's kin prolong.
>   But aged Priam's city hoar
>   A novel hymn doth now intone,

From many a voice; with mighty groan,
 Woe upon Paris' bridal bed
 She utters;—she who long before
 A dirgeful life, alas! had led,
Weeping her sons in wretched slaughter sped.

 So once did wight incautious rear
 A suckling lion, for the breast
 Still yearning, to the house a pest.
 Tame in life's early morning, dear
 To childhood, and by Eld caressed.
 Carried full oft in fondling play,
 Like to a babe in arms he lay;
 The hand with winning glances wooed,
And, smit with pangs of hunger, fawned for food.

 But time the temper doth bewray
 Inherent in his race. Due meed
 Of gentle nurture to repay,
 Rending the flocks with cruel greed,
 Unbidden he prepares the feast,
 And mars with gory stain the halls.
 Resistless, dire, athirst for prey,
 The pest the menial train appals,
Reared for the house by Heaven, fell Atè's priest.

 So came to Troia's walls, in evil hour,
 Spirit of breathless calm, fair pride
 Of riches, love's soul-piercing flower,
 The eyes' soft dart; but from her course aside
 Swerving, to wedlock bitter end she wrought.
 To Priam's offspring came she, mischief fraught,
 Evil companion, bringing evil dower.
 By Zeus escorted, guardian of the guest,
 She sped, dire Fury, bridal pest.

Lives among men this saw, voiced long ago;
 "Success consummate breeds apace,
 Nor childless dies, but to the race
From prosperous Fortune springeth cureless Woe."
Apart I hold my solitary creed.
Prolific truly is the impious deed;
Like to the evil stock, the evil seed;
But fate ordains that righteous homes shall aye
 Rejoice in goodly progeny.

But ancient Arrogance, or soon or late,
    When strikes the hour ordained by Fate,
      Breedeth new Arrogance, which still
Revels, wild wantoner in human ill;
    And the new birth another brood
      Unhallowed, in the house doth bear;—
Gorged Insolence, and, not to be withstood,
Defiant Boldness, demon unsubdued;—
Swart curses twain, their parents' mien that wear.

But Justice doth the smoke-begrimèd cell
    Illumine with celestial sheen,
      And loves with honest worth to dwell.
Gold-spangled palaces with hands unclean,
    Forsaking with averted eyes,
      To holy Innocence she flies.
The power of wealth, if falsely stamped with praise,
With homage she disdains to recognize,
And to their fated issue all things sways.

[*Enter warriors and captives; at last* Agamemnon *appears, seated on a chariot, with* Cassandra *at his side; soon after* Clytemnestra, *accompanied by female attendants, issues from the palace.*]

        Chorus.
Hail, royal lord! Stormer of Ilion, hail!
    Scion of Atreus! How compose my speech,
      How due obeisance render thee,
Yet neither overshoot the mark, nor fail
    The goal of fitting compliment to reach?
For many men, transgressing right, there be
    Semblance who place above reality.
To him who groans beneath affliction's smart,
    All men have prompt condolence; but the sting
Of feignèd sorrow reaches not the heart.
    So men with others' joy rejoicing, bring
Over their visage an enforcèd smile:
    But the discerning shepherd knows his flock,
And his unerring glance detects their guile,
Who simulating love, with glozing art
    And watery kindness fawn, but inly mock.

But thou, O King, (I speak without disguise,)
    In Helen's quarrel lusking war's array,
A mien didst wear unseemly in mine eyes,

Guiding not well the rudder of thy mind,
Who didst, on death-devoted men, essay
    Courage to urge, by sacrifice.
But those who have achieved the great emprize,
Not from the surface of my mind alone,
I welcome now, with feelings not unkind;
And inquest made, in time shall it be known,
Who of thy citizens at home the while
Guarded thy state with truth, and who with guile.

    Agamemnon, *speaking from the chariot.*

First Argos and her tutelary gods,
Who with me wrought to compass my return,
And visit Priam's town with vengeance due,
Justly I hail. For in this cause the gods,
Swayed by no hearsay, in the bloody urn
Without dissentient voice the pebbles cast,
Sealing the doom of Ilion and her sons.
But to the rival urn, by no hand filled,
Hope only came. Smoke still uprising marks
The captured city; Atè's incense-fires
Are living still, but, dying as they die,
The ash sends upward costly fumes of wealth.
Wherefore 'tis meet to render to the gods
Memorial thanks; since round them we have cast
Our vengeful toils, and in a woman's cause
The Argive monster, offspring of the horse,
Host shield-accoutred, made its deadly leap,
And Priam's city levelled to the dust,
What time the Pleiades in ocean waned;
So, bounding o'er the towers, of princely blood
The raw-devouring lion lapped his fill.
This lengthened prelude to the gods! and now
Weighing the judgment ye erewhile expressed,
I say the same, and am with you agreed.
To few is it congenial, envy-free,
To venerate the friend whom Fortune crowns.
The jealous poison, lodged within the heart,
Tortures with twofold pang whom it infects;
By his own griefs oppressed, the envious man
Groans also to behold another's joy.
Out of my proof I speak, for, well I wot,
Who friendship most pretended, only were
Its mirrored image, shadow of a shade.

None but Odysseus, who unwilling sailed.
Once harnessed, was my trusty yoke-fellow;
This I affirm, be he alive or dead.
But for the rest, what to the state pertains,
And to the gods, a full assembly called,
We'll weigh in free debate. Counsel we need.
That where the state is sound, we keep it so;
But where disease the healer's art requires,
By kind excision, or by cautery,
We shall attempt to remedy the harm.
Now to my palace and my household hearth
Returning, first will I the gods salute,
Who forward sped me, and who lead me home;
Since victory so far hath followed me,
Here may she henceforth stedfastly abide!

       Clytemnestra.
Men of our city, Argive elders here,
I shame not in your presence to avow
My wifely temper; bashful Fear in time
From mortals dieth: not by others taught,
But from myself, the wretched life I'll tell
'Twas mine to lead while this man was at Troy.
First, for a woman severed from her mate,
To sit forlorn at home is grievous woe,
Hearing malignant murmurs manifold.
One courier comes, another in his train
Worse tidings brings to echo through the house;
And as for wounds, had my dear lord received
As many as report kept pouring in,
A net methinks had not been more transpierced.
Or had he died oft as reported then,
A second triple-bodied Geryon,
A threefold cloak of earth he must have donned,
Enduring death in every form he wore.
Thus harassed by these ever-rife reports,
Full often from my neck have forceful hands
Seized and untied the beam-suspended noose.
And for this cause our son, pledge of our troth,
Of mine and thine, stands not beside me now,
As stand he should, Orestes. Marvel not,
For him thy trusty spear-guest nourisheth;
Strophius, the Phocian, who hath me forewarned
Of twofold peril, thine 'neath Ilion's wall,
And next lest clamour-fostered Anarchy

Hazard the plot, for 'tis with men inborn
To trample further him already down.
This pretext, trust me, carries no deceit.
But for myself the gushing founts of grief
Are all dried up, no single tear is left;
Sore with late watching are my weary eyes,
Weeping the fiery beacons set for thee
Neglected ever. Often from my dreams
Was I awakened by the tiny hum
Of buzzing gnat, seeing, endured by thee,
More woes than could have filled mine hour of sleep.
These sorrows past, now with a heart unwrung
I hail my husband, watchdog of the fold,
Sure forestay of the ship; of lofty roof
Pillar firm based; Sire's sole-begotten child;
Land beyond hope looming to mariners;
Day after storm most brilliant to behold;
To thirsty wayfarer clear gushing spring.
Sooth, sweet it is to 'scape from harsh constraint;
With such addresses do I honour him.
Let Envy stand aloof! for we have borne
Ere this full many a woe. Now dear my lord
Come from thy car; but on the ground, O King,
Plant not the foot that trampled Ilion.
Maidens, why tarry ye, whose duty 'tis
With carpets to bespread his stepping-floor?
Swift, purple-strew his passage to a home
Unlooked for, e'en as Justice may conduct;
What further she decreeth with the gods,
Thought, not by sleep o'ermastered, shall dispose.

     Agamemnon.
Daughter of Leda! Guardian of my home!
Such as my absence was, is now thy speech,
Drawn out to ample length. With better grace
My praise had come from others than from thee.
And for the rest, seek not in woman's guise
To pamper me, nor, gaping forth loud cries,
Bow down to me, as to barbaric wight.
Make not my path with tapestries bestrewn
A mark for envy. To the gods belong
Such signal honours; but for mortal man,
On bright-hued broidery to plant his foot,
I own it, is to me not free from dread;
As mortal honour me, but not as god;

Without foot-carpeting or gorgeous web,
Glory resounds; a constant mind to keep
Is Heaven's best gift; him only call we blest
Who ends in fair prosperity his days.
If thus I bear myself I need not fear.

> Clytemnestra.

Against my settled purpose speak not thus.

> Agamemnon.

Deem not my sober purpose I will mar.

> Clytemnestra.

Haply thou thus to act hast vowed in fear.

> Agamemnon.

Final and sure my word as man e'er spake.

> Clytemnestra.

What, thinkest thou, had Priam done if victor?

> Agamemnon.

Purples, I ween, he verily had trod.

> Clytemnestra.

Then stand not thou in fear of human blame.

> Agamemnon.

Yet hath the people's rumour mighty power.

> Clytemnestra.

Life envy-free is life unenviable.

> Agamemnon.

'Tis not for woman to be fond of strife.

> Clytemnestra.

But it becomes the fortunate to yield.

> Agamemnon.

Does conquest in this struggle rate so high?

> Clytemnestra.

Yield thee; thy will bend willingly to mine.

> Agamemnon.

If thou wilt have it so, let one with speed
These buskins loosen, vassals of the foot;

Lest, if with them sea-tinctured robes I tread,
Some jealous eye of gods smite me from far.
For much it shameth me, with wanton feet
To mar this wealth of silver-purchased web.
Of this enough. This stranger damsel now
Kindly receive. Zeus, with propitious eye,
Beholds the victor's sway with mercy crowned.
For willingly none bears the captive yoke;
But she, the chosen flower of many a spoil,
Fair present from the host, hath followed me.
But since herein I yield me to thy will,
Treading on purple to my halls I go.

      Clytemnestra.
A sea there is (which who may drain?) that breeds
Abundant purple, fresh from many a shell,
Precious as silver, brilliant dye of robes,
Whereof, through favour of the gods, these halls
May boast, O King, a store right plentiful;
And poverty is stranger to our house
Trampling of many garments had I vowed,
Had thus the oracles our house enjoined,
Ransom devising for this precious life.
For while the root lives on, the leafeage spreads,
Screening the mansion from the dog-star's ray.
So now, returning to thy household hearth,
As warmth in winter doth the presence show.
And when Zeus breweth from the acrid grape
Rich wine, then coolness thro' the halls is shed,
Where, crowner of the home, the husband dwells.
Zeus, Zeus, all-crowner, my petitions crown:
Thine be the care of that which crown thou wilt.

[*Exeunt* Clytemnestra *and* Agamemnon *into the palace.*]

      Chorus.
Whence this dread portent, that untired
Before my bodeful spirit floats?
Wherefore, unbidden and unhired,
Waken these dark prophetic notes?
Why sits not on my bosom's throne
The direful presage to disown
As riddling dream, assurance strong?
      Time's youth hath flown
Since the stern-cables from the boats
Were flung, what time the ship-borne host
Marched on to Ilion from the sandy coast.

After long absence their return
With self-informing eyes I learn;
Yet in its depths my soul, self-taught,
Chanteth Erinys' lyreless strains;
My hopes, of courage reft, depart;
Not vainly throb my inmost reins;

    Whirleth on eddies of dark thought
        My bodeful heart;
    Yet, against hope, the gods I pray,
    That, false to augury, my lay
Futile may fall, with vain foreboding fraught.

    Never will perfect health confess
    Her limit sated; though disease,
Neighbour, with party-wall, against her press.
    Sailing with prosperous course elate,
Strikes on the hidden reef man's proud estate.
Then if reluctant Fear, with well-poised sling,
    His bales doth into ocean fling,
    Riseth once more the bark; and though
    With evil freighted to the full,
    Floateth secure the lightened hull.
    So likewise, gift of ample worth
        From Zeus, the year's increase,
Whose teeming harvests in the furrows grow,
        Quells the disease of dearth.

    But when on earth the crimson gore
    Of man hath fallen, never more
May charm or spell the vanished life evoke;
    Hence he of old, whose mystic lore
Was skilled the dead from Hades to restore,
Fell, blasted by the Thunderer's warning stroke.
    Now did not Fate—a heaven-sent Fate—
    Baffle my impulse, ere too late,
    Leaving behind the lagging tongue,
    My heart its bodeful strain had sung.
    But now it raves; no cheering rays
        My anguished spirit knows,
And hopeless to unravel Fate's dark maze
        With fiery ardour glows.

[*Enter* Clytemnestra, *stepping hastily out of the palace.*]

    Clytemnestra.
Come thou too in, Cassandra, thee I mean;

For not in wrath Zeus placed thee in our house
A sharer in our lustral rites to stand,
With many slaves beside his household altar.
Now from this car descend; be not too proud,
For e'en Alcmena's son,—so runs the tale,—
Sold as a slave, endured the forceful yoke;
But if such fate befal thee, great the boon
Heirs of ancestral wealth to own as lords;
For upstarts, beyond hope who fortune reap,—
These reckless are and cruel to their slaves.
From us thou hast what usuage warranteth.

Chorus.

Thee in clear words she hath addressed, and thou,
Meshed as thou art within the toils of Fate,
Yield if thou canst; mayhap thou wilt not yield.

Clytemnestra.

Nay, an she be not, swallow-like, possessed
Of an unknown, barbaric tongue, my words,
Reaching her mind, must move her to comply.

Chorus.

*Follow! She counsels for thy need the best: Be thou persuaded;—leave
thy chariot-seat.*

Clytemnestra.

No leisure have I here before the gates
To linger; for, beside the central hearth,
The victims wait the sacrificial fire;
A favour that our fondest hope transcends.
But thou, if aught wilt do of what I say,
Make no delay; but if, of sense bereft,
Thou canst not catch the meaning of my words,
In lieu of voice, speak with barbarian hand.

Chorus.

A clear interpreter the stranger needs:
Distraught she seems, like creature newly caught.

Clytemnestra.

Nay, she is mad; to her distempered thoughts
She listens; from a newly-captured town
She cometh here, nor knows the yoke to bear,
Till quelled in foam the passion of her blood.
But words I'll waste no more, thus to be scorned.

[*Exit.*

Chorus.

But I, by pity moved, will not be wroth;
    Come, wretched sufferer, this car forsake;
    To Fortune yielding, hansel this new yoke.

Cassandra.

Ah me! alas! Gods, Earth!
    Apollo, O Apollo!

Chorus.

Why raise for Loxias these cries of bale?
Not he the god to need the mourner's wail.

Cassandra.

Ah me! alas! Gods, Earth!
    Apollo, O Apollo!

Chorus.

Once more she calleth with ill-omened cry,
The god who hath no part in misery.

Cassandra.

Apollo, O Apollo!
Thou way-god! my destroyer!
Once more thou hast destroyed me utterly.

Chorus.

She seems about to augur her own ills;
Heaven's breathing e'en in bonds her spirit fills.

Cassandra.

Apollo, O Apollo!
Thou way-god! my destroyer!
Ah, whither hast thou led me? to what roof?

Chorus.

To the Atreidan; an thou dost not know
I tell thee; thou'lt not say it is not so.

Cassandra.
Ah! Ah!

A heaven-detested house, whose walls of yore
Halters have seen, and streams of kindred gore;
A human shambles with blood-reeking floor.

Chorus.
Keen scented seems the stranger, like a hound;
Ay, and the blood she's tracking will be found.

Cassandra.
Ah! Ah!
Lo! witnesses trust-worthy! Vouchers dire!
These babes, who weep their death-wound, faith inspire,
Their roasted members eaten by their sire!

Chorus.
Thy fame oracular hath reached our ear;
But certes seek we now no prophet here.

Cassandra.
Alas! ye gods!
What is she plotting? what new blow?
A mighty mischief plots she 'neath this roof;
An unimaginable cureless woe,
Unbearable to friends. Help stands aloof.

Chorus.
Dark are these oracles; the first I knew;
For, them the city voucheth wholly true.

Cassandra.
Ah wretched one!
The deed wilt consummate? With guile
Wilt in the bath thy wedded consort cheer?
How speak the issue? Soon it will be here;—
Hand after hand is lifted. Woe the while!

Chorus.
I comprehend her not; this mystic lore,
These blear-eyed oracles perplex me sore.

Cassandra.
Woe! woe! Look! look! What see I there?
Is it, ye gods, a net of hell?
The wife herself, joint-slayer, is the snare.
Now o'er the accursèd rite
Let the dread brood of Night,
Unglutted with the race, their chorus swell!

Chorus.

What Fury 'gainst this house doth summon? What,
The shriek to raise? Such utt'rance cheers me not.
  Pallid through every vein
   Blood to my heart doth run,
  Which to the battle-slain
   Quencheth life's sun;
  But Atè comes amain.

Cassandra.

Hold! hold! Woe! woe! The heifer there
  Keep from the bull. In meshes fell
Of black-woofed garb entangled,—guileful snare,—
  Catching,—she smites him dead;—
  Prone in his watery bed
He falls. The laver's guileful doom I tell.

Chorus.

I boast not to be skilled in auguries,
Yet mischief here I cannot but surmise.
  Through spells, say, if ye know,
  To mortals here below,
  What grateful cheer is sent?
  Their wordy arts from human woe
  Breed dark presentiment.

Cassandra.

Woe! woe! my wretched ill-starred lot!
  Wailing another's fate mine own I mourn;
  Why hast thou led me hither, all forlorn,
Unless with thee to perish? Wherefore not?

Chorus.

Thou'rt frenzied, by some god possest,
  And tuneless quirest forth thy doom,
  Like nightingale, with dusky plume
Sateless of song. From heart opprest,
  Ceaseless her Itys, Itys, flows,
Her life bewailing, rich alone in woes.

Cassandra.

Woe! woe! Clear-voicèd bird, arrayed
  In plumèd shape, by powers divine;
   Sweet life, unmarred by tears, is thine:
But me awaits the double-edged blade.

Chorus.

Whence hast thou these prophetic throes,
    Rushing athwart thy soul, in vain?
    Why body forth in dismal strain,
Blent with shrill cries, these direful woes?
    Whence cometh thus to vex thy soul
Of prophecy the dark, ill-omened goal?

Cassandra.

Oh, nuptial rite, oh, nuptial rite,
    Of Paris, fraught with doom!
    Scamander! whence my fathers drank,
Nourished of yore upon thy bank,
    I throve in youthful bloom.
Me now Cocytos and the streams of night
To augur on their dismal shores invite.

Chorus.

    What thought has uttered all too clear?
    An infant might interpret here.
Smitten within am I with gory sting,
    The while thy bird-like cry to hear
    My heart doth wring.

Cassandra.

Oh deadly coil, oh, deadly coil
    Of Ilion, doomed to fall!
    Alas, the flower-cropping kine
Slain by my father at the shrine
    To save her sacred wall!
But cure was none: she perished; vain the toil!
I too, soul-kindled, soon shall press the soil.

Chorus.

    This tallies with thy former strain;
    Sure some ill demon smites thy brain,
And falling on thee moves thee thus to tell
    In piteous chant thy doleful pain.
    The end I cannot spell.

Cassandra.

In sooth the oracle no more shall peer
Forth from a veil, like newly wedded bride;
But flashing on the soul, like wind that blows
Sunward, it dasheth 'gainst the orient beams

A mighty surge that doth this grief o'ertop.
No more through dark enigmas will I teach!
And bear me witness, how in eager chase
The track I scent of crimes wrought long ago.
For from this roof departeth never more
A choir, concordant but unmusical,
To evil tuned. Ay, drunk with human blood,
And by the draught made bold, within these halls
Abides a rout, not easy to eject,
Of sister Furies; lodged within these walls
They chant in chorus the primeval curse.
Hostile to him his brother's couch who trod,
In turn they tell their loathing. Have I missed,
Or, like the true archer, have I hit the mark?
Or strolling cheat, or lying prophet am I?
Before I die, attest ye now on oath
That of these halls the hoary crimes I know.

Chorus.
And how can oath be healer of woe
Inherent in the race? Yet marvel I
That, nurtured o'er the sea, thou know'st to speak
Of foreign city as though native there.

Cassandra.
Loxias, the seer, me with this grace endowed.

Chorus.
How! passion-smitten was he, though a god?

Cassandra.
Till now it shamed me to speak of this.

Chorus.
True; for who fareth well grows over-nice.

Cassandra.
Love-wrestler was he, warm his favour breathed.

Chorus.
Came ye in course ro rite conjugial?

Cassandra.
Consent I gave, but cheated Loxias.

Chorus.
Mistress already of presaging art?

Cassandra.
Ay, to the townsmen all their woes I spelled.

Chorus.
How then by wrath of Loxias unharmed?

Cassandra.
No credence won I after this offence.

Chorus.
To us thy oracles seem all too true.

Cassandra.
Woe! woe! alas! alas! ye miseries!
Of faithful augury the direful toil
Racks me once more, with bodeful preludings
Vexing my soul—Seated within these halls,
See, tender boys, like dreamy phantoms; children,
As by their dear ones done to death, their hands
Filled with their proper flesh, for nutriment;
Their heart and vitals,—loathsome, piteous, meal,—
Look, how they hold,—their sire has tasted, look!
For these, I say, vengeance devising, waits
A dastard lion, wallowing in bed;
House-warden, sooth, to him that's come, my master,
For the slave's yoke, alas! I needs must bear.
The naval leader, leveller of Troy,
He knows not that the fell she-dog, whose tongue
Spoke words of guileful welcome, long drawn out,
Like lurking Atè, will achieve his doom.
Such things she dares; the female slays the male!
Her,—what detested monster may I name
And hit the mark?—Some basilisk, or Scylla
Housing in rocks, deadly to mariners,
Infuriate dam of Hades, breathing forth,
Against her dearest, curse implacable?
What triumph-notes exultantly she raised,
All daring one, as in the turn of fight,
Feigning to gratulate his safe return!
What boots it whether I persuade or no?
The doomed must come; ere long to pity moved,
Me thou wilt own a prophet all too true.

Chorus.
Thyestes' banquet of his children's flesh
I knew and shudder at; fear takes my soul,

Hearing the truth, no imaged counterfeit.
The rest I heard, but follow not the track.

Cassandra.
On Agamemnon dead, I say, thou'lt look.

Chorus.
Lull, poor forlorn one, thy ill-omened tongue.

Cassandra.
Yet o'er this speech no healing god presides.

Chorus.
If be it must; but may it never be;

Cassandra.
The while thou prayest, theirs it is to slay.

Chorus.
What man deviseth this accursèd deed?

Cassandra.
Widely thy glance hath missed mine oracles.

Chorus.
Ay, for the plotter's scheme to me is dark.

Cassandra.
Yet in Hellenic speech my words are couched.

Chorus.
So too are Pythian chants, yet hard to spell.

Cassandra.
Alas! what fire is this! It seizes me.
Woe! woe! Lykeian god! Apollo! Woe!
The biped lioness, that with the wolf
In absence of the noble lion couched,
Will me, her victim, slaughter, and as one
Poison who mixeth, she my doom will add
To crown her vengeance; whetting 'gainst her lord
The murderous knife, she boasteth to exact
His death, as payment for escorting me.
Why longer wear this scorn-provoking gear,
This wand, these wreaths prophetic round my neck?

Thee I will shatter ere myself am doomed.
Hence to destruction: I will follow soon;
Another, in my place, enrich with woes.
Behold, Apollo's self doth strip me bare
Of the prophetic robe; coldly he gazed,
What time, in these adornments vainly tricked,
To friends and enemies, with one consent,
All undeserved, a laughter I became:
Vagrant yclept, poor hunger-stricken wretch,
A strolling mountebank, I bare it all;
And now the seer (his vengeance wreaked on me
The seeress) calls me to this deadly fate.
My father at the altar fell, but me
The slaughter-block awaiteth, smitten down
By stroke relentless, reeking with hot gore.
Yet not unhonoured of the gods we fall;
For other champion of our cause shall come,
Seed matricidal, venger of his sire.
An exiled wanderer, from this land estranged,
Returns, this vengeance for his friends to crown.
For, lo, the gods a mighty oath have sworn,
His father's prostrate form shall lead him home.
But why, an alien here, pour I my wail?
When that I first have seen my Ilion fare
As fared it hath, and they who won the town
In sorry plight, through judgment of the gods.
I'll do! I'll suffer! I will dare to die.
These gates, as gates of Hades, I adjure,
One prayer I offer, "mortal be the stroke;"
Free from convulsive throes, in easy death,
While ebbs my life blood, may I close mine eyes.

Chorus.
Oh woman, thou most wretched and most wise;
Lengthy thy speech hath been; but if thou knowest
Truly thine own sad doom, how walkest thou
Like heaven-led victim, boldly to the altar?

Cassandra.
There's no escape; brief respite, nothing more.

Chorus.
Yet to be last is gain at least of time.

Cassandra.
The day is come, small were my gain by flight.

Chorus.

Enduring art thou, and of dauntless mind.

Cassandra.

Yet dear to mortals is a glorious death.

Chorus.

Such words none heareth from the fortunate.

Cassandra.

Alas, my sire, for thee and thy brave sons!

[*She suddenly starts back.*

Chorus.

What may this mean? What terror drives thee back?

Cassandra.

Alas! alas!

Chorus.

Why this alas, unless some horror scare thee?

Cassandra.

Blood-reeking murder breatheth from these halls.

Chorus.

'Tis but the scent of victims at the hearth.

Cassandra.

Nay, but such breath as issues from a tomb.

Chorus.

No Syrian odour tell'st thou for the house.

Cassandra.

Well! I will go, within these palace halls
To wail mine own and Agamemnon's doom.
Enough of life! Strangers! Alas! Alas!
Yet quail I not, as birdé at the brake,
Idly; in death my vouchers be in this,
When, in my place, woman for woman dies,
And when for man ill-wedded, man shall fall.
Dying, this hospitable grace I crave.

Chorus.
Poor wretch; Thy fateful doom my pity moves.

Cassandra.
Once more I fain would speak, but not to pour
Mine own funereal wail; but to the Sun,
Looking my last upon his beams, I pray
That my avengers pay my murderers back,
Requiting me, poor slave, their easy prey.
Alas, for man's estate! If Fortune smile,
A show may o'erturn it; should she frown,
A moistened sponge the picture doth destroy.
More than the first this doom my pity moves.

[*Exit into the palace.*

Chorus.
All are of boundless weal insatiate;—
    None warneth from his halls
Him at whom Envy points, as rich or great,
    Saying, "Come here no more."—
So to this man the Blessed Ones have given
    To capture Priam's walls;—
    Home he returns, beloved of Heaven;—
    But must he now the blood repay
    Of ancient murder; must he die,
        And dying expiate,
With his own death, their deaths who died of yore;
Who, being mortal, this can hear, nor pray,
That he were born to scathless destiny?

Agamemnon.

[*In the palace.*

Woe's me! I'm smitten with a deadly blow!

Chorus.
Hush! Wounded unto death who lifts this cry.

Agamemnon.
Woe's me! Again! a second time I'm struck.

Chorus.
By the groaning of the monarch, wrought methinks is
now the deed;
But together taking counsel, weave we now some
prudent scheme.

Chorus.

  I. To you my counsel is to raise the cry,
     And to the palace call the citizens.
 II. To me seems best, at quickest, breaking in,
     To prove the deed by newly-dripping blade.
III. I, this opinion sharing, give my vote
     For action;—not to dally is the point.
 IV. 'Tis manifest; for they, thus preluding,
     Give to the city signs of tyranny.
  V. Ay, we delay;—they, treading under foot
     All thoughts of dalliance, sleep not with the hand.
 VI. No plan I know to fashion or propose;
     Against the guilty doer we must plot.
VII. That view I share, for no device I know,
     By words, the dead man to restore to life.
VIII. What! dragging on our lives, shall we obey
     These home-polluters? Them our leaders make?
 IX. That were past hearing, better far to die;
     For milder doom were death than tyranny.
  X. How! may we not on evidence of groans
     Augur full surely that the man is dead?
 XI. Ere we can argue, we must know the facts;
     Assurance differs widely from surmise.
XII. This I commend, taking the general vote,
     Plainly to know how fareth Atreus' son.

[*The doors of the royal palace are thrown open;* Clytemnestra *is discovered standing with the axe over her shoulder. Behind her, under a cover, are the bodies of* Agamemnon *and* Cassandra.]

Clytemnestra.
Though much to suit the times before was said,
It shames me not the opposite to speak:
For, plotting against foes,—our seeming friends,—
How else contrive with Ruin's wily snare,
Too high to overleap, to fence them round?
To me, not mindless of an ancient feud,
Hath come at last this contest;—late indeed.
The deed achieved, here stand I, where I slew.
So was it wrought (and this I'll not deny),
That he could neither 'scape, nor ward his doom;
Around him, like a fish-encircling net,
This garment's deadly splendour did I cast;—
Him twice I smote, and he, with twofold groan,
His limbs relaxed;—then, prostrate where he lay,
Him with third blow I dowered, votive gift

To nether Hades, saviour of the dead.
Thus as he fell he chafed his soul away;
And gurgling forth the swift death-tide of blood,
He smites me with black drops of gory dew,
Not less exultant than, with heaven-sent joy
The corn-sown land, in birth-hour of the ear.
For this great issue, Argive Senators,
Joy ye, if joy ye can, but I exult.
Nay, o'er the slain were off'rings meet,—with right
Here were they poured,—with emphasis of right.
Such goblet having filled with cursed ills
At home,—himself on his return drains off.

> *Chorus.*
We marvel at thy tongue, how bold thy speech,
Who o'er thy husband makest so thy vaunt.

> Clytemnestra.
As witless woman are ye proving me;
But I with steadfast heart, to you who know,
Proclaim,—and whether ye will praise or blame,
It recks me not,—this man is Agamemnon,—
My husband, dead, the work of this right hand,
Doer of righteous deed;—so stands the case.

> *Chorus.*
O woman, what earth-nurtured bane,
What potion, upsent from the wind-ruffled sea,
Hast tasted, that on thine own head dost heap
Curses, for incense, folk-mutter'd and deep!
   Hast cast off, hast slain;—
Out-cast, uncitied, thyself shalt be,
Huge hate of the townsmen blasting thee.

> Clytemnestra.
Me thou dost doom to exile,—to endure
The people's hate, their curse deep-muttered,—thou,
Who 'gainst this man of yore hadst naught to urge.
He, all unmoved, as though brute life he quenched,
The while his fleecy pastures teem'd with flocks,
His own child slaughtered,—of my travail throes
To me the dearest,—charm for Thracian blasts.
Him shouldst thou not have chased from land and home
Just guerdon for foul deed? Stern judge thou art
When me thou dost arraign;—but, mark my words,

(Nerved as I am to threat on equal terms,)
If with strong hand ye conquer me, then rule;—
But should the god decree the opposite,
Though late, to sober sense shalt thou be schooled.

Chorus.

O haughty of council art thou;—
And haughtily-minded thou vauntest amain,
As raveth thy mind neath blood-reeking fate.
Calling for vengeance, glares forth on thy brow
        Of blood the foul stain;—
Forsaken of friends, the common hate,
Death-blow with death-blow shalt expiate.

Clytemnestra.

This solemn sanction of mine oaths thou hearest;—
By the accomplished vengeance of my child,
By Até, by Erinyes, unto whom
I slew this man,—Expectancy for me
Treads not the halls of Fear, while on my hearth,
Aegisthos, kind as heretofore, burns fire;—
For he of boldness is no puny shield.
There prostrate lies this woman's outrager,
Minion to each Chryseis under Troy.
There too, this captive slave, this auguress,
And this man's concubine,—this prophetess,
His faithful bedfellow, who shared with him
The sailor's bench. Not unrequited wrought they;
For he lies—thus. While she, in swan-like fashion,
Having breathed forth her last, her dying wail,
Lies here, to him a paramour, and so
Adds keener relish to my sweet revenge.

Chorus.

        Oh might some sudden Fate
        Not tethered to a weight
Of couch-enchaining anguish, hither waft
        The boon of endless sleep!
For our most gracious guardian slain we weep,
        In woman's cause of yore
        Full many a pang who bore,
And now lies smitten by a woman's craft.
        Woe! frenzied Helen, woe!
        Through thee alone, through one,
How many souls, how many, were undone;

What havoc dire 'neath Troia thou hast wrought.
    And now the cureless woe,
    Heirloom of blood, shed long ago,
    Through thee hath blossomed, causing strife
Unquenchable, with husband-murder rife.

    Clytemnestra.
    Bowed beneath sorrow's weight,
    Invoke not deadly Fate,
Nor in thine anger Helen thus arraign,
    As though through her, through one,
    Fell many a Danaan son;—
She-man-destroyer, working cureless bane!

    Chorus.
    Demon, who now dost fall
    Ruthless on Atreus' hall
Making the twin Tantalidae thy prey,
    Through women's haughty reign,
Gnawing my heart, thou dost confirm thy sway.
    Like bodeful raven hoarse,
    She standeth o'er the corse,
And chants exulting her discordant strain.

    Clytemnestra.
    Ay now thy speech in sooth
    Runs even with the truth,
Calling the thrice-dread demon of this race;
    For in their veins is nursed,
    By him, the quenchless thirst
    For blood; ere pales the trace
Of ancient pang, new ichor flows apace.

    Chorus.
    Mighty the demon, dire his hate,
    Whom here thou boastest to preside;
    Woe! woe! ill-omened praise of Fate,
    Baneful and still unsatisfied!
    Alas! 'Tis Zeus, in will, in deed,
    Sole cause, sole fashioner; for say
    What comes to mortals undecreed
By Zeus, what here, that owneth not his sway?

    Woe! woe!
    King! King! how thee shall I bewail?

How voice my heartfelt grief? Thou liest there
Entangled in the spider's guileful snare;
In impious death thy life thou dost exhale.

    Ah me! ah me! to death betrayed,
    Sped by the two-edged blade,
On servile couch now ignominious laid.

      Clytemnestra.
    Dost boast as mine this deed?
    Then wrongly thou dost read,
To count me Agamemnon's wife;—not so;
    Appearing in the mien
    Of this dead monarch's queen,
The ancient fiend of Atreus dealt the blow;—
    Requiting his grim feast,
    For the slain babes, as priest,
The full-grown victim now he layeth low.

      Chorus.
    That thou art guiltless of this blood
    Who will attest? Yet by thy side,
    Haply, as thy accomplice, stood
    The Fury who doth here preside.
    Through streams of kindred gore
    Presseth grim Ares on to claim
    Requital for the deed of shame;—
The clotted blood of babes devoured of yore.

      Woe! woe!
    King! King! thee how shall I bewail?
How voice my heartfelt grief? Thou liest there
Entangled in the spider's guileful snare,
In impious death thy life thou dost exhale.

    Ah me! ah me! to death betrayed,
    Sped by the two-edged blade;
On servile couch now ignominious laid.

      Clytemnestra.
    By no unjust decree
    Perished this man, for he
Through guile hath household death enacted here:—
    His proper child he slew,
    Sweet bud from me that grew,

Iphigenia, wept with many a tear.
    Foul quittance for foul deed;—
       He reaped the sword's due meed,
Hence no proud boast from him let Hades hear!

    Chorus.
    Perplexed I am, bewildered sore
    Which way to turn; escape is vain;
Totters the house; I dread the crimson rain
That with loud plashing shakes these walls; no more
Falleth in niggard droppings now the gore.
And bent on deed of mischief, Fate anew
On other whetstones, whetteth vengeance due.

    Earth! Earth! oh hadst thou been
    My shroud ere I my king
Prone in the silver-sided bath had seen!
Who will inter him? Who his dirge shall sing?
So hardy thou? Wilt thou who didst assail
Thy husband's life, thyself uplift the wail?
Wilt to his shade, for the great deeds he wrought,
Render a graceless grace, with malice fraught?

    With tears of honest grief
    Weeping the godlike chief,
Above the tomb who now shall raise
The funeral hymn? Who speak the hero's praise?

    Clytemnestra.
    Not thine the task to counsel here.
    By us he fell: this man we slew;
    Ours be it to inurn him too;
    Borne from the palace, o'er the bier
    Shall sound no notes of wailing;—no,
    But him, with blandishments, shall meet
Iphigenia; by the rapid streams
Of Acheron, his daughter, as beseems,
Facing her father, shall around him throw
Her loving arms, and him with kisses greet.

    Chorus.
    That taunt still answers taunt we see.
    Here to adjudge is hard indeed.
Spoiled be the spoiler; who sheds blood must bleed.
While Zeus surviveth shall this law survive.

Doer must suffer; 'tis the Fates' decree;
Who from the house the fated curse may drive?
The race is welded to calamity.

       Clytemnestra.
    Ay! now on Truth thou dost alight!
    I with the demon of this race—
    The Pleisthenid—an oath will plight.
    My doom, though grievous, I embrace.
    But for the rest, hence let him haste!
Leaving this house, let him another race
Harass with kindred murders. For myself,
When from these halls blood-frenzy I have chased,
Small pittance shall I crave of worldly pelf.

[*Enter* Aegisthos, *arrayed in royal robes, and with armed attendants.*]

       Aegisthos.
Hail, joyous light of justice-bearing day!
At length I can aver that Gods supernal,
Judges of men, look down on earthly woes,
Beholding, in the Erinyes' woven robes,
This man, thus prostrate, welcome sight to me,
The wiles atoning compassed by his sire.
For Atreus, Argos' ruler, this man's father,
Did from the city and his home expel
Thyestes, rival in the sovereignty,—
My father, to be plain, and his own brother.
But coming back, a suppliant of the hearth,
Wretched Thyestes found a lot secure,
Not doomed his natal soil with blood to stain,
Here in his home: but this man's godless sire,
Atreus, with zeal officious more than kind,
Feigning a joyous banquet-day to hold,
Served to my sire, for food, his children's flesh.
Their feet indeed, the members of their hands,—
Seated aloof, in higher place, he hides.
Partaking of the undistinguished parts,
In ignorance, Thyestes eats the food,
Curse-laden, as thou seest, to the race.
Discerning then the impious deed, he shrieked,
And back recoiling the foul slaughter spewed.
Spurning, with righteous curse, th' insulted board

Dread doom he vows to the Pelopidae;—
"So perish the whole race of Pleisthenes."
Hence is it that ye see this man laid low;
The righteous planner of his death am I.
For me, the thirteenth child, in swathing clothes,
He with my wretched sire, to exile drove.
But, grown to manhood, Justice led me back,
And I, although aloof, have reached this man,
The threads combining of the fatal plot.
Now for myself 'twere glorious to die,
Seeing this man entrapped in Justice' toils.

> ### *Chorus.*
> To honour insolence in guilt, Aegisthos,
> I know not;—that with purpose thou didst kill
> This man, thou boastest; of his piteous doom
> Sole author thou:—I tell thee thine own head
> To Justice brought, be sure shall not escape
> The curse of stoning by the people's hand.

> ### Aegisthos.
> Plying the lowest oar, dost menace us
> Who from the upper benches sway the helm?
> Being old thou know'st how bitter at thy years
> Wisdom by stern necessity to learn.
> But bonds and hunger-pangs, to cure the mind
> Of stubborn eld, are skillful leeches found.
> Hast eyes, yet seest not this? Against the pricks
> Kick not, lest stumbling, thou shouldst come to grief.

> ### *Chorus.*
> Woman, house-mate to him from recent war
> Return'd,—defiler of thy husband's bed,
> Death thou didst plot against this warrior chief.

> ### Aegisthos.
> These words will fountains be of bitter tears.
> Thy tongue the opposite to Orpheus is;
> For he drew all by rapture of his voice,
> While thou, by idle bark, dost all things stir
> To hate;—when conquered, thou wilt tamer show.

> ### *Chorus.*
> Shalt thou be ruler of the Argives, thou,

Who, when that thou hadst plotted this man's death,
Didst courage lack to strike the blow thyself?

> Aegisthos

To spread the snare was plainly woman's part,
For I, his ancient foeman, was suspect;
But armed with this man's treasure, be it mine
To rule the citizens. Th' unruly colt
That, barley-fed, turns restive, I will bind
With heavier thong than yokes the trace-horse;
　　—him,
Darkness' grim comrade, Famine, shall see tamed.

> *Chorus.*

This man why didst thou not, O base of soul,
Slaughter thyself? But him his wife, with thee,
The land polluting, and her country's gods,
Hath slain. Orestes, sees he still the light,
That, home-returning with auspicious Fate,
He may, with mighty stroke, deal death to both?

> Aegisthos.

Since thou art minded thus to act, not talk alone, know quickly.
　　　　　　　　　　　　　　　　　　　[*To his attendants.*
Come on, my faithful body-guard, the fray is not far distant.

> *Chorus.*

Come on then, and with hand on hilt, his sword let each make ready.

> Aegisthos.

Be well assured, with hand on hilt, to die I too refuse not.

> *Chorus.*

To die,—thine utterance we accept, and take as thy death-omen.

> Clytemnestra.

Dearest of husbands let us not, I pray, work further mischief.
Already in our many woes reaped have we wretched harvests.
Of sorrow there hath been enough; let us forbear more bloodshed.
Go thou, and ye too aged men, seek your appointed mansions,
Ere aught ye do to work mischance. As fate enjoined we've acted.
If trouble is the lot of man, enough have we encountered;
Sore smitten by the heavy hoof of some avenging demon.
Thus ye a woman's counsel have, if any deign to hearken.

Aegisthos.

To think that their vain tongue 'gainst me into such speech should
blossom;—

That they should hurl forth words like these, their proper doom thus tempting:
They against sober reason err, thus to insult their ruler.

Chorus.

Upon the evil man to fawn is not the wont of Argives.

Aegisthos.

But, be assured, some future day, I yet shall overtake you.

Chorus.

Not so if hither to return some god should guide Orestes.

Aegisthos.

Full well I know that exiles still on hopes are wont to batten.

Chorus.

Work as thou listest. Gorge thy fill. Stain justice. Thou canst do it.

Aegisthos.

Be sure that thou to me shalt pay the forfeit of thy folly.

Chorus.

Be boastful and be bold, like cock beside his partner strutting.

Clytemnestra.

These senseless barkings heed not thou; thyself and I together,
Ruling within these royal halls, will all things wisely order.

[*Exeunt.*

Aeschylus:
The Eumenides

Athena.

I do command you, as your judgment leads,
Just verdict give,—of pleadings now enough.

Chorus (the Eumenides or Furies).

By us in sooth our shafts have all been shot,
The issue of the cause I wait to hear.

Athena.

How may I rule the cause, unblamed by you?

Chorus.

Ye heard what ye have heard;—now in your hearts,
Your oaths revering, strangers, give your votes.

Athena.

Hear ye my statute, men of Attica,—
Ye who of bloodshed judge this primal cause.
And for the host of Aegeus shall abide
This court of jurors, sacred evermore.
The Hill of Ares this, of Amazons
The seat and camping ground, what time of old,
In hate of Theseus, waging war they came,
And 'gainst this city, newly fortified,
A counter-fortress for themselves upreared.
To Ares they did sacrifice, and hence
This rock is titled Areopagus.
Here then shall sacred Awe, and Fear, her kin,
By day and night my lieges hold from wrong,
Save if themselves do innovate my laws.
With influx base or mud, if thou defile
The sparkling water, thou no drink shalt find.
Nor Anarchy, nor Tyrant's lawless rule
Commend I to my people's reverence;—
Nor let them from their city banish Fear
For who 'mong men, uncurbed by fear, is just?
Thus holding Awe in seemly reverence,

Reprinted from Anna Swanwick, trans., *The Dramas of Aeschylus* (London: George Bell and Sons, 1886), pp. 172-187.

A bulwark for your state shall ye possess,
A safeguard to protect your city-walls,
Such as no mortals other-where can boast,
Neither in Scythia, nor in Pelops' realm.
Behold! This court august, untouched by bribes,
Sharp to avenge, wakeful for those who sleep,
Establish I, a bulwark to this land.
This charge, extending to all future time,
I give my lieges. Meet it is ye rise,
Assume the pebbles, and decide the cause,
Your oath revering. All hath now been said.

[*The first Areopagite rises, takes a pebble from the altar, and drops it into the urn. The rest follow in succession between the following distichs.*]

Chorus.
This sisterhood, oppressive to the land,
My council is that ye in no wise shame.

Apollo.
And I enjoin you, fear mine oracles;
From Zeus they issue, fruitless make them not.

Chorus.
Usurping championship of bloody suit,
No longer shall thine oracles be pure.

Apollo.
Did then my Father towards Ixion err,
Who first as blood-stained suppliant, sued for aid?

Chorus.
Say on! but I, defrauded in my suit,
In turn will haunt the land, dread visitant.

Apollo.
Alike of younger and of elder gods
Art thou unhonoured. I the cause shall win.

Chorus.
So whilom wroughtest thou in Pheres' house,
Moving the Fates mortals from death to free.

Apollo.
Was it not just my votary to aid,
Then chiefly in his hour of sorest need?

Chorus.

But thou the prime allotments didst o'errule
With wine deluding the hoar goddesses.

Apollo.

But thou, full soon, defeated in thy suit,
Wilt spew thy venom, harmless to thy foes.

Chorus.

Since thou, young god, o'erridest my hoar age,
The issue I await with list'ning ear,
And doubtful stay my wrath against the town.

[*After the twelfth Areopagite has dropped his pebble into the urn,* Athena *takes one from the altar, and holds it in her hand.*]

Athena.

With me it rests to give the casting vote,
And to Orestes I may suffrage pledge.
For to no mother do I owe my birth;
In all, save wedlock, I approve the male,
And am, with all my soul, my father's child.
Nor care I to avenge a woman's death
Who slew her husband, guardian of the house.
Orestes, judged by equal votes prevails.
The pebbles now pour quickly from the urns,
Judges, to whom this office is assigned.

Orestes.

Phoebos Apollo, how will end this suit?

Chorus.

O Night, dark mother, seest thou these things?

Orestes.

The noose awaits me, or to see the light.

Chorus.

Ruin for us, or firm prerogative.

[*The pebbles are poured out of the urn and counted.*]

Apollo.

Now strangers, count the pebbles with due care;
And while ye tell them o'er, let justice reign;

Lack of right judgment breedeth mighty woe,
Tho while one suffrage hath a house restored.

> Athena.

This man acquitted is from charge of blood,
For equal are the numbers of the votes.

> Orestes.

Hail Pallas! Hail thou saviour of my house!
Me, when bereft of my paternal land,
Thou leadest home: haply some Greek will say,
"The man an Argive is once more, and dwells
On his paternal heritage, by aid
Of Pallas, and of Loxias, and Him,
Third Saviour, mighty consummator, Zeus,"—
Who, honouring my father's death, saves me,
Beholding these my mother's advocates,
Now to my native Argos I depart,
Pledged to this country and thy lieges here
By oath to be revered for evermore,
That never helmsman of the Argive State
Shall hither bear the well-appointed spear.
For we, ourselves, though couching in the grave,
On those who violate these present oaths
By sore perplexities will work, and send
In march despondency, in crossing streams
Omens averse, till they repent their toil.
But unto those who keep this pledge, and honour
Athena's city with confederate spear,
To them will we be gracious evermore.
Hail goddess, and these city-wardens, hail!
Still may your grip be fatal to your foes,
While victory and safety crown your spear.

> Chorus.

1. Ye upstart gods, time-honoured laws
   Down-riding, ye have seized my prey.
2. But I, dishonoured, stung by grief,
   Woe, woe, my torture to allay,
   On all the ground, will cast around
   Venom, whose baleful drops shall cause
   Where it doth light a sterile blight,
   Fatal alike to germ, to leaf.

The pest, O Justice, scouring o'er the plain,
Shall fling abroad its man-destroying stain.

3. I groan anew; what dare? what do?
   My pangs the citizens shall rue;
Alas, most wretched are thy daughters, Night!
Enduring this dishonourable slight.

Athena.

Be moved by me to stay these heavy groans;
Not vanquished are ye, nor to your disgrace
Fell justice, equal-voted, from the urn.
Besides from Zeus clear oracles were sent,
And he who uttered them himself avouched,
Orestes for this deed should know no scath.
Hurl not your heavy wrath upon this land;
Your rage abate, cause not sterility,
Nor rain your poison-drops, like venomed darts,
Ruthless devourers of each tender germ.
For I most righteously do promise you
Both sanctuaries and shrines in this just land;
Seated at hearths with unctuous off'rings fed,
And held in honour by my lieges here.

Chorus.

1. Ye upstart gods, time-honoured laws
   Down-riding, ye have seized my prey.
2. But I, dishonoured, stung by grief,
   Woe, woe, my torture to allay,
   On all the ground, will cast around
   Venom, whose baleful drops shall cause
   Where it doth light a sterile blight,
   Fatal alike to germ, to leaf.
The pest, O Justice, scouring o'er the plain,
Shall fling abroad its man-destroying stain.
3. I groan anew; what dare? what do?
   My pangs the citizens shall rue;
Alas, most wretched are thy daughters Night!
Enduring this dishonourable slight.

Athena.

Not slighted are ye, powers august! through rage
Curse not with hopeless blight the abode of man.
I too on Zeus rely; why speak of that?
And sole among the gods I know the key
That opes the halls where sealèd thunder sleeps.

But such we need not. Be appeased by me,
Nor scatter o'er the land, from froward tongue,
The harmful seed that turneth all to bane.
Of bitter rage lull ye the murky wave;
Be venerated here and dwell with me.
Sharing the first fruits of this ample realm,
For children offered, and for nuptial rite,
This word of mine thou wilt for ever praise.

Chorus.

1. That I should suffer this, oh Fie!
2. That, old in wisdom, I on earth should dwell
   Dishonour'd! Fie! Debasement vile!
3. Rage I breathe forth, and wrath no stint that knows.
4. Fie! Fie! O earth, alas!
5. What agony of pain creeps o'er my heart!
6. Hear, Mother Night, my passion.

7. Mark for scorn,

By crafty gods deluded, held for nought,
Of ancient honour I am basely shorn.

Athena.

I'll bear thine anger, for mine elder thou,
And wiser art, in that regard, than I.
Yet me, with wisdom, Zeus not meanly dowers.
But ye, if now ye seek some alien soil,
will of this land enamour'd be; of this
You I forewarn; for onward-flowing time
Shall these my lieges raise to loftier fame;
And thou, in venerable seat enshrined
Hard by Erectheus' temple, shalt receive
Honours from men and trains of women, such
As thou from other mortals ne'er may'st win.
But cast ye not abroad on these my realms,
To waste their building strength, whetstones of blood,
Evoking frantic rage not born of wine;
Nor, as out-plucking hearts of fighting-cocks,
Plant ye among my townsmen civil strife,
Reckless of kindred blood; let foreign war
Rage without stint, affording ample scope
For him who burns with glory's mighty rage.
No war of home-bred cocks, I ween, is that!
Such terms I proffer, thine it is to choose;

Blessing and blest, with blessed rites revered,
To share this country dear unto the gods.

Chorus.

1. That I should suffer this, oh Fie!
2. That, old in wisdom, I on earth should dwell
   Dishonour'd! Fie! Debasement vile!
3. Rage I breathe forth, and wrath no stint that knows.
4. Fie! Fie! O earth, alas!
5. What agony of pain creeps o'er my heart!
6. Hear, Mother Night, my passion.
          7. Mark for scorn.

By crafty gods deluded, held for nought,
Of ancient honour I am basely shorn.

Athena.

I will not weary to entreat thee fair;
For ne'er with justice shalt thou urge the plaint,
That thou, the elder deity, by me
The younger, and these city-guarding men,
Wert, like an outcast, banished from the land.
But if Persuasion's power ye hold in awe,—
The charm and honeyed sweetness of my tongue,
Tarry thou must; but if thou wilt not tarry,
Not justly wouldst thou on this city hurl
Revenge, or wrath, or do my people wrong;
For thine it is to share with me this land,
In aye-enduring honour justly held.

Chorus.

Athena, queen, what seat dost offer me?

Athena.

One where no sorrow scathes. Receive it thou!

Chorus.

If I consent, what honour waiteth me?

Athena.

No house unblest by thee shall henceforth thrive.

Chorus.

This wilt thou do? endow me with such might?

Athena.

Ay, and will prosper him who worships thee.

Chorus.
Wilt thou sure warrant give me for all time?

Athena.
I may not pledge what I will not perform.

Chorus.
Thine utterance soothes me;—I relax my wrath.

Athena.
Established here thou wilt be rich in friends.

Chorus.
What blessings shall we hymn for this thy land?

Athena.
Such as, with gracious influence, from earth,
From dew of ocean, and from heaven, attend
On conquest not ignoble. That soft airs,
With sunshine blowing, wander o'er the land;
That earth's fair fruit, rich increase of the flocks,
Fail not my citizens for evermore,
With safety of the precious human seed;—
But, for the impious,—weed them promptly out.
For I, like one who tendeth plants, do love
This race of righteous men, by grief unscathed:—
Such be thy charge. Be mine not to endure
That, among mortals, in war's splendid toils,
Athena's city be not conquest-crowned.

Chorus.
Pallas, thy chosen seat henceforth be mine!
        No more the city I despise
Which Zeus omnipotent and Ares prize,
Stronghold of gods, altar-protecting shrine
        Of Hellas' deities,
For which, with friendly augury I pray;
        Springing to light from earth's dark womb,
        May life's fair germs prolific bloom,
            Lured by the solar ray.

Athena.
I for my citizens with gracious mind
        These blessings mediate; these deities
Installing here, mighty and hard to please.
        For unto them hath Fate assigned

The destinies to fix of human kind.
    But whoso findeth them severe
Knows not whence come life's strokes; for crime,
Dread heritage from bygone time,
Doth lead him to these powers august.
Him noiseless Ruin, midst his proud career,
With hostile anger, levels with the dust.

      Chorus.
Here may no tree-destroying mildew sweep,—
      (So show I forth my grace),
May no fierce heat within these bounds alight,
Blasting the tender buds; no sterile blight,
      Disastrous, onward creep.
But in due season here may flocks of worth
    Twin yeanlings bear; and may this race,
    Enriched with treasures of the earth,
    Honour the Heaven-sent grace!

      Athena.
Ye city-guardians do ye hear aright
What thus she promises. For great the might
Erinys wields—dread brood of night—
Alike with Hades and the Olympian Powers;
O'er men confessed and absolute her reign,
To some she giveth song, and some she dowers
    With life, tear-blinded, marred by pain.

      Chorus.
Here may there fall no man-destroying blight!
And ye, great Powers, o'er marriage who preside,
In wedlock bands each lovely maid unite;—
Ye too, dread sisters, to ourselves allied,
    Awful dispensers of the Right,
    In every human home confessed,
    In every age made manifest,
By righteous visitations;—aye revered,
And, everywhere, of deities most feared.

      Athena.
While thus ye ratify with friendly zeal
These blessings to my country, I rejoice,
And love Persuasion's eye, who moved my voice
To soothe these stern refusers, passion-stung.
But Zeus hath conquered, swayer of the tongue,

God of the Forum. Triumphs now for aye
In noble benefits our rivalry.

      Chorus.
Within this city ne'er may civil strife,
Insatiate of ill, tumultuous roar;
Nor thirsty dust quaff deep the purple gore
Of citizens; nor rage, with murder rife,
     Snatch greedily the vengeful knife!
     But studious of the common weal
     May each to each in turn be kind,
Hate may they ever with one common mind;
This among mortals many a woe can heal.

      Athena.
Grow they not wise, as they the pathway find
Of tongue propitious? From these shapes of fear,
I to my lieges see rich gain. For here,
If ye these gracious ones with gracious mind
Adore and magnify,—your state and town
Ye shall for evermore with justice crown.

      Chorus.
Farewell, farewell, enriched with wealth's fair prize,
Farewell, ye people of the city, near
To Zeus himself who dwell, to Pallas dear,
Friends to the friendly Virgin;—timely wise;
'Neath Pallas' wings who rest, her father doth revere.

[Athena *stations herself at the head of the Chorus in the orchestra, where they
    are joined by the escort of females with torches.*]

      Athena.
Ye too farewell! Mine is it first to show
Your destined seats and thitherward to lead.
Escorted by the torchlight's sacred glow,
The while in sacrifice the victims bleed
     The downward slope descend.
Whate'er is baneful to the land restrain,
And conquest's gracious ministry upsend
To this my city. Tutelary train,
Children of Cranaos, it belongs to you,
These alien settlers to their homes to guide;
And with my lieges may there aye abide,
Discernment rightful of the Right and True.

Chorus.

Farewell once more, my farewell I repeat,
All ye, or gods or mortals, who reside
In Pallas' city, and who here preside.
Holding in pious awe my hallow'd seat,
The fortunes of your life ye never-more shall chide.

Athena.

The utt'rance of your pious vows I praise;—
I will escort you with the flashing light
Of torches, to your cavernous abodes
Beneath the earth, with sacred ministers,
And those mine image loyally who guard.
For now, of all the land of Theseus let
The eye come forth,—a glorious company
Of girls, of wives, of matrons hoar with eld,
In festive garb apparelled, vermeil-hued,—
Proceed and let the torch-flame lead the way,
That evermore this gracious sisterhood
May, with events auspicous, bless this land.

[*During the following Chant the procession leaves the temple and descends escorting the Erinnyes to their Shrines.*]

Chorus of the Escort.

Night's hoary children, venerable train,
With friendly escort leave the hallowed fane.

All.
Rustics, glad shouts of triumph raise.

Chorus.
In ancient crypts remote from light,
Victims await you and the hallowed rite.

All.
People, ring out your notes of praise.

Chorus.
With promise to this land of blessings rare,
Down the steep path ye awful beings wend,
Rejoicing in the torchlight's dazzling glare.

All.
Your cries of jubilee ring out amain.

Chorus.
Let torchlights and libations close the rear.
Thus Zeus, all-seeing, and the Fates descend,
To bless these citizens to Pallas dear.

All.
Your cry of jubilee ring out amain.

3

The
Greek Dramatists:
Morality – Individual
Responsibility
or Obedience to Law?

What passes for perhaps an overly simple solution to the problem of the relationship of human justice to divine justice in the Oresteia—the location of justice in the laws of the *polis*—becomes in Sophocles' tragedy *Antigone* a problem without a simple resolution. First performed in 442 B.C., *Antigone* was one of three plays by Sophocles (496–406) dealing with the royal family of Thebes. Antigone was the daughter of the ill-fated Oedipus, the subject of *Oedipus Rex,* and *Oedipus at Colonus.*

Creon, King of Thebes, identified justice with the welfare of the state over which he ruled, and therefore he refused burial to one of Antigone's brothers who had rebelled against the state. Antigone located justice in her personal understanding of the will of the gods, quite apart from the welfare of the state. One may look upon the play as either the tragedy of Antigone—the struggle of the moral individual against the immoral requirements of the state—or as the tragedy of Creon—who leads his state into blasphemy against the law of the gods. Is Antigone guilty of self-will and egoism in preferring her private feelings to the laws of the state? Or is Creon guilty of pride and impiety? Modern readers usually see it as Antigone's tragedy and emphasize her battle on behalf of individual rights and feeling, but if we recall that the play was produced at a time when the *polis* was becoming the locus of all political and religious loyalty in Athens, we can perhaps understand the play as the struggle between the requirements of customary religion and the demands of the new state-centered public cult. In any case, both Antigone and Creon demonstrate

Reprinted from E. H. Plumptre, trans., *The Tragedies of Sophocles* (Boston: D.C. Heath and Co., 1894), pp. 127–177.

personal weaknesses, and they both raise the question of how to reconcile the needs of man with the will of the gods. Evidently the solution proposed by Aeschylus in *The Eumenides* could easily break down or become inadequate, either as individuals refused to submit to the laws of the land or when political authority acted without due reverence for the will of the people and the dictates of the gods. Creon is portrayed as the tyrant, and it is noteworthy that Sophocles, as he praised democracy and attacked one-man rule at the height of the Athenian democracy, could at least dimly foresee that even democracy, indeed any form of government, could raise the irreconciliable problems of public morality versus public expediency. The tragedy of Antigone and Creon is analogous in many ways to the tragic history of the fall of Athens as described by Thucydides. Classical man was evidently conscious of the effect of human passion on social order, and a dominant note of pessimism about man's limitations appears throughout.

Sophocles: Antigone

Dramatis Personae

Creon, King of Thebes.
Haemon, son of Creon.
Teiresias, a seer.
Guard.
First Messenger.
Second Messenger.
Eurydike, wife of Creon.
Antigone, daughter of Oedipus.
Ismene, daughter of Oedipus.
Chorus of Theban Elders
Scene: Thebes, in front of the Palace.

Antigone.
Ismene, mine own sister, darling one!
Is there, of ills that sprang from Oedipus,
One left that Zeus will fail to bring on us,
The two who yet remain? Nought is there sad,
Nought full of sorrow, steeped in sin or shame,
But I have seen it in thy woes and mine.
And now, what new decree is this they tell,
Our captain has enjoined on all the State?
Know'st thou? Hast heard? Or are they hid from thee,
The ills that come from foes upon our friends?

Ismene.

No tidings of our friends, Antigone,
Pleasant or painful, since that hour have come,
When we, two sisters, lost our brothers twain,
In one day dying by a twofold blow.
And since in this last night the Argive host
Has left the field, I nothing further know,
Nor brightening fortune, nor increasing gloom.

Antigone.

That knew I well, and therefore sent for thee
Beyond the gates, that thou may'st hear alone.

Ismene.

What meanest thou? It is but all too clear
Thou broodest darkly o'er some tale of woe.

Antigone.

And does not Creon treat our brothers twain
One with the rites of burial, one with shame?
Eteocles, so say they, he interred
Fitly, with wonted rites, as one held meet
To pass with honour to the dead below.
But for the corpse of Polyneikes, slain
So piteously, they say, he has proclaimed
To all the citizens, that none should give
His body burial, or bewail his fate,
But leave it still unwept, unsepulchred,
A prize full rich for birds that scent afar
Their sweet repast. So Creon bids, they say,
Creon the good, commanding thee and me,—
Yes, me, I say,—and now is coming here,
To make it clear to those who know it not,
And counts the matter not a trivial thing;
But whoso does the things that he forbids,
For him there waits within the city's walls
The death of stoning. Thus, then, stands thy case;
And quickly thou wilt show, if thou art born
Of noble nature, or degenerate liv'st,
Base child of honoured parents.

Ismene.
How could I,
O daring in thy mood, in this our plight,
Or breaking law or keeping, aught avail?

Antigone.
Wilt thou with me share risk and toil? Look to it.

Ismene.
What risk is this? What purpose fills thy mind?

Antigone.
Wilt thou help this my hand to lift the dead?

Ismene.
Mean'st thou to bury him, when law forbids?

Antigone.
He is my brother; yes, and thine, though thou
Would'st fain he were not. I desert him not.

Ismene.
O daring one, when Creon bids thee not?

Antigone.
He has no right to keep me from mine own.

Ismene.
Ah me! remember, sister, how our sire
Perished, with hate o'erwhelmed and infamy,
From evils that himself did bring to light,
With his own hand himself of eyes bereaving,
And how his wife and mother, both in one,
With twisted cordage, cast away her life;
And thirdly, how our brothers in one day
In suicidal conflict wrought the doom,
Each of the other. And we twain are left;
And think, how much more wretchedly than all
We twain shall perish, if, against the law,
We brave our sovereign's edict and his power.
This first we need remember, we were born
Women; as such, not made to strive with men.
And next, that they who reign surpass in strength,
And we must bow to this, and worse than this.
I then, entreating those that dwell below,
To judge me leniently, as forced to yield,
Will hearken to our rulers. Over-zeal
That still will meddle, little wisdom shows.

Antigone.
I will not ask thee, nor though thou should'st wish

To do it, should'st thou join with my consent.
Do what thou wilt, I go to bury him;
And good it were, in doing this, to die.
Loved I shall be with him whom I have loved,
Guilty of holiest crime. More time is mine
In which to share the favour of the dead,
Than that of those who live; for I shall rest
For ever there. But thou, if thus thou please,
Count as dishonoured what the Gods approve.

Ismene.
I do them no dishonour, but I find
Myself too weak to war against the State.

Antigone.
Make what excuse thou wilt, I go to rear
A grave above the brother whom I love.

Ismene.
Ah, wretched me! how much I fear for thee!

Antigone.
Fear not for me. Thine own fate raise safety.

Ismene.
At any rate, disclose this deed to none;
Keep it close hidden: I will hide it too.

Antigone.
Speak out! I bid thee. Silent, thou wilt be
More hateful to me, if thou fail to tell
My deed to all men.

Ismene.
        Fiery is thy mood,
Although thy deeds the very blood might chill.

Antigone.
I know I please the souls I ought to please.

Ismene.
Yes, if thou canst; thou seek'st the impossible.

Antigone.
When strength shall fail me, then I'll cease to strive.

Ismene.
We should not hunt the impossible at all.

Antigone.
If thou speak thus, my hatred wilt thou gain,
And rightly wilt be hated of the dead.
Leave me and my ill counsel to endure
This dreadful doom. I shall not suffer aught
So evil as a death dishonourable.

Ismene.
Go, then, if so thou wilt. Of this be sure,
Wild as thou art, thy friends must love thee still.

[Exeunt.

Chorus of Elders:
O light of yon bright sun,
Fairest of all that ever shone on Thebes,
Thebes with her seven high gates,
Thou didst appear that day,
Eye of the golden dawn,
O'er Dirké's streams advancing,
Driving with quickened curb,
In haste of headlong flight,
The warrior who, in panoply of proof,
From Argos came, with shield of glittering white;
Whom Polyneikes brought,
Roused by the strife of tongues
Against our fatherland,
As eagle shrieking shrill,
He hovered o'er our land,
With snow-white wing bedecked,
Begirt with myriad arms,
And flowing horsehair crests.

He stood above our towers,
Encircling, with his spears all blood-bestained,
The portals of our gates;
He went, before he filled
His jaws with blood of men,
Ere the pine-fed Hephaestos
Had seized our crown of towers.
So loud the battle din
That Ares loves was raised around his rear,
A conflict hard e'en for his dragon foe.

For breath of haughty speech
Zeus hateth evermore;
And seeing them advance,
With mighty rushing stream,
And clang of golden arms,
With brandished fire he hurls
One who rushed eagerly
From topmost battlement
To shout out, "Victory!"

Crashing to earth he fell,
Down-smitten, with his torch,
Who came, with madman's haste,
Drunken, with frenzied soul,
And swept o'er us with blasts,
The whirlwind blasts of hate.
Thus on one side they fare,
And Ares great, like war-horse in his strength,
Smiting now here, now there,
Brought each his several fate.
For seven chief warriors at the seven gates met,
Equals with equals matched,
To Zeus, the Lord of War,
Left tribute, arms of bronze;
All but the hateful ones,
Who, from one father and one mother sprung,
Stood wielding, hand to hand,
Their two victorious spears,
And had their doom of death as common lot.

But now, since Victory,
Of mightiest name, hath come
To Thebes, of chariots proud,
Joying and giving joy,
After these wars just past,
Learn ye forgetfulness,
And all night long, with dance and voice of hymns,
Let us go around in state
To all the shrines of Gods,
While Bacchos, making Thebes resound with dance,
Begins the strain of joy;
But, lo! our country's king,
Creon, Menoekeus' son,
New ruler, by new change,

And providence of God,
Comes to us, steering on some new device;
      For, lo! he hath convened,
      By herald's loud command,
This council of the elders of our land.

      Enter Creon.

            Creon.
My friends, for what concerns our commonwealth,
The Gods who vexed it with the billowing storms
Have righted it again; and I have sent,
By special summons, calling you to come
Apart from all the others. This, in part,
As knowing ye did all along uphold
The might of Laios' throne, in part again,
Because when Oedipus our country ruled,
And, when he perished, then towards his sons
Ye still were faithful in your steadfast mind.
And since they fell, as by a double death,
Both on the selfsame day with murderous blow,
Smiting and being smitten, now I hold
Their thrones and all their power of sov'reignty
By nearness of my kindred to the dead.
And hard it is to learn what each man is,
In heart and mind and judgment, till he gain
Experience in princedom and in laws.
For me, whoe'er is called to guide a State,
And does not catch at counsels wise and good,
But holds his peace through any fear of man,
I deem him basest of all men that are,
And so have deemed long since; and whosoe'er
As worthier than his country counts his friend,
I utterly despise him. I myself,
Zeus be my witness, who beholdeth all,
Would not keep silence, seeing danger come,
Instead of safety, to my subjects true.
Nor could I take as friend my country's foe;
For this I know, that there our safety lies,
And sailing while the good ship holds her course.
We gather friends around us. By these rules
And such as these do I maintain the State.
And now I come, with edicts, close allied
To these in spirit, for my citizens,

Concerning those two sons of Oedipus.
Eteocles, who died in deeds of might
Illustrious, fighting for our fatherland,
To honour him with sepulture, all rites
Duly performed that to the noblest dead
Of right belong. Not so his brother; him
I speak of, Polyneikes, who, returned
From exile, sought with fire to desolate
His father's city and the shrines of Gods,
Yea, sought to glut his rage with blood of men,
And lead them captives to the bondslave's doom;
Him I decree that none shall dare entomb,
That none shall utter wail or loud lament,
But leave his corpse unburied, by the dogs
And vultures mangled, foul to look upon.
Such is my purpose. Ne'er, if I can help,
Shall the vile have more honour than the just;
But whoso shows himself my country's friend,
Living or dead, from me shall honour gain.

> Chorus.
This is thy pleasure, O Menoekeus' son,
For him who hated, him who loved our State;
And thou hast power to make what laws thou wilt,
Both for the dead and all of us who live.

> Creon.
Be ye then guardians of the things I speak.

> Chorus.
Commit this task to one of younger years.

> Creon.
Nay, watchmen are appointed for the corpse.

> Chorus.
What other task then dost thou lay on us?

> Creon.
Not to consent with those that disobey.

> Chorus.
None are so foolish as to seek for death.

> Creon.
Yet that shall be the doom; but love of gain
Hath oft with false hopes lured men to their death.

Enter Guard.

Guard.

I will not say, O king, that I have come
Panting with speed, and plying nimble feet,
For I had many halting-points of thought,
Backwards and forwards turning, round and round:
For now my mind would give me sage advice;
"Poor wretch, why go where thou must bear the blame?
Or wilt thou tarry, fool? Shall Creon know
These things from others? How wilt thou 'scape grief?"
Revolving thus, I came in haste, yet slow,
And thus a short way finds itself prolonged;
But, last of all, to come to thee prevailed.
And though I tell of nought, yet I will speak;
For this one hope I cling to, might and main,
That I shall suffer nought but destiny.

Creon.

What is it then that causes such dismay?

Guard.

First, for mine own share in it, this I say,
The deed I did not, do not know who did,
Nor should I rightly come to ill for it.

Creon.

Thou feel'st thy way and fencest up thy deed
All round and round. 'Twould seem thou hast some news.

Guard.

Yea, news of fear engenders long delay.

Creon

Wilt thou not speak, and then depart in peace?

Guard.

Well, speak I will. The corpse. . . . Some one has been
But now and buried it, a little dust
O'er the skin scattering, with the wonted rites.

Creon.

What say'st thou? What man dared this deed of guilt?

Guard.

I know not. Neither was there stroke of axe,
Nor earth cast up by mattock. All the soil

Was dry and hard, no track of chariot wheel;
But he who did it went and left no sign.
And when the first day-watchman showed it us,
The sight caused wonder and sore grief to all;
For he had disappeared: no tomb indeed
Was over him, but dust all lightly strown,
As by some hand that shunned defiling guilt;
And no sign was there of wild beast or dog
Having come and torn him. Evil words arose
Among us, guard to guard imputing blame,
Which might have come to blows, and none was there
To check its course, for each to each appeared
The man whose hand had done it. Yet not one
Had it brought home, but each disclaimed all knowledge;
And we were ready in our hands to take
Bars of hot iron, and to walk through fire,
And call the Gods to witness none of us
Were privy to his schemes who planned the deed,
Nor his who wrought it. Then at last, when nought
Was gained by all our searching, some one speaks,
Who made us bend our gaze upon the ground
In fear and trembling; for we neither saw
How to oppose it, nor, accepting it,
How we might prosper in it. And his speech
Was this, that all our tale should go to thee,
Not hushed up anywise. This gained the day;
And me, ill-starred, the lot condemns to win
This precious prize. So here I come to thee
Against my will; and surely do I trow
Thou dost not wish to see me. Still 'tis true
That no man loves the messenger of ill.

      Chorus.
For me, my prince, my mind some time has thought
If this perchance has some divine intent.

      Creon.
Cease then, before thou fillest me with wrath,
Lest thou be found, though full of years, a fool.
For what thou say'st is most intolerable,
That for this corpse the providence of Gods
Has any care. What! have they buried him,
As to their patron paying honours high,
Who came to waste their columned shrines with fire,

To desecrate their offerings and their lands,
And all their wonted customs? Dost thou see
The Gods approving men of evil deeds?
It is not so; but men of rebel mood,
Lifting their head in secret long ago,
Still murmured thus against me. Never yet
Had they their neck beneath the yoke, content
To bear it with submission. They, I know,
Have bribed these men to let the deed be done.
No thing in use by man, for power of ill,
Can equal money. This lays cities low,
This drives men forth from quiet dwelling-place,
This warps and changes minds of worthiest stamp,
To turn to deeds of baseness, teaching men
All shifts of cunning, and to know the guilt
Of every impious deed. But they who, hired,
Have wrought this crime, have laboured to their cost,
Or soon or late to pay the penalty.
But if Zeus still claims any awe from me,
Know this, and with an oath I tell it thee,
Unless ye find the very man whose hand
Has wrought this burial, and before mine eyes
Present him captive, death shall not suffice,
Till first, hung up still living, ye shall show
The story of this outrage, that henceforth,
Knowing what gain is lawful, ye may grasp
At that, and learn it is not meet to love
Gain from all quarters. By base profit won
You will see more destroyed than prospering.

> Guard.

May I then speak? Or shall I turn and go?

> Creon.

See'st not e'en yet how vexing are thy words?

> Guard.

Is it thine ears they trouble, or thy soul?

> Creon.

Why dost thou gauge my trouble where it is?

> Guard.

The doer grieves thy heart, but I thine ears.

Creon.
Pshaw! what a babbler, born to prate art thou!

Guard.
May be; yet I this deed, at least, did not.

Creon.
Yes, and for money; selling e'en thy soul.

Guard.
Ah me!
How dire it is, in thinking, false to think!

Creon.
Prate about thinking: but unless ye show
To me the doers, ye shall say ere long
That scoundrel gains still work their punishment. [*Exit.*

Guard.
God send we find him! Should we find him not,
As well may be, (for this must chance decide,)
You will not see me coming here again;
For now, being safe beyond all hope of mine,
Beyond all thought, I owe the Gods much thanks. [*Exit.*

Chorus.
Many the forms of life,
Wondrous and strange to see,
But nought than man appears
More wondrous and more strange.
He, with the wintry gales,
O'er the white foaming sea,
'Mid wild waves surging round,
Wendeth his way across:
Earth, of all Gods, from ancient days the first,
Unworn and undecayed.
He, with his ploughs that travel o'er and o'er,
Furrowing with horse and mule,
Wears ever year by year.

The thoughtless tribe of birds,
The beasts that roam the fields,
The brood in sea-depths born,
He takes them all in nets
Knotted in snaring mesh,
Man, wonderful in skill.

And by his subtle arts
He holds in sway the beasts
That roam the fields, or tread the mountain's height;
    And brings the binding yoke
Upon the neck of horse with shaggy mane,
    Or bull on mountain crest.
    Untameable in strength.
    And speech, and thought as swift as wind,
And tempered mood for higher life of states,
    These he has learnt, and how to flee
    Or the clear cold of frost unkind,
    Or darts of storm and shower,
Man all-providing. Unprovided, he
Meeteth no chance the coming days may bring;
    Only from Hades, still
    He fails to find escape,
    Though skill of art may teach him how to flee
    From depths of fell disease incurable.
    So, gifted with a wondrous might,
Above all fancy's dreams, with skill to plan,
    Now unto evil, now to good,
    He turns. While holding fast the laws,
    His country's sacred rights,
That rest upon the oath of Gods on high,
High in the State: an outlaw from the State,
    When loving, in his pride,
    The thing that is not good;
Ne'er may he share my hearth, nor yet my thoughts,
Who worketh deeds of evil like to this.

    Enter Guards, *bringing in* Antigone

As to this portent which the Gods have sent,
I stand in doubt. Can I, who know her, say
That this is not the maid Antigone?
O wretched one of wretched father born,
Thou child of Oedipus,
What means this? Surely 'tis not that they bring
Thee as a rebel 'gainst the king's decree,
And taken in the folly of thine act?

      Guard.
Yes! She it was by whom the deed was done.
We found her burying. Where is Creon, pray?

      Chorus.
Back from his palace comes he just in time.

Enter Creon.

Creon.
What chance is this, with which my coming fits?

Guard.
Men, O my king, should pledge themselves to nought;
For cool reflection makes their purpose void.
I surely thought I should be slow to come here,
Cowed by thy threats, which then fell thick on me;
But now persuaded by the sweet delight
Which comes unlooked for, and beyond our hopes,
I come, although I swore the contrary,
Bringing this maiden, whom in act we found
Decking the grave. No need for lots was now;
The prize was mine, and not another man's.
And now, O king, take her, and as thou wilt,
Judge and convict her. I can claim a right
To wash my hands of all this troublous coil.

Creon.
How and where was it that ye seized and brought her?

Guard.
She was in act of burying. Thou knowest all.

Creon.
Dost know and rightly speak the tale thou tell'st?

Guard.
I saw her burying that self-same corpse
Thou bad'st us not to bury. Speak I clear?

Creon.
How was she seen, and taken in the act?

Guard.
The matter passed as follows:—When we came,
With all those dreadful threats of thine upon us,
Sweeping away the dust which, lightly spread,
Covered the corpse, and laying stript and bare
The tainted carcase, on the hill we sat
To windward, shunning the infected air,
Each stirring up his fellow with strong words,

If any shirked his duty. This went on
Some time, until the glowing orb of day
Stood in mid heaven, and the scorching heat
Fell on us. Then a sudden whirlwind rose,
A scourge from heaven, raising squalls on earth,
And filled the plain, the leafage stripping bare
Of all the forest, and the air's vast space
Was thick and troubled, and we closed our eyes,
Until the plague the Gods had sent was past;
And when it ceased, a weary time being gone,
The girl is seen, and with a bitter cry,
Shrill as a bird's, when it beholds its nest
All emptied of its infant brood, she wails;
Thus she, when she beholds the corpse all stript,
Groaned loud with many moanings, and she called
Fierce curses down on those who did the deed.
And in her hand she brings some fine, dry dust,
And from a vase of bronze, well wrought, upraised,
She pours the three libations o'er the dead.
And we, beholding, give her chase forthwith,
And run her down, nought terrified at us.
And then we charged her with the former deed,
As well as this. And nothing she denied.
But this to me both bitter is and sweet,
For to escape one's-self from ill is sweet,
But to bring friends to trouble, this is hard
And painful. Yet my nature bids me count
Above all these things safety for myself.

      Creon. [*To* Antigone]
Thou, then—yes, thou, who bend'st thy face to earth—
Confessest thou, or dost deny the deed?

      Antigone.
I own I did it, and will not deny.

      Creon. [*To Guard*]
Go thou thy way, where'er thy will may choose,
Freed from a weighty charge.

                   [*Exit Guard*

      [*To* Antigone]
      And now for thee.
Say in few words, not lengthening out thy speech,
Knew'st thou the edicts which forbade these things?

Antigone.
I knew them. Could I fail? Full clear were they.

Creon.
And thou did'st dare to disobey these laws?

Antigone.
Yes, for it was not Zeus who gave them forth,
Nor Justice, dwelling with the Gods below,
Who traced these laws for all the sons of men;
Nor did I deem thy edicts strong enough,
That thou, a mortal man, should'st over-pass
The unwritten laws of God that know not change.
They are not of to-day nor yesterday,
But live for ever, nor can man assign
When first they sprang to being. Not through fear
Of any man's resolve was I prepared
Before the Gods to bear the penalty
Of sinning against these. That I should die
I knew, (how should I not?) though thy decree
Had never spoken. And, before my time
If I shall die, I reckon this a gain;
For whoso lives, as I, in many woes,
How can it be but he shall gain by death?
And so for me to bear this doom of thine
Has nothing painful. But, if I had left
My mother's son unburied on his death,
In that I should have suffered; but in this
I suffer not. And should I seem to thee
To do a foolish deed, 'tis simply this,—
I bear the charge of folly from a fool.

Chorus.

The maiden's stubborn will, of stubborn sire
The offspring shows itself. She knows not yet
To yield to evils.

Creon.
Know then, minds too stiff
Most often stumble, and the rigid steel
Baked in the furnace, made exceeding hard,
Thou see'st most often split and shivered lie;
And I have known the steeds of fiery mood
With a small curb subdued. It is not meet
That one who lives in bondage to his neighbours
Should think too proudly. Wanton outrage then

This girl first learnt, transgressing these my laws;
But this, when she has done it, is again
A second outrage, over it to boast,
And laugh as having done it. Surely, then,
She is the man, not I, if, all unscathed,
Such deeds of might are hers. But be she child
Of mine own sister, or of one more near
Than all the kith and kin of Household Zeus,
She and her sister shall not 'scape a doom
Most foul and shameful; for I charge her, too,
With having planned this deed of sepulture.
Go ye and call her. 'Twas but now within
I saw her raving, losing self-command.
And still the mind of those who in the dark
Plan deeds of evil is the first to fail,
And so convicts itself of secret guilt.
But most I hate when one found out in guilt
Will seek to gloze and brave it to the end.

Antigone.
And dost thou seek aught else beyond my death?

Creon.
Nought else for me. That gaining, I gain all.

Antigone.
Why then delay? Of all thy words not one
Pleases me now, (and may it never please!)
And so all mine must grate upon thine ears.
And yet how could I higher glory gain
Than placing my true brother in his tomb?
There is not one of these but would confess
It pleases them, did fear not seal their lips.
The tyrant's might in much besides excels,
And it may do and say whate'er it will.

Creon.
Of all the race of Cadmos thou alone
Look'st thus upon the deed.

Antigone.
They see it too
As I do, but their tongue is tied for thee.

Creon.
Art not ashamed against their thoughts to think?

Antigone.
There is nought base in honouring our own blood.

Creon.
And was he not thy kin who fought against him?

Antigone.
Yea, brother, of one father and one mother.

Creon.
Why then give honour which dishonours him?

Antigone.
The dead below will not repeat thy words.

Creon.
Yes, if thou give like honour to the godless.

Antigone.
It was his brother, not his slave that died.

Creon.
Wasting this land, while *he* died fighting for it.

Antigone.
Yet Hades still craves equal rites for all.

Creon.
The good craves not the portion of the bad.

Antigone.
Who knows if this be holy deemed below?

Creon.
Not even when he dies can foe be friend.

Antigone.
My nature leads to sharing love, not hate.

Creon.
Go then below; and if thou must have love,
Love them. While I live, women shall not rule.

Enter Ismene, *led in by* Attendants

Chorus.
And, lo! Ismene at the gate
Comes shedding tears of sisterly regard,
And o'er her brow a gathering cloud
    Mars the deep roseate blush,
    Bedewing her fair cheek.

Creon. [*To* Ismene]
And thou who, creeping as a viper creeps,
Did'st drain my life in secret, and I knew not
That I was rearing two accursèd ones,
Subverters of my throne,—come, tell me, then,
Wilt thou confess thou took'st thy part in this,
Or wilt thou swear thou did'st not know of it?

Ismene.
I did the deed, if she did, go with her,
Yea, share the guilt, and bear an equal blame.

Antigone.
Nay, justice will not suffer this, for thou
Did'st not consent, nor did I let thee join.

Ismene.
Nay, in thy troubles, I am not ashamed
In the same boat with thee to share thy fate.

Antigone.
Who did it, Hades knows, and those below:
I do not love a friend who loves in words.

Ismene.
Do not, my sister, put me to such shame,
As not to let me join in death with thee,
And so to pay due reverence to the dead.

Antigone.
Share not my death, nor make thine own this deed
Thou had'st no hand in. My death shall suffice.

Ismene.
What life to me is sweet, bereaved of thee?

Antigone.
Ask Creon there, since thou o'er him dost watch.

Ismene.

Why vex me so, in nothing bettered by it?

Antigone.

'Tis pain indeed, to laugh my laugh at thee.

Ismene.

But now, at least, how may I profit thee?

Antigone.

Save thou thyself. I grudge not thy escape.

Ismene.

Ah, woe is me! and must I miss thy fate?

Antigone.

Thou mad'st thy choice to live, and I to die.

Ismene.

'Twas not because I failed to speak my thoughts.

Antigone.

To these did'st thou, to those did I seem wise.

Ismene.

And yet the offence is equal in us both.

Antigone.

Take courage. Thou dost live. My soul long since
Hath died to render service to the dead.

Creon.

Of these two girls the one goes mad but now,
The other ever since her life began.

Ismene.

E'en so, O king; no mind that ever lived
Stands firm in evil days, but goes astray.

Creon.

Thine did, when, with the vile, vile deeds thou chosest.

Ismene.

How could I live without her presence here?

Creon.
Speak not of presence. She is here no more.

Ismene.
And wilt thou slay thy son's betrothèd bride?

Creon.
Full many a field there is which he may plough.

Ismene.
None like that plighted troth 'twixt him and her.

Creon.
Wives that are vile I love not for my sons.

Ismene.
Ah, dearest Haemon, how thy father shames thee!

Creon.
Thou with that marriage dost but vex my soul.

Chorus.
And wilt thou rob thy son of her he loved?

Creon.
'Tis Death, not I, shall break the marriage off.

Chorus.
Her doom is fixed, it seems, then. She must die.

Creon.
Fixed, yes, by me and thee. No more delay,
Lead them within, ye slaves. These must be kept
Henceforth as women, suffered not to roam;
For even boldest natures shrink in fear
When they see Hades overshadowing life.

[*Exeunt Guards with* Antigone *and* Ismene.

Chorus.
Blessed are those whose life no woe doth taste!
    For unto those whose house
The Gods have shaken, nothing fails of curse
Or woe, that creeps to generations far.

E'en thus a wave, (when spreads,
With blasts from Thrakian coasts,
The darkness of the deep,)
Up from the sea's abyss
Hither and thither rolls the black sand on,
And every jutting peak,
Swept by the storm-wind's strength,
Lashed by the fierce wild waves,
Re-echoes with the far-resounding roar.
I see the woes that smote, in ancient days,
The seed of Labdacos,
Who perished long ago, with grief on grief
Still falling, nor does this age rescue that;
Some God still smites it down,
Nor have they any end:
For now there rose a gleam,
Over the last weak shoots,
That sprang from out the race of Oedipus;
Yet this the blood-stained scythe
Of those that reign below
Cuts off relentlessly,
And maddened speech, and frenzied rage of heart.
Thy power, O Zeus, what haughtiness of man.
Yea, what can hold in check?
Which neither sleep, that maketh all things old,
Nor the long months of Gods that never fail,
Can for a moment seize.
But still as Lord supreme,
Waxing not old with time,
Thou dwellest in Thy sheen of radiancy
On far Olympos' height.
Through future near or far as through the past,
One law holds ever good,
Nought comes to life of man unscathed throughout by woe.
For hope to many comes in wanderings wild,
A solace and support;
To many as a cheat of fond desires,
And creepeth still on him who knows it not,
Until he burn his foot
Within the scorching flame.
Full well spake one of old,
That evil ever seems to be as good
To those whose thoughts of heart
God leadeth unto woe,
And without woe, he spends but shortest space of time.

And here comes Haemon, last of all thy sons:
 Comes he bewailing sore
The fate of her who should have been his bride,
 The maid Antigone,
 Grieving o'er vanished joys?

   Enter Haemon.

   Creon.
Soon we shall know much more than seers can tell.
Surely thou dost not come, my son, to rage
Against thy father, hearing his decree,
Fixing her doom who should have been thy bride;
Or dost thou love us still, whate'er we do?

   Haemon.
My father, I am thine; and thou dost guide
With thy wise counsels, which I gladly follow.
No marriage weighs one moment in the scales
With me, while thou dost guide my steps aright.

   Creon.
This thought, my son, should dwell within thy breast,
That all things stand below a father's will;
For so men pray that they may rear and keep
Obedient offspring by their hearths and homes,
That they may both requite their father's foes,
And pay with him like honours to his friend.
But he who reareth sons that profit not,
What could one say of him but this, that he
Breeds his own sorrow, laughter to his foes?
Lose not thy reason, then, my son, o'ercome
By pleasure, for a woman's sake, but know,
A cold embrace is that to have at home
A worthless wife, the partner of thy bed.
What ulcerous sore is worse than one we love
Who proves all worthless? No! with loathing scorn,
As hateful to thee, let that girl go wed
A spouse in Hades. Taken in the act
I found her, her alone of all the State,
Rebellious. And I will not make myself
False to the State. She dies. So let her call
Oh Zeus, the lord of kindred. If I rear
Of mine own stock things foul and orderless,
I shall have work enough with those without.

For he who in the life of home is good
Will still be seen as just in things of state;
I should be sure that man would govern well,
And know well to be governed, and would stand
In war's wild storm, on his appointed post,
A just and good defender. But the man
Who by transgressions violates the laws,
Or thinks to bid the powers that be obey,
He must not hope to gather praise from me.
No! we must follow whom the State appoints
In things or just and trivial, or, may be,
The opposite of these. For anarchy
Is our worst evil, brings our commonwealth
To utter ruin, lays whole houses low,
In battle strife hurls firm allies in flight;
But they who yield to guidance,—these shall find
Obedience saves most men. Thus help should come
To what our rulers order; least of all
Ought men to bow before a woman's sway.
Far better, if it must be so, to fall
By a man's hand, than thus to bear reproach.
By woman conquered.

    Chorus.
    Unto us, O king,
Unless our years have robbed us of our wit,
Thou seemest to say wisely what thou say'st.

    Haemon.
The Gods, my father, have bestowed on man
His reason, noblest of all earthly gifts;
And that thou speakest wrongly these thy words
I cannot say, (God grant I ne'er know how
Such things to utter!) yet another's thoughts
May have some reason. 'Tis my lot to watch
What each man says or does, or blames in thee,
For dread thy face to one of low estate,
Who speaks what thou wilt not rejoice to hear.
But I can hear the things in darkness said,
How the whole city wails this maiden's fate,
As one "who of all women most unjustly,
For noblest deed must die the foulest death,
Who her own brother, fallen in the fray,
Would neither leave unburied, nor expose
To carrion dogs, or any bird of prey,

May she not claim the meed of golden praise?"
Such is the whisper that in secret runs
All darkling. And for me, my father, nought
Is dearer than thy welfare. What can be
A nobler prize of honour for the son
Than a sire's glory, or for sire than son's?
I pray thee, then, wear not one mood alone,
That what thou say'st is right, and nought but that;
For he who thinks that he alone is wise,
His mind and speech above what others have,
Such men when searched are mostly empty found.
But for a man to learn, though he be wise,
Yea to learn much, and know the time to yield,
Brings no disgrace. When winter floods the streams,
Thou see'st the trees that bend before the storm,
Save their last twigs, while those that will not yield
Perish with root and branch. And when one hauls
Too tight the mainsail rope, and will not slack,
He has to end his voyage with deck o'erturned.
Do thou then yield; permit thyself to change.
Young though I be, if any prudent thought
Be with me, I at least will dare assert
The higher worth of one, who, come what will,
Is full of knowledge. If that may not be,
(For nature is not wont to take that bent,)
'Tis good to learn from those who counsel well.

> Chorus.

My king! 'tis fit that thou should'st learn from him,
If he speaks words in season; and, in turn,
That thou [*To* Haemon] should'st learn of him, for both speak well.

> Creon.

Shall we at our age stoop to learn from him,
Young as he is, the lesson to be wise?

> Haemon.

Learn nought thou should'st not learn. And if I'm young,
Thou should'st my deeds and not my years consider.

> Creon.

Is that thy deed to reverence rebel souls?

> Haemon.

I would bid none waste reverence on the base.

Creon.
Has not that girl been seized with that disease?

Haemon.
The men of Thebes with one accord say, No.

Creon.
And will my subjects tell us how to rule?

Haemon.
Dost thou not see thou speakest like a boy?

Creon.
Must I then rule for others than myself?

Haemon.
That is no State which hangs on one man's will.

Creon.
Is not the State deemed his who governs it?

Haemon.
Brave rule! Alone, and o'er an empty land!

Creon.
This boy, it seems, will be his bride's ally.

Haemon.
If thou art she, for thou art all my care.

Creon.
Basest of base, against thy father pleading!

Haemon.
Yea, for I see thee sin a grievous sin.

Creon.
And do I sin revering mine own sway?

Haemon.
Thou show'st no reverence, trampling on God's laws.

Creon.
O guilty soul, by woman's craft beguiled!

Haemon.
Thou wilt not find me slave unto the base.

Creon.
Thy every word is still on her behalf.

Haemon.
Yea, and on thine and mine, and Theirs below.

Creon.
Be sure thou shalt not wed her while she lives.

Haemon.
Then she must die, and, dying, others slay.

Creon.
And dost thou dare to come to me with threats?

Haemon.
Is it a threat against vain thoughts to speak?

Creon.
Thou to thy cost shalt teach me wisdom's ways,
Thyself in wisdom wanting.

Haemon.
                          I would say
Thou wast unwise, if thou wert not my father.

Creon.
Thou woman's slave, I say, prate on no more.

Haemon.
Wilt thou then speak, and, speaking, listen not?

Creon.
Nay, by Olympos! Thou shalt not go free
To flout me with reproaches. Lead her out
Whom my soul hates, that she may die forthwith
Before mine eyes, and near her bridegroom here.

Haemon.
No! Think it not! Near me she shall not die,

And thou shalt never see my face alive,
That thou may'st storm at those who like to yield. [*Exit.*

Chorus.
The man has gone, O king, in hasty mood.
A mind distressed in youth is hard to bear.

Creon.
Let him do what he will, and bear himself
As more than man, he shall not save those girls.

Chorus.
What! Dost thou mean to slay them both alike?

Creon.
Not her who touched it not; there thou say'st well.

Chorus.
What form of death mean'st thou to slay her with?

Creon.
Leading her on to where the desert path
Is loneliest, there alive, in rocky cave
Will I immure her, just so much food
Before her set as may avert pollution,
And save the city from the guilt of blood;
And there, invoking Hades, whom alone
Of all the Gods she worships, she, perchance,
Shall gain escape from death, or then shall know
That Hades-worship is but labour lost.

[*Exit.*

Chorus.
O Love, in every battle victor owned;
        Love, rushing on thy prey,
Now on a maiden's soft and blooming cheek,
        In secret ambush hid;
Now o'er the broad sea wandering at will,
        And now in shepherd's folds;
Of all the Undying Ones none 'scape from thee,
        Nor yet of mortal men
Whose lives are measured as a fleeting day;
And who has thee is frenzied in his soul.
Thou makest vile the purpose of the just,
        To his own fatal harm;

Thou hast stirred up this fierce and deadly strife,
    Of men of nearest kin;
The charm of eyes of bride beloved and fair
    Is crowned with victory,
And dwells on high among the powers that rule,
    Equal with holiest laws;
For Aphrodite, she whom none subdues,
Sports in her might and majesty divine,
    I, even I, am borne
    Beyond the appointed laws;
    I look on this, and cannot stay
    The fountain of my tears.
    For, lo! I see her, see Antigone
    Wend her sad, lonely way
To that bride-chamber where we all must lie.

        Antigone.
Behold, O men of this my fatherland,
    I wend my last lone way,
Seeing the last sunbeam, now and nevermore;
    He leads me yet alive,
    Hades that welcomes all,
    To Acheron's dark shore,
    With neither part nor lot
    In marriage festival,
    Nor hath the marriage hymn
    Been sung for me as bride,
But I shall be the bride of Acheron.

        Chorus.
And hast thou not all honour, worthiest praise,
Who goest to the home that hides the dead,
Not smitten by the sickness that decays,
    Nor by the sharp sword's meed,
But of thine own free will, in fullest life,
    Alone of mortals, thus
    To Hades tak'st thy way?

        Antigone.
I heard of old her pitiable end,
    On Sipylos' high crag,
The Phrygian stranger from a far land come,
    Whom Tantalos begat;
    Whom growth of rugged rock,
    Clinging as ivy clings,

Subdued, and made its own:
And now, so runs the tale,
There, as she melts in shower,
The snow abideth aye,
And still bedews yon cliffs that lie below
Those brows that ever weep.
With fate like hers God brings me to my rest.

Chorus.
A Goddess she, and of the high Gods born;
And we are mortals, born of mortal seed.
And lo! for one who liveth but to die,
To gain like doom with those of heavenly race,
Is great and strange to hear.

Antigone.
Ye mock me then. Alas! Why wait ye not,
By all our fathers' Gods, I ask of you,
Till I have passed away,
But flout me while I live?
O city that I love,
O men that claim as yours
That city stored with wealth,
O Dirkè, fairest fount,
O grove of Thebes, that boasts her chariot host,
I bid you witness all,
How, with no friends to weep,
By what stern laws condemned,
I go to that strong dungeon of the tomb,
For burial strange, ah me!
Nor dwelling with the living, nor the dead.

Chorus.
Forward and forward still to farthest verge
Of daring hast thou gone,
And now, O child, thou hast rushed violently
Where Right erects her throne;
Surely thou payest to the uttermost
Thy father's debt of guilt.

Antigone.
Ah! thou hast touched the quick of all my grief,
The thrice-told tale of all my father's woe,
The fate which dogs us all,
The old Labdakid race of ancient fame.

Woe for the curses dire
Of that defilèd bed,
With foulest incest stained,
My mother's with my sire,
Whence I myself have sprung, most miserable.
And now, I go to them,
To sojourn in the grave,
Accursèd, and unwed;
Ah, brother, thou did'st find
Thy marriage fraught with ill,
And thou, though dead, hast smitten down my life.

Chorus.
Acts reverent and devout
May claim devotion's name,
But power, in one to whom power comes as trust,
May never be defied;
And thee, thy stubborn mood,
Self-chosen, layeth low.

Antigone.
Unwept, without a friend,
Unwed, and whelmed in woe,
I journey on this road that open lies.
No more shall it be mine (O misery!)
To look upon yon daylight's holy eye;
And yet, of all my friends,
Not one bewails my fate,
No kindly tear is shed.

Enter Creon.

Creon.
And know ye not, if men have leave to speak
Their songs and wailings thus to stave off death,
That they will never stop? Lead, lead her on,
Without delay, and, as I said, immure
In yon cavernous tomb, and then depart.
Leave her to choose, or drear and lonely death,
Or, living, in the tomb to find her home.
Our hands are clean in all that touches her;
But she no more shall dwell on earth with us.

Antigone.
[*Turning towards the cavern*]
O tomb, my bridal chamber, vaulted home,

Guarded right well for ever, where I go
To join mine own, of whom the greater part
Among the dead doth Persephassa hold;
And I, of all the last and saddest, wend
My way below, life's little span unfilled.
And yet I go, and feed myself with hopes
That I shall meet them, by my father loved,
Dear to my mother, well-beloved of thee,
Thou darling brother: I, with these my hands,
Washed each dear corpse, arrayed you, poured libations,
In rites of burial; and in care for thee,
Thy body, Polyneikes, honouring,
I gain this recompense. [And yet in sight
Of all that rightly judge the deed was good;
I had not done it had I come to be
A mother with her children,—had not dared,
Though 'twere a husband dead that mouldered there,
Against my country's will to bear this toil.
And am I asked what law constrained me thus?
I answer, had I lost a husband dear,
I might have had another; other sons
By other spouse, if one were lost to me;
But when my father and my mother sleep
In Hades, then no brother more can come.
And therefore, giving thee the foremost place,
I seemed in Creon's eyes, O brother dear,
To sin in boldest daring. Therefore now
He leads me, having taken me by force,
Cut off from marriage bed and marriage song,
Untasting wife's true joy, or mother's bliss,
With infant at her breast, but all forlorn,
Bereaved of friends, in utter misery,
Alive, I tread the chambers of the dead.]
What law of Heaven have I transgressed against?
What use for me, ill-starred one, still to look
To any God for succour, or to call
On any friend for aid? For holiest deed
I bear this charge of rank unholiness.
If acts like these the Gods on high approve,
We, taught by pain, shall own that we have sinned;
But if these sin, [*Looking at* Creon,] I pray they suffer not
Worse evils than the wrongs they do to me.

     Chorus.
Still do the same wild blasts
   Vex her who standeth there.

Creon.
Therefore shall these her guards
    Weep sore for this delay.

Chorus.
Ah me! this word of thine
    Tells of death drawing nigh.

Creon.
I cannot bid thee hope
    For other end than this.

Antigone.
O citadel of Thebes, my native land,
    Ye Gods of ancient days,
    I go, and linger not.
Behold me, O ye senators of Thebes,
The last, lone scion of the kingly race,
What things I suffer, and from whom they come,
Revering still the laws of reverence.

                [*Guards lead* Antigone *away.*

Chorus.
So did the form of Danae bear of old,
    In brazen palace hid,
    To lose the light of heaven,
And in her tomb-like chamber was enclosed:
Yet she, O child, was noble in her race,
And well she stored the golden shower of Zeus.
But great and dread the might of Destiny;
    Nor kingly wealth, nor war,
    Nor tower, nor dark-hulled ships
    Beaten by waves, escape.
So too was shut, enclosed in dungeon cave,
    Bitter and fierce in mood,
    The son of Dryas, king
Of yon Edonian tribes, for vile reproach,
By Dionysos' hands, and so his strength
And soul o'ermad wastes drop by drop away,
And so he learnt that he, against the God,
    Spake his mad words of scorn;
    For he the Maenad throng
    And bright fire fain had stopped,
    And roused the Muses' wrath.
And by the double sea of those Dark Rocks
    Are shores of Bosporos,

And Thrakian isle, as Salmydessos known,
　　Where Ares, whom they serve,
　　God of the region round,
　　Saw the dire, blinding wound,
　　That smote the twin-born sons
Of Phineus by relentless step-dame's hand,—
　　Dark wound, on dark-doomed eyes,
　　Not with the stroke of sword,
But blood-stained hands, and point of spindle sharp.

And they in misery, miserable fate,
　　Wasting away, wept sore,
Born of a mother wedded with a curse.
　　And she who claimed descent
　　From men of ancient fame,
　　The old Erechtheid race,
　　Amid her father's winds,
Daughter of Boreas, in far distant caves
　　Was reared, a child of Gods,
　　Swift moving as the steed
　　O'er lofty crag, and yet
The ever-living Fates bore hard on her.

Enter Teiresias, *guided by a Boy.*

Teiresias.
Princes of Thebes, we come as travellers joined,
One seeing for both, for still the blind must use
A guide's assistance to direct his steps.

Creon.
And what new thing, Teiresias, brings thee here?

Teiresias.
I'll tell thee, and do thou the seer obey.

Creon.
Of old I was not wont to slight thy thoughts.

Teiresias.
So did'st thou steer our city's course full well.

Creon.
I bear my witness from good profit gained.

Teiresias.
Know, then, thou walk'st on fortune's razor-edge.

Creon.
What means this? How I shudder at thy speech!

Teiresias.
Soon shalt thou know, as thou dost hear the signs
Of my dread art. For sitting, as of old,
Upon my ancient seat of augury,
Where every bird finds haven, lo! I hear
Strange cry of winged creatures, shouting shrill,
With inarticulate passion, and I knew
That they were tearing each the other's flesh
With bloody talons, for their whirring wings
Made that quite clear: and straightway I, in fear,
Made trial of the sacrifice that lay
On fiery altar. And Hephaestos' flame
Shone not from out the offering; but there oozed
Upon the ashes, trickling from the bones,
A moisture, and it smouldered, and it spat,
And, lo! the gall was scattered to the air,
And forth from out the fat that wrapped them round
The thigh bones fell. Such omens of decay
From holy sacrifice I learnt from him,
This boy, who now stands here, for he is still
A guide to me, as I to others am.
And all this evil falls upon the State,
From out thy counsels; for our altars all,
Our sacred hearths are full of food for dogs
And birds unclean, the flesh of that poor wretch
Who fell, the son of Oedipus. And so
The Gods no more hear prayers of sacrifice,
Nor own the flame that burns the victim's limbs;
Nor do the birds give cry of omen good,
But feed on carrion of a slaughtered corpse.
Think thou on this, my son: to err, indeed,
Is common unto all, but having erred,
He is no longer reckless or unblest,
Who, having fallen into evil, seeks
For healing, nor continues still unmoved.
Self-will must bear the charge of stubbornness:
Yield to the dead, and outrage not a corpse.
What prowess is it fallen does to slay?

Good counsel give I, planning good for thee,
And of all joys the sweetest is to learn
From one who speaketh well, should that bring gain.

        Creon.

Old man, as archers aiming at their mark,
So ye shoot forth your venomed darts at me;
I know your augur's tricks, and by your tribe
Long since am tricked and sold. Yes, gain your gains,
Get Sardis' amber metal, Indian gold;
That corpse ye shall not hide in any tomb.
Not though the eagles, birds of Zeus, should bear
Their carrion morsels to the throne of God,
Not even fearing this pollution dire,
Will I consent to burial. Well I know
That man is powerless to pollute the Gods.
But many fall, Teiresias, dotard old,
A shameful fall, who gloze their shameful words
For lucre's sake, with surface show of good.

        Teiresias.

Ah me! Does no man know, does none consider . . .

        Creon.

Consider what? What trite poor saw comes now?

        Teiresias.

How far good counsel is of all things best?

        Creon.

So far, I trow, as folly is worst ill.

        Teiresias.

Of that disease thy soul, alas! is full.

        Creon.

I will not meet a seer with evil words.

        Teiresias.

Thou dost so, saying I divine with lies.

        Creon.

The race of seers is ever fond of gold.

        Teiresias.

And that of tyrants still loves lucre foul.

Creon.
Dost know thou speak'st thy words of those that rule?

Teiresias.
I know. Through me thou rul'st a city saved.

Creon.
Wise seer art thou, yet given o'ermuch to wrong.

Teiresias.
Thou'lt stir me to speak out my soul's dread secrets.

Creon.
Out with them; only speak them not for gain.

Teiresias.
So is't, I trow, in all that touches thee.

Creon.
Know that thou shalt not bargain with my will.

Teiresias.
Know, then, and know it well, that thou shalt see
Not many winding circuits of the sun,
Before thou giv'st as quittance for the dead,
A corpse by thee begotten; for that thou
Hast to the ground cast one that walked on earth,
And foully placed within a sepulchre
A living soul; and now thou keep'st from them,
The Gods below, the corpse of one unblest,
Unwept, unhallowed, and in these things thou
Can'st claim no part, nor yet the Gods above;
But they by thee are outraged; and they wait,
The sure though slow avengers of the grave,
The dread Erinnyes of the mighty Gods,
For thee in these same evils to be snared.
Search well if I say this as one who sells
His soul for money. Yet a little while,
And in thy house the wail of men and women
Shall make it plain. And every city stirs
Itself in arms against thee, owning those
Whose limbs the dogs have buried, or fierce wolves,
Or wingèd birds have brought that accursèd taint
To region consecrate. Doom like to this,
Sure darting as an arrow to its mark,
I launch at thee, (for thou dost vex me sore,)

An archer aiming at the very heart,
And thou shalt not escape its fiery sting.
And now, O boy, lead thou me home again,
That he may vent his spleen on younger men,
And learn to keep his tongue more orderly,
With better thoughts than this his present mood.

[*Exit.*

Chorus.

The man has gone, O king, predicting woe,
And well we know, since first our raven hair
Was mixed with grey, that never yet his words
Were uttered to our State and failed of truth.

Creon.

I know it too, 'tis that that troubles me.
To yield is hard, but, holding out, to smite
One's soul with sorrow, this is harder still.

Chorus.

We need wise counsel, O Menoekeus' son.

Creon.

What shall I do? Speak thou, and I'll obey.

Chorus.

Go then, and free the maiden from her tomb,
And give a grave to him who lies exposed.

Creon.

Is this thy counsel? Dost thou bid me yield?

Chorus.

Without delay, O king, for lo! they come,
The Gods' swift-footed ministers of ill,
And in an instant lay the self-willed low.

Creon.

Ah me! 'tis hard; and yet I bend my will
To do thy bidding. With necessity
We must not fight at such o'erwhelming odds.

Chorus.

Go then and act! Commit it not to others.

Creon.
E'en as I am I'll go. Come, come, my men,
Present or absent, come, and in your hands
Bring axes: come to yonder eminence.
And I, since now my judgment leans that way,
Who myself bound her, now myself will loose,
Too much I fear lest it should wisest prove
Maintaining ancient laws to end my life.

[*Exit.*

Chorus.
O Thou of many names,
    Of that Cadmeian maid
    The glory and the joy,
    Whom Zeus as offspring owns,
    Zeus, thundering deep and loud,
Who watchest over famed Italia,
And reign'st o'er all the bays that Deo claims
    On fair Eleusis' coast.
Bacchos, who dwell'st in Thebes, the mother-town
    Of all thy Bacchant train,
    Along Ismenos' stream,
    And with the dragon's brood;

    Thee, o'er the double peak
    Of yonder height the blaze
    Of flashing fire beholds,
    Where nymphs of Corycos
    Go forth in Bacchic dance,
And by the flowery stream of Castaly,
And Thee, the ivied slopes of Nysa's hills,
    And vine-clad promontory,
(While words of more than mortal melody
    Shout out the well-known name,)
    Send forth, the guardian lord
    Of the wide streets of Thebes.

    Above all cities Thou,
With her, thy mother whom the thunder slew,
    Dost look on it with love;
And now, since all the city bendeth low
    Beneath the sullen plague,
    Come Thou with cleansing tread
    O'er the Parnassian slopes,

Or o'er the moaning straits.
O Thou, who lead'st the band,
The choral band of stars still breathing fire,
    Lord of the hymns of night,
The child of highest Zeus; appear, O king,
    With Thyian maidens wild,
    Who all night long in dance,
    With frenzied chorus sing
    Thy praise, their lord, Iacchos.

    Enter Messenger.

    Messenger.
Ye men of Cadmos and Amphion's house,
I know no life of mortal man which I
Would either praise or blame. 'Tis Fortune's chance
That raiseth up, and Fortune bringeth low,
The man who lives in good or evil plight;
And prophet of men's future there is none.
For Creon, so I deemed, deserved to be
At once admired and envied, having saved
This land of Cadmos from the hands of foes;
And, having ruled with fullest sovereignty,
He lived and prospered, joyous in a race
Of goodly offspring. Now, all this is gone;
For when men lose the joys that sweeten life,
I cannot deem they live, but rather count
As if a breathing corpse. His heaped-up stores
Of wealth are large, so be it, and he lives
With all a sovereign's state; and yet, if joy
Be absent, all the rest I count as nought,
And would not weigh them against pleasure's charm,
More than a vapour's shadow.

    Chorus.
    What is this?
What new disaster tell'st thou of our chiefs?

    Messenger.
Dead are they, and the living cause their death.

    Chorus.
Who slays, and who is slaughtered? Tell thy tale.

    Messenger.
Haemon is dead, slain, weltering in his blood.

Chorus.
By his own act, or by his father's hand?

Messenger.
His own, in wrath against his father's crime.

Chorus.
O prophet! true, most true, those words of thine.

Messenger.
Since things stand thus, we well may counsel take.

Chorus.
Lo! Creon's wife comes, sad Eurydike.
She from the house approaches, hearing speech
About her son, or else by accident.

Enter Eurydike.

Eurydike.
I on my way, my friends, as suppliant bound,
To pay my vows at Pallas' shrine, have heard
Your words, and so I chanced to draw the bolt
Of the half-opened door, when lo! a sound
Falls on my ears, of evil striking home,
And terror-struck I fall in deadly swoon
Back in my handmaids' arms; yet tell it me,
Tell the tale once again, for I shall hear,
By long experience disciplined to grief.

Messenger.
Dear lady, I will tell thee: I was by,
And will not leave one word of truth untold.
Why should we smooth and gloze, where all too soon
We should be found as liars? Truth is still
The only safety. Lo! I went with him,
Thy husband, in attendance, to the edge
Of yonder plain, where still all ruthlessly
The corpse of Polyneikes lay exposed,
Mangled by dogs. And, having prayed to her,
The Goddess of all pathways, and to Pluto,
To temper wrath with pity, him they washed
With holy washing; and what yet was left
We burnt in branches freshly cut, and heaped
A high-raised grave from out his native soil,
And then we entered on the stone-paved home,

Death's marriage-chamber for the ill-starred maid.
And some one hears, while standing yet afar,
Shrill voice of wailing near the bridal bower,
By funeral rites unhallowed, and he comes
And tells my master, Creon. On his ears,
Advancing nearer, falls a shriek confused
Of bitter sorrow, and with groaning loud,
He utters one sad cry, "Me miserable!
And am I then a prophet? Do I wend
This day the dreariest way of all my life?
My son's voice greets me. Go, my servants, go,
Quickly draw near, and standing by the tomb,
Search ye and see; and where the stone torn out
Shall make an opening, look ye in, and say
If I hear Haemon's voice, or if my soul
Is cheated by the Gods." And then we searched,
As he, our master, in his frenzy bade us;
And, in the furthest corner of the vault,
We saw her hanging by her neck, with cord
Of linen threads entwined, and him we found
Clasping her form in passionate embrace,
And mourning o'er the doom that robbed him of her,
His father's deed, and that his marriage bed,
So full of woe. When Creon saw him there,
Groaning aloud in bitterness of heart,
He goes to him, and calls in wailing voice,
"Poor boy! what hast thou done? Hast thou then lost
Thy reason? In what evil sinkest thou?
Come forth, my child, on bended knee I ask thee."
And then the boy, with fierce, wild-gleaming eyes,
Glared at him, spat upon his face, and draws,
Still answering nought, the sharp two-handled sword.
Missing his aim, (his father from the blow
Turning aside,) in anger with himself,
The poor ill-doomed one, even as he was,
Fell on his sword, and drove it through his breast,
Full half its length, and clasping, yet alive,
The maiden's arm, still soft, he there breathes out
In broken gasps, upon her fair white cheek,
Swift stream of bloody shower. So they lie,
Dead bridegroom with dead bride, and he has gained,
Poor boy, his marriage rites in Hades' home,
And left to all men witness terrible,
That man's worst ill is want of counsel wise.

[*Exit* Eurydike

Chorus.
What dost thou make of this? She turneth back,
Before one word, or good or ill, she speaks.

Messenger.
I too am full of wonder. Yet with hopes
I feed myself, she will not think it meet,
Hearing her son's woes, openly to wail
Out in the town, but to her handmaids there
Will give command to wail her woe at home.
Too trained a judgment has she so to err.

Chorus.
I know not. To my mind, or silence hard,
Or vain wild cries, are signs of bitter woe.

Messenger.
Soon we shall know, within the house advancing,
If, in the passion of her heart, she hides
A secret purpose. Truly dost thou speak;
There is a terror in that silence hard.

Chorus. [*Seeing* Creon *approaching with the corpse of* Haemon
in his arms.]
And lo! the king himself if drawing nigh,
And in his hands he bears a record clear,
No woe (if I may speak) by others caused,
        Himself the great offender.

Enter Creon, *bearing* Haemon's *body*

Creon.
Woe! for the sins of souls of evil mood,
        Stern, mighty to destroy!
    O ye who look on those of kindred race,
        The slayers and the slain,
Woe for mine own rash plans that prosper not!
Woe for thee, son; but new in life's career,
        And by a new fate dying!
            Woe! woe!
        Thou diest, thou art gone,
Not by thine evil counsel, but by mine.

Chorus.
Ah me! Too late thou seem'st to see the right.

Creon.
Ah me!
I learn the grievous lesson. On my head,
God, pressing sore, hath smitten me and vexed,
In ways most rough and terrible, (Ah me!)
Shattering my joy, as trampled under foot.
Woe! woe! Man's labours are but labour lost.

Enter Second Messenger.

Second Messenger.
My master! thou, as one who hast full store,
One source of sorrow bearest in thine arms,
And others in thy house, too soon, it seems,
Thou need'st must come and see.

Creon.
And what remains
Worse evil than the evils that we bear?

Second Messenger.
Thy wife is dead, that corpse's mother true,
Ill starred one, smitten with a blow just dealt.

Creon.
O agony!
Haven of Death, that none may pacify,
        Why dost thou thus destroy me?
    [*Turning to* Messenger.] O thou who comest, bringing in thy train
        Woes horrible to tell,
Thou tramplest on a man already slain.
What say'st thou? What new tidings bring'st to me?
        Ah me! ah me!
Is it that now there waits in store for me
My own wife's death to crown my misery?

Chorus.
Full clearly thou may'st see. No longer now
Does yon recess conceal her.

[*The gates open and show the dead body of* Eurydike.]

Creon.
Woe is me!
This second ill I gaze on, miserable,

What fate, yea, what still lies in wait for me?
Here in my arms I bear what was my son;
And there, O misery! look upon the dead.
Ah, wretched mother! ah, my son! my son!

Second Messenger.
In frenzy wild she round the altar clung,
And closed her darkening eyelids, and bewailed
The noble fate of Megareus, who died
Long since, and then again that corpse thou hast;
And last of all she cried a bitter cry
Against thy deeds, the murderer of thy sons.

Creon.
Woe! woe! alas!
I shudder in my fear. Will no one strike
A deadly blow with sharp two-edgèd sword?
Fearful my fate, alas!
And with a fearful woe full sore beset.

Second Messenger.
She in her death charged thee with being the cause
Of all their sorrows, these and those of old.

Creon.
And in what way struck she the murderous blow?

Second Messenger.
With her own hand below her heart she stabbed,
Hearing her son's most pitiable fate.

Creon.
Ah me! The fault is mine. On no one else,
Of all that live, the fearful guilt can come;
I, even I, did slay thee, woe is me!
I, yes, I speak the truth. Lead me, ye guards,
Lead me forth quickly; lead me out of sight,
More crushed to nothing than is nothing's self.

Chorus.
Thou counsellest gain, if gain there be in ills,
For present ills when shortest then are best.

Creon.
Oh, come thou then, come thou,

The last of all my dooms, that brings to me
Best boon, my life's last day. Come then, oh come,
That never more I look upon the light.

Chorus.
These things are in the future. What is near,
That we must do. O'er what is yet to come
They watch, to Whom that work of right belongs.

Creon.
I did but pray for what I most desire.

Chorus.
Pray thou for nothing then: for mortal man
There is no issue from a doom decreed.

Creon. [*Looking at the two corpses.*]
Lead me then forth, vain shadow that I am,
Who slew thee, O my son, unwillingly,
And thee too—(O my sorrow!)—and I know not
Which way to look or turn. All near at hand
Is turned to evil; and upon my head
There falls a doom far worse than I can bear.

Chorus.
Man's highest blessedness,
    In wisdom chiefly stands;
And in the things that touch upon the Gods,
    'Tis best in word or deed,
    To shun unholy pride;
Great words of boasting bring great punishments,
    And so to grey-haired age
    Teach wisdom at the last.

4

Classical Philosophy: The Good Is the Rational

Along with the *Euthyphro,* the *Apology,* and the *Crito,* the *Phaedo* (excerpts of which follow) is a dialogue of Plato's dealing with the career, trial, and death of Socrates. Socrates (470–399 B.C.) was an Athenian citizen and philosopher during the century of Athens' greatest development and her tragic decline in the Peloponnesian War. He probably practiced a trade like any ordinary citizen and fulfilled all of his civic responsibilities in political and military life on behalf of his *polis.* He chose to devote himself to the education of the young, but he took no fee for his services and left no writings to posterity. His fame rests solely on the elevated impression which he made on certain of his disciples, particularly on Plato, a young aristocrat whose dialogues are a poetic recreation of Socrates' life and philosophy.

Socrates taught by a method of questioning and logical inquiry, and he avoided the concern with physical nature demonstrated by earlier Greek philosophers; Socrates preferred investigating the ethical rather than the physical nature of life. He lived in an environment in which traditional religious beliefs had been weakened and in which political democracy had fallen into factionalism and demagoguery. Because of his personal association with figures in the aristocratic party and the possibly antidemocratic implications of his ethical philosophy, Socrates was in 399 accused by the restored Athenian democracy of impiety; he was convicted and sentenced to death. This was more than enough reason for Plato, Socrates' devoted follower, to withdraw from the evil life of democratic politics and to search for a higher life. In a sense, Plato's whole philosophy and career was a defense of Socrates' quest for truth and a search for a way of organizing men so that wisdom would no longer be at the mercy of the mob. Plato founded the Academy of Athens, the first institution in the ancient world approaching what we mean by a university. His philosophy is generally referred to as idealistic, giving precedence to abstract ideas or forms over sensory matter. Plato's philosophy—and it is difficult to discover to what extent he went significantly beyond the conclusions of Socrates—provided one important foundation for the view of classical man, particularly in its identification of God with reason and its dualism between mind and body, in which the body became identified with the transitory and evil, and mind or soul with the good and the true.

The final pages of the *Phaedo* convey the saintliness of Socrates' personality as it impressed his closest followers. Indeed, Platonism has often in its long history seemed as much a religion as a philosophy, for it sanctions a contemplative and ascetic withdrawal from the world of matter and ordinary affairs. In this, Platonism has affinities with various philosophies and religions of the Far East, but idealism in its Platonic form is thoroughly western in its thrust. It is also somewhat pessimistic about the ability of the majority of men to attain truth, this higher life being restricted to the few who are philosophers.

Plato:
The Phaedo

... When I was young, Cebes, I had a prodigious desire to know that department of philosophy which is called the investigation of nature; to know the causes of things, and why a thing is and is created or destroyed, appeared to me to be a lofty profession; and I was always agitating myself with the consideration of questions such as these: —Is the growth of animals the result of some putrefaction which the hot and the cold principle suffer, as some have said? Is the blood the element with which we think, or the air, or the fire? or perhaps nothing of the kind—but the brain may be the originating power of the perceptions of hearing and sight and smell, and memory and opinion may come from them, and knowledge from memory and opinion when they have attained fixity. And then I went on to examine the corruptions of them, and then to the things of heaven and earth, and at last I concluded myself to be utterly and absolutely incapable of these inquiries, as I will satisfactorily prove to you. For I was fascinated by them to such a degree that my eyes grew blind to things which I had seemed to myself, and also to others, to know quite well; I unlearned what I had before thought self-evident truths; e.g. such a fact as that the growth of man is the result of eating and drinking; for when by the digestion of food flesh is added to flesh and bone to bone, and when by the same process each tissue has received its appropriate accretion, then the lesser bulk

Excerpted from *The Phaedo* in Benjamin Jowett, trans., *The Dialogues of Plato,* Vol. I (Oxford: The Clarendon Press, 1953), pp. 453–477. Reprinted by permission of the Clarendon Press.

becomes larger and so the small man becomes big. Was not that a reasonable notion?

Yes, said Cebes, I think so.

Well; but let me tell you something more. There was a time when I thought that I understood the meaning of greater and less pretty well; and when I saw a big man standing by a little one, I fancied that one was taller than the other just by the head, and similarly with horses: and still more clearly did I seem to perceive that ten is more than eight because it has two additional units, and that two cubits are more than one because it is larger by a half of itself.

And what is now your notion of such matters? said Cebes.

I should be far enough from imagining, he replied, that I knew the cause of any of them, by heaven I should; for I cannot satisfy myself that, when one is added to one, either the one to which the addition is made or the one which is added becomes two, or that the two units added together make two by reason of the addition. I cannot understand how, when separated from the other, each of them was one and not two, and now, when they are brought together, the mere juxtaposition or meeting of them should be the cause of their becoming two. Neither can I believe that the division of one is the way to make two; for then an opposite cause would produce the same effect,—as in the former instance the addition and juxtaposition of one to one was the cause of two, in this the separation and subtraction of one from the other would be the cause. Nor am I any longer satisfied that I understand how the unit comes into being at all, or in short how anything else is either generated or destroyed or exists, so long as this is the method of approach; but I have in my mind some confused notion of a new method, and can never admit the other.

Then I heard someone reading, as he said, from a book of Anaxagoras, that mind was the disposer and cause of all, and I was delighted at this notion, which appeared quite admirable, and I said to myself: If mind is the disposer, mind will dispose all for the best, and put each particular in the best place; and I argued that if anyone desired to find out the cause of the generation or destruction or existence of anything, he must find out what state of being or doing or suffering was best for that thing, and therefore a man had only to consider what was best and most desirable both for the thing itself and for other things, and then he must necessarily also know the worse, since the same science comprehended both. Arguing in this way, I rejoiced to think that I had found in Anaxagoras a teacher of the causes of existence such as I desired, and I imagined that he would tell me first whether the earth is flat or round; and after telling me this, he would proceed to explain the cause and the necessity of this being so, starting from the greater good, and demonstrating that it is better for the earth to be such as it is; and if he said that the earth was in the centre, he would further explain that this position was the better, and I should be satisfied with the explanation given, and not want any other sort of cause. And I thought that I would then go on and ask him about the sun and moon and stars, and that he would explain to me their comparative swiftness, and their returnings and various states, active and passive, and in what way all of them were for the best. For I could not imagine that when he spoke of mind as the disposer of them, he would give any other account of their being as they are, except that this was best; and I thought that while explaining to me in detail the cause of each and the cause of all, he would also explain to me what was best for each and what was good for all. These hopes I would not have sold for a large sum of money, and I seized the books and started to read them as fast as I could in my eagerness to know the best and the worse.

How high were my hopes, and how quickly were they lost to me! As I proceeded, I found my philosopher altogether forsaking mind and making no appeal to any other principle of order, but having recourse to air, and ether, and water, and many other eccentricities. I might compare him to a person who began by maintaining generally that mind is the cause of the actions of Socrates, but who, when he endeavoured to explain the causes of my several actions in detail, went on to show that I sit here because my body is made up of bones and muscles; and the bones, as he would say, are hard and have joints which divide them, and the muscles are elastic, and they cover the bones, which have also a covering or environment of flesh and skin which contains them; and as the bones swing in their sockets, through the contraction or relaxation of the muscles I am able to bend my limbs, and this is why I am sitting here in a curved posture—that is what he would say; and he would have a similar explanation of my talking to you, which he would attribute to sound, and air, and hearing, and he would assign ten thousand other causes of the same sort, forgetting to mention the true cause, which is, that the Athenians have thought it better to condemn me, and accordingly I have thought it better and more right to remain here and undergo my sentence; for I strongly suspect that these muscles and bones of mine would long ago have been in Megara or Boeotia, borne there by their own idea of what was best, if I did not think it more right and honourable to endure any penalty ordered by the state, instead of running away into exile. There is surely a strange confusion of causes and conditions in all this. It may be said, indeed, that without bones and muscles and the other parts of the body I cannot execute my purposes. But to say at the same time that I act from mind, and that I do as I do because of them and not from the choice of the best, is a very careless and idle mode of speaking. I wonder that they cannot distinguish the cause from the condition without which the cause would never be the cause; it is the latter, I think, which the many, feeling about in the dark, are always mistaking and misnaming 'cause'. And thus one man sets the earth within a cosmic whirling, and steadies it by the heaven; another gives the air as a support to the earth, which is a sort of broad trough. They never look for the power which in arranging them as they are arranges them for the best; and instead of ascribing to it any superhuman strength, they rather expect to discover another Atlas who is stronger and more everlasting than this earthly Atlas, and better able to hold all things together. That it is really the good and the right which holds and binds things together, they never reflect. Such then is the principle of causation which I would faiñ learn if anyone would teach me. But as I have failed either to discover it myself, or to learn it of anyone else, I will exhibit to you, if you like, the method I have followed as the second best mode of inquiring into the cause.

I should very much like to hear, he replied.

Socrates proceeded:—I thought that as I had failed in the study of material things, I ought to be careful that I did not lose the eye of my soul; as people may injure their bodily eye by observing and gazing on the sun during an eclipse, unless they take the precaution of only looking at the image reflected in the water, or in some similar medium. So in my own case, I was afraid that my soul might be blinded altogether if I looked at things with my eyes or tried to apprehend them by the help of particular senses. And I thought that I had better retreat to the domain of reasoning and seek there the truth of existence. I dare say that the simile is not perfect—for I do not quite agree that he who contemplates things through the medium of thought, sees them only 'through a glass darkly', more so than he who considers them in their material existence. However, this was the method which I adopted: I first assumed some proposition, which I judged to be the strongest, and then I affirmed as true whatever seemed to agree with this, whether relating to causation or to anything else; and that which disagreed I regarded as untrue. But I should like to explain my meaning more clearly, as I do not think that you as yet understand me.

No indeed, replied Cebes, not very well.

There is nothing new, he said, in what I am about to tell you; but only what I have been always and everywhere repeating in the previous discussion and on other occasions: I shall try to show you the sort of causation which has occupied my thoughts. I shall have to go back to those familiar theories which are in the mouth of everyone, and first of all assume that there is an absolute beauty and goodness and greatness, and the like; grant me these and admit that they exist, and I hope to be able to show you the nature of cause, and to prove the immortality of the soul.

Cebes said: You may proceed at once with the proof, for I grant you this.

Well, he said, then I should like to know whether you agree with me in the next step; for I cannot help thinking that if there be anything beautiful other than absolute beauty it is beautiful only in so far as it partakes of absolute beauty—and I should say the same of everything. Do you agree in this notion of the cause?

Yes, he said, I agree.

He proceeded: I no longer look for, nor can I understand, those other ingenious causes which are alleged; and if a person says to me that the bloom of colour, or form, or any such thing is a source of beauty, I dismiss all that, which is only confusing to me, and simply and singly, and perhaps foolishly, hold and am assured in my own mind that nothing makes a thing beautiful but the presence or participation of beauty in whatever way or manner obtained; for as to the manner I am uncertain, but I stoutly contend that by beauty all beautiful things become beautiful. This appears to me to be the safest answer which I can give, either to myself or to another, and to this I cling, in the persuasion that this principle will never be overthrown, and that to myself or to anyone who asks the question, I may safely reply, That by beauty beautiful things become beautiful. Do you not agree with me?

I do.

And that by greatness great things become great and greater greater, and by smallness the less become less?

True.

Then if a person were to remark that A is taller by a head than B, and B less by a head than A, you would refuse to admit his statement, and would stoutly contend that what you mean is only that the greater is greater by, and by reason of, greatness, and the less is less only by, and by reason of, smallness. I imagine you would be afraid of a counter-argument that if the greater is greater and the less less by the head, then, first, the greater is greater and the less less by the same thing; and, secondly, the greater man is greater by the head which is itself small, and so you get the monstrous absurdity that a man is great by something small. You would be afraid of this, would you not?

Indeed I should, said Cebes, laughing.

In like manner you would think it dangerous to say that ten exceeded eight by, and by reason of, two; but would say by, and by reason of, number; or you would say that two cubits exceed one cubit not by a half, but by magnitude?—for there is the same danger in all these cases.

Very true, he said.

Again, would you not be cautious of affirming that the addition of one to one, or the division of one, is the cause of two? And you would loudly asseverate that you know of no way in which anything comes into existence except by participation in the distinctive reality of that in which it participates, and consequently, as far as you know, the only cause of two is the participation in duality—this is the way to make two, and the participation in unity is the way to make one. You would say: 'I will let alone all subtleties like these of division and addition—wiser heads than mine may answer them; inexperienced as I am, and ready to start, as the proverb says, at my own shadow, I cannot afford to give up the sure ground of the original postulate.' And if anyone fastens on you there, you would not mind him, or answer him until you could see whether the consequences which follow agree with one another or not, and when you are further required to give an account of this postulate, you would give it in the same way, assuming some higher postulate which seemed to you to be the best founded, until you arrived at a satisfactory resting-place; but you would not jumble together the fundamental principle and the consequences in your reasoning, like the eristics—at least if you wanted to discover real existence. Not that this confusion signifies to them, who probably never care or think about the matter at all, for they have the wit to be well pleased with themselves however thorough may be the muddle of their ideas. But you, if you are a philosopher, will certainly do as I say.

What you say is most true, said Simmias and Cebes, both speaking at once.

Ech. Yes, Phaedo; and I do not wonder at their assenting. Anyone who has the least sense will acknowledge the wonderful clearness of Socrates' reasoning.

Phaed. Certainly, Echecrates; and such was the feeling of the whole company at the time.

Ech. Yes, and equally of ourselves, who were not of the company, and are now listening to your recital. But what followed?

Phaed. After all this had been admitted, and they had agreed, that the forms exist individually, and that other things participate in them and derive their names from them, Socrates, if I remember rightly, said:—

This is your way of speaking; and yet when you say that Simmias is greater than Socrates and less than Phaedo, do you not predicate of Simmias both greatness and smallness?

Yes, I do.

But still, he continued, you allow that Simmias does not in fact exceed Socrates, as the words may seem to imply, essentially because he is Simmias, but by reason of the size which he happens to have; exactly as on the other hand he does not exceed Socrates because Socrates is Socrates, but because Socrates has smallness when compared with the greatness of Simmias?

True.

And if Phaedo exceeds him in size, this is not because Phaedo is Phaedo, but because Phaedo has greatness relatively to Simmias, who is comparatively smaller?

That is true.

And therefore Simmias is said to be small, and is also said to be great, because he is in a mean between them, submitting his smallness to be exceeded by the greatness of the one, and presenting his greatness to the other to exceed that other's smallness. He added, laughing, I am speaking like a book, but I believe that what I am saying is true.

Simmias assented.

I speak as I do because I want you to agree with me in thinking, not only that absolute greatness will never be simultaneously great and small, but also that the greatness in us will never admit the small or consent to be exceeded; instead of this, one of two things will happen, either it will fly and retire before its opposite, the small, or at the approach of its opposite it has already ceased to exist; but it refuses to become other than what it was by staying and receiving smallness. For instance, I having received and admitted smallness remain as I was, and am the same person and small: but greatness has not condescended to become small. In like manner the smallness in us refuses to be or become great; nor can any other opposite which remains the same ever be or become its own opposite, but either goes away or perishes in the change.

That, replied Cebes, is quite my notion.

Hereupon one of the company, though I do not exactly remember which of them, said: In heaven's name, is not this the direct contrary of what was admitted before—that out of the greater came the less and out of the less the greater, and that opposites were simply generated from opposites; but now this principle seems to be utterly denied.

Socrates turned his head to the speaker and listened. I like your courage, he said, in reminding us of this. But you do not observe that there is a difference in the two cases. For then we were saying that an opposite thing comes into being from its opposite; now, however, speaking of bare opposites, and taking them either as they are realized in us or as they exist in themselves, we say that one of them can never become the other: then, my friend, we were speaking of things in which opposites are inherent and which are called after them, but now about the opposites which are inherent in them and which give their name to them; and these essential opposites will never, as we maintain, admit of generation into or out of one another. At the same time, turning to Cebes, he said: Are you at all disconcerted, Cebes, at our friend's objection?

No, not by this one, said Cebes; and yet I cannot deny that I am often disturbed by objections.

Then we are agreed after all, said Socrates, that the opposite will never in any case be opposed to itself?

To that we are quite agreed, he replied.

Yet once more let me ask you to consider the question from another point of view, and see whether you agree with me:—There is a thing which you term heat, and another thing which you term cold?

Certainly.

But are they the same as fire and snow?

Most assuredly not.

Heat is a thing different from fire, and cold is not the same with snow?

Yes.

And yet I fancy you agree that when snow receives heat (to use our previous phraseology), they will not remain snow and heat; but at the advance of the heat, the snow will either retire or perish?

Very true, he replied.

And the fire too at the advance of the cold will either retire or perish; but it will never receive the cold, and yet insist upon remaining what it was, and so be at once fire and cold.

That is true, he said.

And in some cases the name of the form is attached not only to the form in an eternal connexion; but something else which, not being the form, yet never exists without it, is also entitled to be called by that name. I will try to make this clearer by an example:—The odd number is always called by the name of odd?

Very true.

But is this the only thing which is called odd? Here is my point. Are there not other things which have their own name, and yet must be called odd, because, although not the same as oddness, they are essentially never without oddness? I mean such a case as that of the number three, and there are many other examples. Take that case. Would you not say that three may be called by its proper name, and also be called odd, which is not the same with three? and this may be said not only of three but also of five, and of every alternate number—each of them without being oddness is odd; and in the same way two and four, and the other series of alternate numbers, has every number even, without being evenness. Do you agree?

Of course.

Then now mark the point at which I am aiming:—not only do essential opposites seem to exclude one another, but also concrete things, which, although not in themselves opposed, contain opposites; these, I say, likewise reject the form opposed to that which is contained in them, and when it approaches them they either perish or withdraw. For example; Will not the number three endure annihilation or anything sooner than be converted into an even number, while remaining three?

Very true, said Cebes.

And yet, he said, the number two is certainly not opposed to the number three?

It is not.

Then not only do opposite forms repel the advance of one another, but also there are other things which withdraw before the approach of opposites.

Very true, he said.

Suppose, he said, that we endeavour, if possible, to determine what these are.

By all means.

Are they not, Cebes, such as compel anything of which they have possession, not only to take their own form, but also the form of an opposite?

What do you mean?

I mean, as I was just now saying, and as I am sure that you know, that those things which are possessed by the form of the number three must not only be three in number, but must also be odd.

Quite true.

And such things will never suffer the intrusion of the form opposite to that which gives this impress?

No.

And this impress was given by the form of the odd?

Yes.

And to the odd is opposed the even?

True.

Then the form of the even number will never intrude on three?

No.

Then three has no part in the even?

None.

Then the triad or number three is uneven?

Very true.

To return then to my definition of things which are not opposite to one of a pair of opposites, and yet do not admit that opposite—as, in the instance given, three, although not opposed to the even, does not any the more admit of the even, but always brings the opposite into play on the other side; or as two does not receive the odd, or fire the cold—from these examples (and there are many more of them) perhaps you may be able to arrive at the general conclusion, that not only opposites will not receive opposites, but also that nothing which brings an opposite will admit the opposite of that which it brings, in that to which it is brought. And here let me recapitulate—for there is no harm in repetition. The number five will not admit the form of the even, any more than ten, which is the double of five, will admit the form of the odd. The double has itself a different opposite, but nevertheless rejects the odd altogether. Nor similarly will parts in the ratio 3:2 admit the form of the whole, nor will the half or the one-third, or any such fraction: You will agree?

Yes, he said, I entirely agree and go along with you in that.

And now, he said, let us begin again; and do not you answer my question in the words in which I ask it, but follow my example: let me have not the old safe answer of which I spoke at first, but another equally safe, of which the truth will be inferred by you from what has been just said. If you ask me 'what that is, of which the inherence makes the body hot', I shall reply not heat (this is what I call the safe and stupid answer), but fire, a far superior answer, which we are now in a condition to give. Or if you ask me 'why a body is diseased', I shall not say from disease, but from fever; and instead of saying that oddness is the cause of odd numbers, I shall say that the monad is the cause of them: and so of things in general, as I dare say that you will understand sufficiently without my adducing any further examples.

Yes, he said, I quite understand you.

Tell me, then, what is that of which the inherence will render the body alive?

The soul, he replied.

And is this always the case?

Yes, he said, of course.

Then whatever the soul occupies, to that she comes bearing life?

Yes, certainly.

And is there any opposite to life?

There is, he said.

And what is that?

Death.

Then from our previous conclusion it follows that the soul will never admit the opposite of what she always brings.

Impossible, replied Cebes.

And now, he said, what did we just now call that which does not admit the form of the even?

Uneven.

And that which does not admit the musical or the just?

The unmusical, he said, and the unjust.

And what do we call that which does not admit death?

The immortal, he said.

And does the soul admit of death?

No.

Then the soul is immortal?

Yes, he said.

And may we say that this has been proven?

Yes, abundantly proven, Socrates, he replied.

Supposing that the odd were necessarily imperishable, must not three be imperishable?

Of course.

And if that which is cold were necessarily imperishable, when heat came attacking the snow, must not the snow have retired whole and unmelted —for it could never have perished, nor again could it have remained and admitted the heat?

True, he said.

Again, if that which cannot be cooled were imperishable, the fire when assailed by cold would not have perished or have been extinguished, but would have gone away unaffected?

Certainly, he said.

And the same may be said of the immortal: if the immortal is also imperishable, the soul when attacked by death cannot perish; for the preceding argument shows that the soul will not admit death, or exist as dead, any more than three or the odd number will exist as even, or fire, or the heat in the fire, will be cold. Yet a person may say: 'But although the odd will not become even at the approach of the even, why may not the odd perish and the even take the place of the odd?' Now to him who makes this objection, we cannot answer that the odd is imperishable; for this is not the fact. If we had accepted it as a fact, there would have been no difficulty in contending that at the approach of the even the odd and the number three took their departure; and the same argument would have held good of fire and heat and any other thing.

Very true.

And the same may be said of the immortal: if we agree that the immortal is also imperishable, then the soul will be imperishable as well as immortal; but if not, some other proof of her imperishableness will have to be given.

No other proof is needed, he said; for if the immortal, being eternal, is liable to perish, then nothing is imperishable.

Yes, replied Socrates, and all men, I think, will agree that God, and the essential form of life, and the immortal in general, will never perish.

Yes, all men, he said—that is true; and what is more, gods, if I am not mistaken, as well as men.

Seeing then that the immortal is indestructible, must not the soul, if she is immortal, be also imperishable?

Most certainly.

Then when death attacks a man, the mortal portion of him may be supposed to die, but the immortal retires at the approach of death and is preserved safe and indestructible?

Yes.

Then, Cebes, beyond question, the soul is immortal and imperishable, and our souls will truly exist in another world!

I am convinced, Socrates, said Cebes, and have nothing more to object; but if my friend Simmias, or anyone else, has any further objection to make, he had better speak out, and not keep silence, since I do not know to what other season he can defer the discussion if there is anything which he wants to say or to have said.

But I too, replied Simmias, can give no reason for doubting the result of the argument. It is when I think of the greatness of the subject and the feebleness of man that I still feel and cannot help feeling uncertain in my own mind.

Yes, Simmias, replied Socrates, that is well said: and I may add that our first principles, even if they appear to you certain, should be closely examined; and when they are satisfactorily analysed, then you will, I imagine, follow up the argument as far as is humanly possible; and if you make sure you have done so, there will be no need for any further inquiry.

Very true.

But then, O my friends, he said, if the soul is really immortal, what care should be taken of her, not only in respect of the portion of time allowed to what is called life, but of eternity! And the danger of neglecting her from this point of view does indeed now appear to be awful. If death had only been the end of all, dying would have been a godsend to the wicked, for they would have been happily quit not only of their body, but of their own evil together with their souls. But now, inasmuch as the soul is manifestly immortal, there is for her no release or salvation from evil except the attainment of the highest virtue and wisdom. For the soul when on her progress to the world below takes nothing with her but nurture and education; and these are said greatly to benefit or greatly to injure the departed, at the very beginning of his journey thither. . . .

A man of sense ought not to assert that the description which I have given of the soul and her mansions is exactly true. But I do say that, inasmuch as the soul is shown to be immortal, he may venture to think, not improperly or unworthily, that something of the kind is true. The venture is a glorious one, and he ought to comfort himself with words of power like these, which is the reason why I lengthen out the tale. Wherefore, I say, let a man be of good cheer about his soul, who having cast away the pleasures and ornaments of the body as alien to him and working harm rather than good, has sought after the pleasures of knowledge; and has arrayed the soul, not in some foreign attire, but in her own proper jewels, temperance, and justice, and courage, and nobility, and truth—in these adorned she is ready to go on her journey to the world below. You, Simmias and Cebes, and you others, will depart at some time or other. Me already, as a tragic poet would say, the voice of fate calls. Soon I must drink the poison; and I think that I had better repair to the bath first, in order that the women may not have the trouble of washing my body after I am dead.

When he had done speaking, Crito said: And have you any commands for us, Socrates—anything to say about your children, or any other matter in which we can serve you?

Nothing particular, Crito, he replied: only, as I have always told you, take care of yourselves, that is a service which you may be ever rendering to me and mine and to yourselves. whether you promise to do so or not. But if you have no thought for yourselves, and care not to walk in the path of life which I have shown you, not now for the first time, then however much and however earnestly you may promise at the moment, it will be of no avail.

We will do our best, said Crito: And in what way shall we bury you?

In any way that you like; but you must first get hold of me, and take care that I do not run away from you. Then he turned to us, and added with a smile:—I cannot make Crito believe that I am the same Socrates who have been talking and conducting the argument; he fancies that I am the other Socrates whom he will soon see, a dead body—and indeed he asks, How shall he bury me? And though I have spoken many words in the endeavour to show that when I have drunk the poison I shall leave you and go to the joys of the blessed,—these words of mine, with which I was comforting you and myself, have had, as I perceive, no effect upon Crito. And therefore I want you to be surety for me to him now, as at the trial he was surety to the judges for me: but let the promise be of another sort; for he was surety for me to the judges that I would remain, and you must be my surety to him that I shall not remain, but go away and depart; and then he will suffer less at my death, and not be grieved when he sees my body being burned or buried. I would not have him sorrow at my hard lot, or say at the burial, Thus we lay out Socrates, or, Thus we follow him to the grave or bury him; for be well assured, my dear Crito, that false words are not only evil in themselves, but they infect the soul with evil. Be of good cheer then and say that you are burying my body only, and do with that whatever is usual, and what you think best.

When he had spoken these words, he arose and went into a chamber to bathe; Crito followed him and told us to wait. So we remained behind, talking and thinking of the subject of discourse, and also of the greatness of our loss; he was like a father of whom we were being bereaved, and we were about to pass the rest of our lives as orphans. When he had taken the bath his children were brought to him—(he had two young sons and an elder one); and the women of his family also came, and he talked to them and gave them a few directions in the presence of Crito; then he dismissed them and returned to us.

Now the hour of sunset was near, for a good deal of time had passed while he was within. When he came out, he sat down with us again after his bath, but not much was said. Soon the jailer, who was the servant of the Eleven, entered and stood by him, saying:—To you, Socrates, whom after your time here I know to be the noblest and gentlest and best of all who ever came to this place, I will not impute the angry feelings of other men, who rage and swear at me, when, in obedience to the authorities, I bid them drink the poison —indeed, I am sure that you are not angry with me; for others, as you are aware, and not I, are to blame. And so fare you well, and try to bear lightly what must needs be—you know my errand. Then bursting into tears he turned and started on his way out.

Socrates looked up at him and said: I return your good wishes, and will do as you bid. Then turning to us, he said, How charming the man is: since I have been in prison he has always been coming to see me, and at times he would talk to me, and was as good to me as could be, and now see how generously he sorrows on my account. We must do as he says, Crito; and therefore let the cup be brought, if the poison is prepared: if not, let the attendant prepare some.

But, said Crito, the sun is still upon the hill-tops, and is not yet set. I know that many a one takes the draught quite a long time after the announcement has been made to him, when he has eaten and drunk to his satisfaction and enjoyed the society of his chosen friends; do not hurry—there is time enough.

Socrates said: Yes, Crito, and therein they of whom you speak act logically, for they think that they will be gainers by the delay; but I likewise act logically in not following their example, for I do not think that I should gain anything by drinking the poison a little later; I should only be ridiculous in my own eyes for sparing and saving a life which is already down to its dregs. Please then to do as I say, and not to refuse me.

Crito made a sign to the servant, who was standing by; and he went out, and having been absent for some time, returned with the jailer carrying the cup of poison. Socrates said: You, my good friend, who are experienced in these matters, shall give me directions how I am to proceed. The man answered: You have only to walk about until your legs are heavy, and then to lie down, and the poison will act. At the same time he handed the cup to Socrates, who in the easiest and gentlest manner, without the least fear or change of colour or feature, and looking at the man sideways with that droll glance of his, took the cup and said: What do you say about making a libation out of this cup to any god? May I, or not? The man answered: We only prepare, Socrates, just so much as we deem enough. I understand, he said: but a prayer to the gods I may and must offer, that they will prosper my journey from this to the other world—even so—and so be it according to my prayer. Then he held his breath and drank off the poison quite readily and cheerfully. And hitherto most of us had been fairly able to control our sorrow; but now when we saw him drinking, and saw too that he had finished the draught, we could no longer forbear, and in spite of myself my own tears were flowing fast; so that I covered my face and wept, not indeed for him, but at the thought of my own calamity in having to part from such a friend. Nor was I the first; for Crito, when he found himself unable to restrain his tears, had got up, and I followed; and at that moment, Apollodorus, who had been weeping all the time, burst out in a loud and passionate cry which broke us all down. Socrates alone retained his calmness: What is this strange outcry? he said. I sent away the women mainly in order that they might not misbehave in this fashion, for I have been told that a man should die in peace. Be quiet then, and bear yourselves with fortitude. When we heard his words we were ashamed, and refrained our tears; and he walked about until, as he said, his legs began to fail, and then he lay on his back, according to the directions, and the man who gave him the poison now and then looked at his feet and legs; and after a while he pressed his foot hard, and asked him if he could feel; and he said, No; and then his leg, and so upwards and upwards, and showed us that he was becoming cold and stiff. And he felt them himself, and said: When the poison reaches the heart, that will be the end. He was beginning to grow cold about the groin, when he uncovered his face, for he had covered himself up, and said—they were his last words—he said: Crito, I owe a cock to Aesculapius; will you remember to pay the debt? The debt shall be paid, said Crito; is there anything else? There was no answer to this question; but in a minute or two a movement was heard, and the attendant uncovered him; his eyes were set, and Crito closed his eyes and mouth.

Such was the end, Echecrates, of our friend; concerning whom we may truly say that of all the men of his time whom we have known, he was the wisest and justest and best.

5

Classical Philosophy: The Good Life

Aristotle (384–322 B.C.) was a student of Plato and has often been taken as an opponent of Platonic idealism. Where Plato scorned the world of sensory perception and sought the good and the true in the realm of abstract ideas or forms, Aristotle has been credited with an empirical and experimental attitude towards nature and reality. It is true that Aristotle differed with Plato concerning the reality of abstract ideas or forms, but one can exaggerate these differences and distinctions. Plato and Aristotle both contributed importantly to the development of a characteristic viewpoint of classical man: that man is primarily a rational being.

Aristotle was a Macedonian from the northern part of Greece, the son of a physician to the royal house of Macedon from which Alexander the Great would issue. The example of his father and his early education led Aristotle to study medicine and biology, and this initial influence never left him, causing him to emphasize experimentation and observation more than such strictly moral philosophers as Socrates and Plato. But Aristotle did study with Plato for about 20 years and was his most brilliant student. After Plato's death, Aristotle founded a rival institution to the Platonic Academy, the so-called Lyceum. The author of works on ethics, metaphysics, biology, astronomy, physics, logic, poetics, and political science, Aristotle can perhaps be viewed as the first systematic philosopher. So great was his reputation in later years that he was known simply as "the philosopher," and his conclusions, often empirically grounded, about man and nature became rigid dogmas in the hands of lesser men. Aristotle partially relived Socrates' experience, for he too was a victim of Athenian politics. As a Macedonian and former tutor of Alexander the Great, Aristotle was suspected of being an enemy of the Athenian state, and he decided to flee Athens rather than repeat Socrates' fate.

The Nicomachean Ethics express some of the characteristic philosophy of Aristotle and of classical man. Virtue and goodness are generally identified with the rational activity of the mind, while evil is derived from ignorance. The life of virtue—the highest life—is the life of the mind, and only an immoderate concern with the desires of the body and the cares of daily life hamper the pursuit of excellence and virtue. Aristotle investigated the nature of virtue through a combination of inductive observation and abstract logic, but reached conclusions similar to Plato's—that virtue is intellectual and therefore closed to the majority of men. This is an essential ingredient in the outlook of classical man: the good life is only for the few. The many—the masses, whether freemen or slaves—are doomed to lead nearly animalistic lives under the rule of tyrants; neither philosopher could really place much hope in the rule of philosopher–kings, for both Plato and Aristotle had tried and failed to make their royal pupils and friends in politics attentive to the lessons of philosophy.

Aristotle:

The Nicomachean Ethics

Since all our acts, whether intellectual or moral, aim at some good end, what is the end at which we assert that the art political aims,—that is to say, what is the highest of all goods attainable by human action? Upon its name almost all men are agreed. For both the untaught many and the educated few call it Happiness, and understand this same happiness to consist in a good and a prosperous life. But as to what this happiness exactly is they disagree, so that hereupon popular and philosophic views conflict. Some say that it is a something tangible and conspicuous, such as is pleasure, or wealth, or honour,—some, in short, give one account of it, and some another; and often the same man's views will vary, and when seized by sickness he will assert that happiness is health, and when pressed for money that it is wealth; while those, again, who are conscious of their own ignorance, marvel at him who converses upon matters which are great, and too high for them. And some, again, have held that, beyond and beside these many particular goods, there is an absolute and universal good, from which is derived the goodness of these many singulars. To sift so many views were perhaps a purposeless task. It will be sufficient if we examine those which are most widely spread, or which seem to have some foundation upon which to rest. We must further bear in mind the difference between the synthetical method, which proceeds from the universal to the singular, and the analytical, which proceeds from the particular to the univer-

The Nicomachean Ethics of Aristotle, Robert Williams, trans. (London: Longmans, Green, and Co., 1869), pp. 5-8, 13-17, 18-27, 30-34, 372-376.

sal. And, indeed, Plato did well in investigating, and in attempting to solve the question whether method is to be synthetic or analytic,—either being conceivably possible, exactly as in a race-course one can run from the stewards to the goal, or from the goal to the stewards. In either case, however, we must begin with truths taken upon their own evidence. Of these there are two kinds—the universal, which is first in the order of nature; and the particular, which is first for man, or in the order of experience. We then had, perhaps, best begin with those principles which are first for man. And hence he who is to be a competent student of what is noble, and of what is just, or, in a word, of the art political, ought previously to have been trained in good habits. For the first principle from which ethics start is the particular fact of experience, of which if we are perfectly convinced that it is such or such, our conviction is in no way strengthened by knowledge of the why and wherefore. He who has been thus trained will either already know the most general principles of the science, or will with ease acquire them. But he who knows neither the universal rule, nor the particular fact, had best bear in mind the proverb of Hesiod—

> *Wisest is he who of himself hath knowledge,*
> *And wise is he who lists to prudent counsel;*
> *But whoso nor hath knowledge, nor to others*
> *Lendeth his ear, is but an idle dullard.*

But, to return to the point from which we commenced our digression, the many and baser sort give by their lives a fair presumption that their conception of the chief good and of happiness is that it consists in material pleasure: for their only delight is in a life of gross enjoyment. There are, indeed, but three noteworthy modes of life, the one just mentioned, the life of the statesman, and the third, the life of the philosopher. Now the many are clearly in no way better than slaves, in that they deliberately choose the life of brute beasts. Nor would their view call for consideration, were it not that many of those who are high in power are of like passions with Sardanapalus. On the other hand, the better and educated class, who devote themselves to active life, identify the chief good with honour. Honour, indeed, seems upon the whole to be the end of the statesman's life. Yet this is clearly too purely external and superficial a thing to be the good of which we are in quest. For honour would seem to rest rather with those who give than with those who receive it, whereas we divine that the chief good is a something that rests with a man's self, and that is hard to be alienated. Moreover, it would seem that statesmen only pursue honour as a self-convincing proof of virtue: certain at least is it that they seek to be held in honour by the prudent and among those by whom they are known, and for their virtue. And hence it is clear that in their view at least, if not in that of others, virtue must rank the higher. And hence one may perhaps be led to suppose that it is virtue that is the end of the statesman's life. Yet even virtue itself would seem to fall short of being an absolute end. For it is possible that the possessor of virtue should for the whole of his life either sleep, or be otherwise inactive, or, yet more than this, that the greatest evil and misfortune should befall him. And no one, save from pure love of paradox, can maintain that he is happy whose life is such as this. Of these two modes, then, of life enough has now been said: they have, indeed, been adequately discussed in popular treatises. There remains only the third life, the life philosophic, which we shall consider hereafter. As for the money-getting life, it violates the natural fitness of things. Wealth is clearly not the absolute good of which we are in search, for it is a utility, and only desirable as a means. Hence one would be better justified in adopting as the chief good any of the ends mentioned above; for they are choiceworthy in and for themselves. And yet it is evident that the chief good is none of these, although in their behalf many arguments have been constructed. . . .

It is clear that every course of action and every art has its own peculiar good; for the good sought by medicine is one, and the good sought by tactics is another; and of all other arts the same holds good. What, then, is in each case the chief good? Surely it will be that to which all else that is done is but a means. And this in medicine will be health, and in tactics victory, and in architecture a house, and so forth in other cases; and in all free action, that is to say in all purpose or conscious choice of means to a desired end, it will be that end; for it is with this in view that we always take all the other steps in the particular action. And so, if there be but one end of all things that we do, this will be in all human action the chief good; while, if there be more than one, it will be their sum. Our argument, therefore, has now returned to the question from which it originally digressed, and which we must now endeavour yet more thoroughly to clear up. Now since there are clearly many and divers ends, some of which we occasionally choose as means, such as wealth, or pipes, or instruments generally, it is clear that all these ends are not final; whereas the chief good is clearly a something absolutely final. So that, if there be but one thing that is final, this will be the good of which we are in quest; and, if there be more than one, then the most final among them. Now we call that which is pursued for its own sake more final than that which is pursued as a means to something further, and that which is never chosen as a means more final than any such things as are choiceworthy both as ends in themselves and as means to this; while, to sum up, we call that alone absolutely final which is in all cases to be chosen as an end, and never as a means. And happiness would seem to be pre-eminently such; for happiness we always choose as an end, and never as a means; while honour, and pleasure, and intelligence, and all excellence we do indeed choose as ends (for we should choose each one of them even if they bore no good fruit), but we choose them also for the sake of happiness, thinking that by their means we shall be happy. But happiness itself no man ever chooses for the sake of these things, or indeed as a means to aught beyond itself. And the all-sufficiency of happiness clearly leads to the same conclusion; for the final human good is always held to be all-sufficient. Nor do we understand that the range of this all-sufficiency is to be restricted to the individual in a life of isolation, but we hold that it also includes his parents, and his children, and his wife, and indeed his friends and his fellow-citizens, since man's nature is to be citizen of a free state. But herein some limit must be fixed; for were one so to extend this as to take in a man's ancestors, and his descendants, and the friends of his friends, the circle would become infinite. Of this question, however, we will hereafter treat, and for the present will define as all-sufficient that which alone and by itself can make our life desirable, and supply all our needs. And we are of opinion that happiness is such. And, moreover, happiness is the most desirable of all things, in that there is nothing else which is on a par with it, and so capable of being added to it. Were not this so, then the addition of any such other good, no matter how small, would evidently render it more desirable. For any such addition would constitute an excess of good; and of any two goods the greater is always the more choiceworthy. Happiness, then, is clearly a something complete in itself, and all-sufficient, forming the one end of all things done by man.

But still to say nothing more about happiness than that it is the greatest of all goods is clearly but little better than a truism, and one seems to yearn for a yet more definite account. This we shall most probably obtain from the consideration of what it is that man as such has to do. For, as in the case of flute players, and of sculptors, and of all craftsmen, and indeed of all those who have any work of their own to do, or who can originate any peculiar train of action, it is in this their especial work that their chief good and greatest welfare lie, so too ought it to be in the case of man as man, if as man he has any special functions of his own. Are we then to believe that man as carpenter, or that man as cobbler, has a function of his own, and so can originate a course of action; while as man he lacks this, and has no task assigned him by nature? Shall we not rather say that as the eye, and the hand, and the foot, and each of the various members, evidently has its office, so too, beyond and beside all these, must be assigned an office to man as such? And, if so, what are we to say that this office is? Life he has in common even with plants, whereas what we seek is a something peculiar to himself. The life of mere nutrition and growth must therefore be dismissed. Next to this in order is what may be called the life of the senses. But even this is shared by horses, and by oxen, and by all beasts. There is only left what may be described as a life of free moral action, belonging to that part of us which possesses reason, and which may possess it, either as being obedient to its commands, or as properly possessing and exercising it in consecutive thought. And, as this life can be conceived in two aspects, we will take it in its active state, for then more properly is it called life. If, then, the function or office of man as such be an active life or activity of the soul in accordance with reason, or at least not without reason, and if we say that the work of such an one and that of such an one who is good of his sort differ not in kind, as in the case of a harper and of a good harper,—and if we are to say this in every case, our conception of the work itself remaining unaltered by any additional excess of excellence; so that a harper's work is to play the harp, and the work of a good harper is to play it well,—if all this be so, and if we are to take as the function of man a certain kind of life, and to make this life consist in an activity of the soul, that is to say in moral action consciously accompanied by reason; and to take as the function of the good man the doing all this well and perfectly, remembering that it is its own excellence alone that causes each thing to be done well,—then, if all this be so, we shall find that the chief good of man consists in an activity of the soul in accordance with its own excellence (or, in other words, such that the essential conditions of its excellence are fulfilled), and, if there be many such, in accordance with the best and the most perfect among them. And we must further add the condition of a perfect life; for a single day, or even a short period of happiness, no more makes a blessed and a happy man than one sunny day or one swallow makes a spring. . . .

We must investigate the nature of happiness, not only from the point of view afforded us by our conclusion, and by our premises, but also from that of the statements made by others. For with a true theory all facts agree, while with what is false truth is quickly found to conflict. Now there is an old triple division of goods into goods external, goods of the souls, and goods of the body; of which it is held that those of the soul are the highest and the chief. But moral action, inasmuch as we make it an activity of the soul, belongs to the soul; so that our statements hold good by the test of this view, which has been sanctioned by time, and by the assent of philosophers. And we are right, moreover, in that we make the end of life to consist in an activity, that is to say in moral action. For happiness thus becomes a good of the soul, and not a good external. And, again, the proverb that the happy man lives well and fares well is in harmony with our definition. For what we have described is but a sort of fair-living and prosperity.

And, again, all the scientific determinations of happiness are clearly contained in our definition. For some hold that happiness lies in virtue, others that it is prudence, or some kind of philosophic knowledge, or that it is all of these together, or some one of them, accompanied by pleasure, or at least not without pleasure; while others again hold that material prosperity is in it an essential element. And of these views some depend on common experience and old authorities, and others on the authority of a few, but those men of high repute. Nor is it likely that either side are entirely wrong, but rather that in some one point at least they are right, if not in most. Now with those who say that happiness is either virtue as a whole, or some one particular form of virtue, our definition concords. For an activity in accordance with virtue will itself involve such virtue. And it matters perhaps no little whether the chief good be conceived as a mere possession, or as a something of which use is to be made—that is to say as a mere formed habit, or as an activity. For such a habit may possibly exist in a man, and yet bear no good fruit, as when he is asleep, or otherwise inactive. But with the activity it cannot possibly be thus. He who displays this cannot possibly but act, and, what is more, act well. For as at the Olympic games it is not the fairest and the strongest who are crowned, but they that run—for some of these it is that win the victory—so too, among the noble and good in life, it is they that act rightly who become masters of life's prize. And the life of such men has in itself a pleasure of its own. Activities of the soul, no less than those of the body, have their own pleasure; and, since each man takes pleasure in that which he is said to love—as a lover of horses in horses, and a lover of shows in shows—it follows that, in the same way, the lover of justice will take pleasure in justice; and the lover of virtue as a whole, in virtue. Now, for the many, the objects that yield them pleasure are discordant, inasmuch as they are not really pleasant in themselves; but, to those who love what is noble, those things give pleasure that are intrinsically pleasant. And all virtuous acts are such; so that to such men they give a pleasure—and that a pleasure intrinsic to themselves. Such a life then needs no pleasure to deck it like an amulet, for it has in itself a pleasure of its own. And, indeed, we may add that the man who takes no pleasure in noble acts cannot be a good man. For surely no one would call him just who took no pleasure in fair dealing; or him liberal who took no pleasure in liberal acts; and so forth in every virtue. And, if this be so, then virtuous acts cannot but be intrinsically pleasant. Aye, and, more than this, they are also both good and noble; and are moreover preeminently each of these, if the judgment of the upright man about them be true: and his judgment is as ours. Happiness then is the best, and the noblest, and the most pleasant of all goods; nor are these things distinct, as said the inscription at Delos,

> *Justice is noblest; best of goods is health;*
> *Sweetest to win the object of desire;*

for in our best acts all these characteristics are to be found. And it is in these acts, or in that one among them that is the best, that we say that happiness consists. And yet, as we have said, it obviously wants the addition of external goods; for, if not impossible, it is at least difficult to do noble deeds, if bared of all such equipments. Friends, and wealth, and power in the State, serve as instruments by which to win many fair ends. And some things there are to be bereft of which casts a shadow over our happiness—such as are noble birth, fair offspring, or beauty of person. For he surely will not find happiness easy to win who is of utterly mean appearance, or of ignoble birth, or who is childless, and alone in life; and perhaps still less so, should his sons or his friends be utterly depraved, or should they have been noble only to die. As, then, we have said, happiness would seem to need external aids such as these. And hence it is that some have made it identical with mere good fortune,— I say some, for others make it virtue.

Hence, too, arises the doubt whether happiness is to be taught, or to be gained by habituation, or by any other kind of practice, or whether it comes to us by some divine lot, or even perhaps by chance. Most certainly, if there be aught that is a free gift of God to men, it were well to suppose that happiness is such, and the more so as it is the best of all human goods. But still this question would perhaps be more in place in another treatise than the present. Happiness, at all events, even if it be not sent by the Gods, but is acquired by virtuous action, and by a course of teaching, or of some such other practice, is clearly an object most divine. For the prize of all virtue cannot but be the chief and final good, and consequently a something divine and full of joy. And it ought to be widely shared, since it may be won through a course of pupilage and of good practice by all those who are not of their own nature absolutely incapable of virtue. For, if it be better that happiness should come to us thus rather than by chance, it is but reasonable to hold that it does so come; since the works of nature, as a whole, are ordered in the fairest possible way, exactly as are the results of art, and indeed of all causation, and especially those of virtue, the noblest of all causes. So that to intrust to chance the greatest and fairest of all goods would be too sore a discord in Nature's harmony. And, moreover, our own definition of happiness, as an activity of the soul in accordance with virtue, makes the question clear. For, of all other goods, some—those of the body—are necessary for happiness; while others—those external—are fitted by their very nature to be means and instruments for its acquisition. And this, moreover, agrees with what we said at first, when we stated that the end of the art political was the chief good; for this art spares no trouble to inspire the citizens with a definitely virtuous character—such that they may be disposed towards noble deeds. And thus it is with good reason that we never call happy either ox, or horse, or any other beast; for to brute beasts nature has given no share in action such as this. And hence, too, is it that not even a boy is held happy, since his youth puts such acts, as yet, out of his power; so that to call him happy is but a fond expression of hope. For happiness presupposes, as we have said, perfect virtue and a life in all respects complete. But many are the changes and divers the chances in life; and it is possible that he who now flourishes most should, as is fabled of Priam in the epic, stumble in his old age upon great mishaps. And him whose fortunes have been such as this, and his end wretched, no man can call happy.

Are we then to call no man happy while he yet lives, but to wait, as Solon advises, until we have seen the end of his life? And, if we are to adopt this view, are we then to say that the man is actually happy after his death? Or is not this an altogether untenable position, especially for us who have defined happiness as an activity? And if, on the other hand, we do not mean that the man when dead is actually happy, nor must Solon be understood to say this, but rather that it is only when he is dead that we can with safety assert that a man is happy, since then only is he beyond the range of all evil and mishap,—with this view also issue can be joined. For it is held that things good and evil can happen to him who is dead, exactly as they can to him who is alive but not aware of them, such as are the honour or dishonour, and indeed all other good or evil fortune, of his children, and of his descendants generally. And herein arises a fresh difficulty. For, however happy may have been a man's life up to his old age, and however fitting thereunto his death, it is none the less possible that many changes should befall his descendants, and that some among them should be upright, and should meet with a life according to their deserts, while with others of them it should be far otherwise; and it is also clear that in successive generations every possible degree of relationship may arise between descendants and their ancestors. So that, while on the one hand it is absurd to conceive the dead man as sharing all their vicissitudes, and as becoming happy one moment and wretched the next, it is on the other hand equally absurd to suppose that the fortunes of descendants never, for however short a time, reach to their ancestors. Perhaps, however, the solution of the present question will present itself if we return to our original problem. For, if we are to wait that we may see how a man's life ends, and are then, and then only, to call him happy, not as being now actually happy, but as having been such; then surely it is absurd that when a man is actually happy we should hold it premature to predicate of him that which he actually enjoys, merely because the changes of life are such that we are unwilling to call men happy who are still alive; our conception of happiness being that it is abiding and in no way likely to change, while fortune's wheel often rolls many cycles in the same man's lifetime. For it is clear that, if fortune be our test, we shall over and over again have to call a man first happy and then wretched, thus making the happy man

Chameleon-hued; his house upon the sand.

Is it not rather true that fortune must in no way be our guide? For, although man's life needs good fortune, as we have said, yet it is not in fortune that good and evil lie, but it is virtuous acts that determine life for happiness, acts evil for misery. So that our present problem but serves to testify to the accuracy of our definition of happiness. For there is nothing human so surely lasting as are virtuous acts. More lasting are they than even scientific knowledge, and the most precious among them are the most lasting, in that those whose lot is blessed most earnestly and most continuously pass their life in the pursuit of them. And this would seem to be the reason why their practice cannot be forgotten. Thus, then, the happy man will enjoy that security of which we are in quest, and will continue happy throughout his whole life. For most continuously, or at least more continuously than for any other man, will all his acts and all his thoughts be most excellent, and his treatment of fortune most noble and most consistently harmonious, who is

Truly good,
Square-finished, free from every flaw of blame.

But, since the results of fortune are manifold, both great and small, small changes of luck, whether for good or for the reverse, clearly cannot turn the scale of life. But Fortune, if she come for our good in many and in great shapes, will make our life more blessed (for it is in the nature of her gifts thus to add a lustre to our happiness, and to use them well is fair and upright); while, if she come thus for our harm, she crushes and mars our blessedness, bringing with her a sore burden of pains, and hindering many noble acts. But nevertheless even here true nobility shines out, when a man bears calmly many and great mishaps, not through dulness of feeling, but from true high-breeding, and greatness of spirit. And, since, as we have said, it is our own acts that determine our life, no one of the really blessed can ever become wretched, for he will never do hateful and disgraceful deeds. For we hold that the really good and prudent man will bear all changes of fortune with good grace, and will always, as the case may allow, act most nobly; exactly as a good general will use such forces as are at his disposal most skilfully, and even a good cobbler will, out of such leather as he may have, make the most perfect shoe; and of all those who practise any other art the same rule will hold good. And, if this be so, then never will he who is once happy become wretched, though, if he become entangled in a lot such as that of Priam, he can hardly be called blessed. Nor will his life have many shades and changes. For no light thing will move him from his happiness, nor any chance mishap, but only misfortunes great and many: and after such he will not again become happy in a moment, but only in a long and all-adequate time, sufficient to make him master of prizes great and noble. Why, then, should we not call him happy whose acts have been those of consistent and perfect virtue, and whose equipment of external goods has been sufficient, and that not for any chance period, but for a lifetime of fair length? Or must we add that he is to continue so to live, and that his death is to match his life? Since for us the future lies in obscurity, while we hold that happiness is the perfect crown of life, and a thing in all ways absolutely complete. And, since all this is so, we will call those among the living happy whose lot is and will be such as we have said, but happy only in so far as man can be so. . . .

And now, since happiness is an activity of the soul in accordance with perfect virtue, we must inquire what is virtue; for thus perhaps we shall be in a better position to consider the nature of happiness. He who is a political philosopher in the true sense of the word will give virtue his most thorough attention, his object being to make the citizens good, and so obedient to the laws. And, as instances of this, we have the lawgivers of Crete and of Lacedaemon, and all such others as are upon record like to those. And so, since the discussion of virtue is the province of political science, it is clear that the present investigation will harmonise with our original purpose. We have therefore to consider virtue, that is to say, of course, the virtue of man; for it was man's highest good, and man's happiness, of which we were in quest. And by man's virtue we understand not the virtue of the body but the virtue of the soul, since we have defined happiness as an activity of the soul. And, if this be so, it is clear that the politican must no less know about the soul than he who is to heal the eye must know about the body as a whole, and all the more so in that the art political is higher and nobler than is medicine. And indeed physicians of the higher and better sort interest themselves no little in the knowledge of the body as a whole. And hence it follows that the politican must consider about the soul, and must consider it with this end in view, that is to say so far only as is sufficient for our present object; for further minuteness of discussion would only entail more labour than is needed for our purpose. Now concerning the soul even ordinary language lays down certain sufficient distinctions, of which we will make use; as, for example, that the soul has two parts, the one irrational, the other possessed of reason. But whether these parts be distinct in the same sense as are the members of the body, and all else that is capable of physical division, or rather be only distinct in thought, being in their own nature absolutely inseparable, exactly as are concavity and convexity in an arc, is a question immaterial to our purpose. And, again, of the irrational part there is yet a further part that would seem to be common to man with other living things, and to form the soul of plants. I speak of that principle which is the cause of all nutrition and growth. For a vital faculty of this nature one assigns to all things that assimilate nutriment, as even to the foetus; and this self-same faculty one also assigns to the full-grown being, since such a supposition is more reasonable than it is to hold that any substitution has taken place. Any excellence or virtue that this part of our soul may possess is clearly not peculiar to man, but is shared by him with animals and with plants. It is in sleep, indeed, that this part or faculty of our soul is most active, and it is in sleep that the good man and the bad are least distinguishable from one another; whence has come the proverb, that for one half their lives the happy in no way differ from the wretched. Nor could we expect it to be otherwise. For sleep is a torpor of our soul, in so far as it can be called morally good or bad, save only where to some slight extent certain of the movements of active life carry themselves on into our slumber, and so render the dreams of the good better than are those of ordinary men. But on these matters we have now said enough, and here we will close our discussion of the nutritive soul, since nature has given it no part in that virtue which is peculiarly human. And, again, there would seem to be another element in the soul, which also is irrational, and which yet to some extent partakes of reason. For, in the self-restrained, and also in the incontinent man, we give praise to their reason, that is to say to the rational portion of their soul, for that it exhorts them as is right, and to the best course. But there is clearly, in each of them, a something else, of its own nature opposed to reason, which conflicts with reason, and strives to counteract it. For, exactly as a palsied limb, when a man purposes to move it to the right, swings round on the contrary to the left, so too is it with the soul of the incontinent man; for his impulses run counter to his reason. Only, whereas in the body we can see the part that so moves, in the soul we cannot see it. And yet, perhaps, we must none the less on this account hold that there is in the soul an element contradistinguished from reason, which sets itself in opposition to reason, and goes its way against it; although wherein precisely it is distinct from reason concerns us not. And yet even this part too has clearly, as we have said, some share in reason, for in the self-restrained man it certainly obeys his reason. And, in the man who is thoroughly temperate and brave, it is perhaps yet more amenable; for in him all his members are in harmony with reason. Hence, then, it clearly appears that the irrational part of our soul has two members, of which one, the nutritive, is in no way concerned with reason; while the other, the concupiscent, or, more generally, the appetitive part, in a certain sense partakes of reason, in so far as it listens to reason, and obeys its commands. It is in this sense that we speak of showing a rational obedience to one's father or to one's friends, and not in that in which we speak of a rational understanding of mathematical truths. And, that the irrational part of our souls is to some extent amenable to reason, all admonition, all rebuke, all exhortation, is a proof. And hence, since even this part of our soul is in a certain sense to be called rational, it follows that the rational element in us will also have two parts, the one in its own right possessing reason in itself, while the other is obedient to reason, as is a son to his father. And, in accordance with this division, we can classify the virtues, and call some of them intellectual and others moral,—philosophy, appreciation, and prudence being excellences or virtues of the intellect, while liberality and temperance are moral virtues, or virtues of the character. For, when speaking of a man's character, we do not say that he is a philosopher, or a man of quick appreciation, but that he is gentle or temperate. And yet we none the less praise the wise man also for his state of mind, and understand by virtue a praiseworthy state of mind. . . .

Since, then, happiness consists in an activity wherein virtue is consciously manifested, it follows, as a matter of course, that the virtue thus manifested will be the highest which we possess; or that, in other words, it will constitute the highest excellence of the noblest of our faculties. Whether, then, this be our reason, or whether it be a something else, which, in the course of nature, seems to rule in us, and to take the lead, and to occupy itself with the consideration of what is noble and divine, either as being a something absolutely divine in itself, or as being the most divine element in man; the activity in which this part of ourselves so manifests itself that the essential conditions of its own special excellence are fulfilled, will constitute finally perfect happiness. That this activity will consist in the contemplation of abstract truth, we have already said; and it would seem that our statement is consistent with what we said before, and also with the truth. For, in the first place, this activity will be the highest which is possible; inasmuch as reason is the highest of our faculties, and the objects upon which reason exercises itself are the highest of all objects of thought. And, in the second place, it is the most continuous; inasmuch as, of all our acts, the exercise of the pure reason can be the most continuously carried on. We are, moreover, agreed that in all happiness pleasure is an essential element; and, of all those acts in which any human excellence whatsoever is manifested, philosophic speculation upon abstract truth is confessedly the most pleasant. Clear it certainly is that philosophy possesses pleasures of its own, wonderful for their purity and for their certainty; and it is but reasonable to suppose that, for those who are already possessed of the truth, the pursuit of speculation has greater pleasures than it has for those who are still inquirers. Fourthly, it is to the act of philosophic speculation that what

is called "all-sufficiency" most especially belongs. As regards the bare neces-
saries of life, of these the philosopher and the just man, and all others, stand
in equal need. But after that life has been adequately equipped with all that
is absolutely necessary, the just man still stands in further need of persons
towards whom, and in conjunction with whom, he can act justly; and of the
temperate man, and of the brave man, and indeed of all those in whom any
moral virtue manifests itself, a similar rule holds good. Whereas the philosopher can exercise himself in speculation, even although absolutely secluded
from the society of others; and, indeed, the wiser he is the more easy for him
will this be. For, although, perhaps, he may be the better for having fellow-
workers in his speculations, yet none the less he, of all men, is absolutely in
himself the most all-sufficient. Fifthly, it would seem that, of all our acts,
philosophic speculation is the only one which is loved absolutely for itself, and
quite independently of its results. For the contemplation of abstract truth
yields no result whatever beyond and besides itself; whereas every moral action
yields a something, either more or less, over and above the mere act. Then,
again, it would seem that happiness is the very antithesis of a busy life, in that
it is compatible with perfect leisure. And it is with such leisure in view that
a busy life is always led, exactly as war is only waged for the sake of ultimate
peace. Now, the virtues of practical life manifest themselves in the field of
politics or of war, and the acts which they involve are incompatible with
perfect leisure. Of war, indeed, this holds absolutely true; for no one ever
chooses war for its own sake, or for its own sake prepares a war. A man would,
indeed, seem to have an absolute thirst for blood, if he were to make enemies
of his friends, that battle and bloodshed might ensue. Equally incompatible
with leisure are the pursuits of the politican, their object being something more
than the mere pleasure of an active political life, regarded as an end in itself.
The ultimate object of the politican is to secure for himself and for his fellow-
citizens power and honour, or, in a word, happiness; and, that happiness is not
to be identified with an active political life, we have shown by the fact, that
in our search for each we invariably regard it as a something distinct from the
other. Thus, then, of all virtuous action, that which has political life or war
for its field is foremost in beauty and in dignity, but still is none the less
incompatible with perfect leisure, in that it has a further end beyond itself at
which it aims, and is not choiceworthy for its own sake. Whereas the activity
of the intellect, manifesting itself in pure speculation, is in itself preeminently
earnest and good, and has no further end beyond itself at which to aim. It has,
moreover, a pleasure of its own, and that, too, a pleasure by which it is itself
intensified. And, in a word, in this activity alone is to be found absolute
all-sufficiency, and, along with it, the possibility of perfect leisure, and an entire
absence of care, in so far as is compatible with the conditions of human life,
and, indeed, each and all of the essentials of perfect blessedness. And hence
it follows, that it is in this activity that perfectly final human happiness consists, if only the one condition be fulfilled, of a sufficient length of life; for, in
happiness there must be nothing insufficient. Moreover, a life thus passed will

be higher than human; for it will not be in so far as he is human that a man will lead it, but in so far as he has in him a divine element. And, by as much as this is higher than is that compound part of our organisation into which material factors enter, by so much is that activity in which it is manifested higher than is that of any other virtue whatsoever. Since, in other words, the reason is a divine thing if contrasted with human nature as a whole, the life of reason will also be divine, as contrasted with the ordinary and human life. Nor ought we to follow the advice of the old saw, "let not man meddle with great matters which are too high for him," but rather, as far as in us lies, to act as if immortality were our share, by seeking in everything that we do to lead a life in conformity with that element in ourselves which is highest and best. For, although physically it may be insignificant, it is none the less far more powerful and far more precious than is any other part of our nature. In this part, moreover, it is that the true self of each one of us would seem to have its place, since a man's self is identical with that which is supreme in him, and most precious. Strange, indeed, would it be, were a man to choose, not the life which is peculiarly his own, but the life of some other kind of being. And here, again, we may apply what we have said before. For that is, for each being, best and most pleasant, in which its nature finds for itself a fit expression. Sweetest, then, and best of all things for man is the life of reason; since reason it is that constitutes the essence of humanity. And thus the happiest of all lives is the life philosophic.

6

Classical Philosophy:
Inner Tranquility
in the
Midst of Disorder

Cicero (106–43 B.C.) is known largely as the author of Latin prose which intermediate students of Latin have to decipher. He did indeed develop a style of oratory and prose expression which dominated Latin letters for 1500 years, but it is chiefly as a vulgarizer of Greek thought that Cicero contributed to the image of classical man.

The son of provincial, middle-class Romans, Cicero made his way to political importance through a successful legal career. He studied Greek philosophy and rhetoric in Rhodes and Athens and made a name for himself in the Roman legal profession. His middle-class origins did not provide much advantage for one interested in a political career, for in the dying days of the Roman Republic both the aristocratic republicans and the demagogic militarists who struggled for power were men of ancient lineage and connections. Cicero wanted a political career for the wealth and glory it could bring; his motives, revealed in his large correspondence which has survived, were never particularly idealistic or disinterested. In the last 20 years of his life he participated actively in politics—as a senator, a consul, and a provincial governor —but he never achieved more than a subordinate association with the men who really held power. His political wisdom and consistency were never the highest, and he fell afoul of various dangerous enemies, including Julius Caesar, Mark Antony, and Octavian (the future Augustus). In the last year of his life he foolishly allied himself with the reactionary republicans who were hopelessly attempting to restore the corrupt and moribund Roman Republic, and he was finally executed by the successors to Julius Caesar for his support, after the fact, of Caesar's assassin. One can only deem his political career a failure since he failed to save the Republic, but in the story of the transition of the Republic into the rule of one man, Augustus the Emperor, only Augustus came through victorious.

Cicero's personal qualities were not so distinguished that we should admire him unduly, but he has left posterity invaluable information on the social, political, and intellectual life of Rome in the first century before Christ. His philosophical, literary, and political writings were hardly original —like most Romans he had a practical rather than a speculative inclination —but he did serve to popularize and vulgarize Greek learning with lasting benefit to the West which would lose direct contact with the Greek and Hellenistic East. Cicero was particularly attracted to the Hellenistic philosophy of Stoicism, and he found in it a release and asylum from the distress of daily life. Cicero always preferred the active life, but in Stoic philosophy he found the consolation for failure and disappointment that he sought. In the "Tusculan Disputations" he sought a defense against pain and death. Gone is even the possibility for the few, as in Plato and Aristotle, to achieve enlightenment and truth; instead the keynote is resignation. Death and decay were in the air in the late Hellenistic world which corresponded with the rise of the Roman Empire, and Cicero's quest for release in a sense mirrored the search for peace in a civilization which had lost its trust in the future, though it would endure for 300 years more. No view of classical man would be complete without the resignation preached by Stoicism: the pall of meaninglessness does lie over the image of classical man, and Cicero's last years were devoted less to learning how to live than how to die.

Cicero:
The Tusculan Disputations

5. *A.* Death I certainly consider a bane.

M. For those who are dead, or for those who have to die?

A. For both.

M. And if a bane, then a form of misery?

A. Undoubtedly.

M. And therefore both they whose lot it has already been, and they whose lot it will some day be, to die, are miserable.

A. That is how it seems to me.

M. There is none, then, who is not miserable?

A. Not one.

M. And in fact—if you mean to be consistent—all who ever have been or will be born are not only miserable, but everlastingly miserable. For if you were to confine yourself to the statement that they only are miserable

From *Basic Works of Cicero*, edited with Introduction and Notes by Moses Hadas. Copyright 1951 by Random House, Inc., pp. 66; 71-75; 78-80; 102-103; 105-106; 108; 123. Reprinted by permission of the publisher.

who have to die, you would even then except nobody who has ever lived (for all must die); still there would be an end of the misery at the hour of death. If, however, the dead also are miserable, we are born to misery everlasting; for they who were born a hundred thousand years ago, nay, all who have ever been born, must continue in their misery.

    A. Quite so. . . .

    M. The first point for consideration, then, is, what death, which seems to be a thing perfectly well understood, really is. For, notwithstanding that it seems to be perfectly well understood, there are some who think that death is the departure of soul from body; others, that no departure at all takes place, but that soul and body succumb together, and that the soul is extinguished in the body. Of those who hold that the soul departs, there are some who think that it is instantly dispersed; others, that it endures for a while; others, that it endures for ever. Moreover, as regards soul itself, there is a great variety of opinion as to what, where, and whence it is. Some have an idea that the heart is the actual soul, and so we get the words "without heart," "wanting heart," and "of one heart," meaning "senseless," "feebleminded," and "of one mind"; and the wise statesman Nasica, twice consul, got the name of "Good heart" or "Sagacious," and so too "the man of matchless heart, Aelius Sextus." According to Empedocles the blood suffusing the heart is the soul. Others fancy that the sovereignty which we attribute to the soul is vested in a portion of the brain. Others again do not like the idea which makes the heart absolutely, or a part of the brain absolutely, the soul; but have maintained, some of them, that the soul's abiding-place is *in* the heart, others *in* the brain. Others again, as our own people pretty generally do, consider the breath of life to be the soul. The word speaks for itself; for we talk of *giving up the ghost,* and *breathing out the breath of life;* and so on in other instances. In fact the actual word for "soul" in Latin has come from the word for "breath." Zeno, the Stoic, considers soul to be fire.

    10. Now what I have just mentioned, the heart, the blood, the brain, the breath of life, and fire, these are the commonly received theories. The rest are confined pretty nearly to single individuals. As many of the ancients had done before him, Aristoxenus, a musician as well as a philosopher, held, and was the most recent instance of so holding, that the soul is a sort of attunement (or *intension*) of the body itself: that, just as in vocal and instrumental music what is called harmony is produced, so by the nature and conformation of the whole body various vibrations are caused, like sounds in music. He clung to his own art; and yet what he maintained was almost identical with what had been noticed in all its bearings, and exploded, long before, by Plato in the *Phaedo.* Xenocrates denied that there was any form or substance, as it were, of the soul, asserting that it was number, whereof, as Pythagoras had previously declared, the power was the greatest in the whole range of nature. His master, Plato, propounded a tri-partite soul, whereof he placed the dominant part, reason, to wit, in the head, as in a citadel; and the other two parts, passion and appetite, he made subordinate, and located them

in two separate spots, placing passion in the breast, and appetite below the midriff. Dicaearchus, on the contrary, in that debate between sundry learned persons which he represents to have taken place at Corinth, and which he published in three books, having in the first book introduced several speakers, in the other two puts forward one Pherecrates, an elder of Phthia or Phthiotis, and a descendant, he says, of Deucalion, who argues that there is no such thing at all as soul, that it is but an empty term, and that *animal* and *animate* are vain appellations; that there is neither in men nor brute any *living soul* (*animus*) or *breath of life* (*anima*), and that all that influence whereby we do or perceive anything is equally diffused among all bodies that are quick; and that it is not separable from the body, inasmuch as it *is* not at all, and there *is* not anything but body, one and uncompounded, with such conformation as to derive vitality and perception from its own natural organization. Aristotle, who far excels all others (Plato always excepted) in genius and research, whilst admitting those four commonly received elements—first propounded by Empedocles—whence everything was supposed to spring, suggests a fifth natural essence, to which belongs the mind or soul (*mens*). For thinking and foreseeing and learning and teaching and inventing and ever so many other properties— such as remembering, for instance, and loving and hating and desiring and fearing and feeling joy and anguish—these and others like them he considers inherent in none of those four elements; he therefore adds a fifth, which has no name, and so he calls the soul continuance—"uninterrupted and perennial movement."

11. These, unless there be some which have accidentally escaped my notice, are pretty nearly the opinions held about the soul. For we may pass by Democritus, who—great man as he certainly was—makes up his soul of smooth, round corpuscles on the theory of a fortuitous concurrence. Indeed, with this school, there is nothing for which a concourse of atoms does not account. As to which of these opinions is absolutely true, let some god see to that. Which is most truth-*like* is the main question. Which would you prefer, then? To decide between these conflicting opinions, or to return to our original argument?

A. If it were possible, I should like both; but it is difficult to fuse the two. If, therefore, without discussing these theories, we can be delivered from fear of death, let us get on with that at once. But, if that be impossible without clearing up this question about souls and their nature, let us, if you please, have that now, and the other anon.

M. The course which I understand you to prefer, is, I think, the more convenient. For, no matter which—if any—of the opinions I have set before you be correct, reason will show that death either is not a bane, or— better still—is a blessing. For, if heart, or blood, or brain, be the soul, undoubtedly—being body—it will perish with the rest of the body. But, if it be breath, peradventure it will be dispersed; if fire, quenched; if the harmony of Aristoxenus, distuned. As for Dicaearchus, who says that there is absolutely no soul, why mention him at all? According to every one of these said opinions, there is not, after death, anything whatever to concern anybody. For simultaneously with life consciousness is lost; and nothing can make any difference to the unconscious. As for the other opinions, they give hope that souls, after their departure from the body, may make their way to heaven as their own proper abode, if peradventure that idea causes you any delight.

A. Yes, indeed; and that it may be really so is my foremost wish; my next is 'that, even if it be not really so, yet I may be made to entertain a conviction that it is.

M. What need, then, of such aid as *ours?* Can we surpass Plato in eloquence? Peruse with care that work of his which relates to the soul, and you will require nothing beyond.

A. I have done so, I assure you, and pretty frequently too. But, somehow, as I read I assent, but when I lay the book aside and begin reflecting by myself upon the immortality of souls, all that assent slips gradually away.

M. How is that? Do you admit that souls either endure after death, or perish at the moment of death?

A. I do.

M. Suppose that they endure?

A. I admit that they are happy.

M. Suppose that they perish?

A. They are not miserable, since they *are* not at all: so much you just now compelled me to conclude.

M. How or why, then, say you that death appears to you an evil, since it will either make us happy, if souls endure, or not miserable, because unconscious?

12. *A.* Then, if it be not too much trouble, make it quite clear to me first—if you can—that souls do endure; next, if you do not completely establish that (for it certainly is difficult), you shall prove to me that death is devoid of bane. For what I have my fears about, is just this: whether it be not a bane, I will not say to *be* without consciousness, but to be obliged to lack it. . . .

14. But the most cogent argument is this: that nature herself pronounces a silent verdict in favour of the immortality of souls, inasmuch as all feel an interest and a very great interest in what shall be after their death. "He planteth trees t' enrich a future age," sings the poet in the *Synephebi.* Why plants he them, and on what ground, but that he feels some link between himself and posterity? So then the thrifty husbandman shall plant trees of which himself will never see the fruit; and shall not a great man plant laws and institutions, and governments? The procreation of children, the extension of a family name, the adoption of sons, the care in testamentary dispositions, and even the decorations and inscriptions on tombs—what is the meaning of all these, but that the future also shares our thoughts? And what then? Can you doubt but that the beau-ideal of a nature should be formed upon the lines of the best natures? Now amongst mankind, what nature is superior to theirs who consider themselves born to aid, protect, and preserve their fellowmen? Hercu-

les went up to join the gods in Heaven: but this he never would have done, but that, whilst he was in the world, he secured for himself a way thither. Such legends are of olden date, and hallowed by the religious belief of all.

15. Take the case of this Republic. What must we suppose to have been the reflections of those many, those mighty men, who laid down their lives for the commonwealth? That their fame would be bounded by the same limits as their life? Nobody, without great hopes of immortality, would ever court death for the sake of his country. Themistocles, Epaminondas, I myself—not to seek for examples in antiquity and foreign lands—might all have lived at ease; but, somehow or other, there is inherent in the mind a forecast of times to come, and this is especially the case and most readily exhibits itself in the highest characters and the loftiest souls. But were this withdrawn, who would be such a simpleton as to live continually amidst toil and danger? I refer now to active leaders of men. But what of poets? Do they not yearn to be famous after death? Else what mean lines like these

> Look on this form—here agèd Ennius stands,
> Who sang the deeds wrought by your fathers' hands?

He demands his meed of glory from them whose fathers he had covered with glory. And again:

> Mourn not for me—no tearful tribute give,
> For on the lips of living men I live!

But why confine myself to poets? Artists (which word includes sculptors) yearn to be famous after death: else, why did Pheidias insert a likeness of himself on the shield of his Minerva, when he was not permitted to place an inscription? What! Do not our philosophers inscribe their names upon those very books which they write about despising glory? But if universal consent be the voice of nature, and all without exception agree that there is something still appertaining to those who have departed this life; we must needs think the same. And if we may suppose that they whose souls are pre-eminent for genius or virtue see farthest into nature's properties, inasmuch as they possess the most perfect natures, it is likely to be true—as all the best men are the most zealous to serve posterity—that there is a something of which they will be conscious after death. . . .

34. *M.* I see that you fix your eyes above, and desire a move to Heaven. And I have hopes that such will be our lot. But suppose—as they whom you wot of maintain—that souls do not endure after death: then evidently, if so it be, we are deprived of our hope of a happier existence. Still, what bane does that opinion entail? For, suppose that the soul does perish, just like the body: is there any sense of pain or any feeling at all remaining in the body?

Nobody asserts *that,* though Epicurus charges Democritus with asserting it; a charge which the followers of Democritus deny. And so in the soul likewise there remains no consciousness, for itself has become null and nowhere. Where, then, is the bane? For there is no intermediate condition between existence and non-existence. Is it in the fact that the actual severance of soul and body does not take place without pain? Even if it be so, how insignificant is it! Moreover, I do not think that it is so generally; it generally takes place unconsciously, sometimes even pleasurably. In point of fact, whatever the true state of the case may be, it is a perfectly unimportant matter, for it takes place in the twinkling of an eye. What causes pain, or rather torture, is severance from all the blessings which life bestows; if it would not be more correct to say, from all the banes. But why should I now mourn over the life of man? I could do so, with truth and justice; but what need is there—when my object is to prevent us from supposing that we shall be miserable after death—to make even life more miserable than it is by lamentation? I have done all that in the book in which, so far as I could, I endeavoured to find consolation. It is from banes then, and not from blessings, that death removes us, if we would but have the truth. . . .

38.Wherefore the wise man is not deterred by thoughts of death (which, because of accidents, is ever impending over us, and, because of the shortness of life, can never be very far off) from studying to promote, to all futurity, the welfare of the State and of his own people, and from feeling that between posterity—though he may be unconscious of it—and himself there is some sort of connecting link. Therefore, even he who opines that the soul is mortal may act with an eye to eternity; not from a passion for glory, of which he will not be conscious, but of virtue—in the wake whereof glory, though you heed not *that,* inevitably follows.

If then the course of nature is on this wise: that, as birth introduces us to the beginning of things, so does death to the end, it follows that, as before birth there was nothing which concerned us, so there will be nothing that concerns us after death. What bane, then, can there be in this, inasmuch as death concerns neither living nor dead? . . . As for ourselves, however, should anything happen of such a nature, that we seem to have received from the deity an order to depart this life—let us obey with joy and giving of thanks, and look upon ourselves as discharged from prison, and released from bonds; that either we may return to that home eternal which is our proper abode, or else be free from consciousness and cease from trouble. But if no such order come, let us be so minded as to think the awful day (as it is to others) a day of felicitation for us, and count nothing to be a bane which hath been appointed for us either by the immortal gods or by Nature the mother of all. For we are not born or created idly or fortuitously; but doubtless there is some power which takes thought for the race of men, and which was not likely to create and foster what —when it had accomplished all its toils—would sink into everlasting misery in death. Let us rather regard it as a haven and a refuge prepared for us: whither may we arrive with swelling sails! But if we be beaten back by adverse winds, still, sooner or later, we must bring up there. Besides, what is necessary for all, can that be a bane for any one? . . .

But even if it be granted that men are deprived by death of good fortune, does it follow that the dead *lack* the blessings of life, and that this is misery? Yet such must be the argument. But *can* he who *is* not, "lack" anything at all? For a pathetic term is this same "lack," because there is at the bottom of it an idea of "having not, after having had," of "missing," of "wanting back again," of "needing." These, to my mind, are the grievances of him who "lacks." One would "lack" eyes, for instance, for blindness is decidedly grievous; or children, for so is bereavement. This is applicable enough in the case of the quick; but of the dead none "lacks," not only the advantages of life, but even life itself. I am speaking now of the dead, who *are not.* As for us, who *are,* do we "lack" either horns or wings? Would anybody use such an expression? Certainly not; and why? Because from not having that which is neither by your habits nor your nature adapted for you, you would feel no "lack," though perfectly conscious that you have it not. This argument must be urged again and again, when we have once established the point (as to which there can be no doubt, if souls be mortal) that in death there is so thorough a perishing that there is not left the very faintest suspicion of consciousness. When, then, this point is once properly and thoroughly fixed, the other must be discussed, in order to perfectly understand what is meant by "lack," that there may be no mistake about terms. To "lack," then, means this: to be without that which you would wish to have. For there is a notion of wishing in "lack," unless when it is used in quite a different fashion, as in the case of fever (when you say that a patient "lacks," that is, "is free from," fever. For, in common parlance, "lack" is something used in this other sense; when you "have not" something or other, and are perfectly conscious of not having it, though you are quite content to be without it). In the case of death, you cannot so use the word "lack," properly speaking, for it would not indicate any possible grievance. Properly, you "lack" what is a blessing; which lack is a bane. Not even the quick, however, "lack" even a blessing which they do not want. Nevertheless, in the case of the quick, the expression would no doubt be intelligible; as, for instance, that you yourself "lack" a kingdom: though it cannot be so accurately predicated in your case as it could have been in that of Tarquinius, when he was driven from his dominions. But in the case of the dead it is quite unintelligible; for "lack" is said of the conscious, and, as there is no consciousness in the dead, there is consequently no "lack" at all in the case of the dead. . . .

Contents of Volume 2

General Introduction   1

Introduction   3

1   Man's Dialogue with God   5
Selections from the Hebrew and Christian Scriptures: *Genesis*   6;
Exodus   18; *Psalms*   33; *Isaiah*   36; *Job*   52; *Mark*
69; *Matthew*   94; *John*   100; *Acts of the Apostles*   100;
The Epistle to the Romans   111

2   The Meaning of History in Man's Journey into Eternity
    124
St. Augustine: *City of God*   125

3   The Christian Knight: Warrior of God   132
The Song of Roland   133

4   The Christian Beggar: Follower of Christ   147
St. Francis of Assisi: *Canticle of the Sun*   148; *The Little Flowers*
    149

5   The Christian Philosopher: The Baptism of Reason
154
St. Thomas Aquinas: *Summa Contra Gentiles*   155

6   The Christian Humanist: The Day-to-Day Philosophy
of Christ   173
Erasmus: *Familiar Colloquies: A Lover and Maiden*   174; *Familiar
Colloquies: The Funeral*   184

7   Christian Faith and Man's Liberation   199
Martin Luther: *On Christian Liberty*   200

8   Service to the Sovereignty of God   208
John Calvin: *Commentaries on the Psalms*   209

9   Mystical Union with God   220
St. Teresa of Avila: *Autobiography*   *221*

10   The Leap of Faith   232
Soren Kierkegaard: *Fear and Trembling*   *233*

11   Christ and the Secular World   249
Dietrich Bonhoeffer: *Letters from Prison*   *250*

Contents of Volume 3

General Introduction   1

Introduction   3

1 *Man, A Political Animal*   *5*
Niccolò Machiavelli: *The Prince*   7

2 *Society: A Rational Human Contrivance*   *21*
John Locke: *On Civil Government*   23

3 *The Scientific Manifesto*   *39*
Jean d'Alembert: *Preliminary Discourse to the Encyclopedia of Diderot and d'Alembert*   40

4 *Moral Doubts in an Age of Progress*   *47*
Jean-Jacques Rousseau: *Discourse on the Sciences and Arts*   48

5 *The Liberal Ideology*   *66*
Marquis de Condorcet: *Outlines of an Historical View of the Progress of the Human Mind*   67

6 *Material Man*   *83*
Karl Marx and Friedrich Engels: *The German Ideology*   85

7 *Man and the Natural Order*   *96*
Charles Darwin: *The Origin of Species*   98; *The Descent of Man*   115

8 *Liberation from Christianity*   *121*
Friedrich Nietzsche: *The Genealogy of Morals*   122

9 *"If There Is No God . . ."*   *139*
Fyodor Dostoyevsky: *The Brothers Karamazov*   140

10 *The Price of Civilization*   *151*
Sigmund Freud: *The Future of an Illusion*   152; *Civilization and Its Discontents*   155; Why War? (Letter to Einstein, 1932)   158

11 *Man in an Unfriendly Universe* *161*
Jean-Paul Sartre, *The Flies* 162

Epilogue 169